Business as Usual

Business as Usual

How Sponsored Media Sold American Capitalism in the Twentieth Century

CAROLINE JACK

THE UNIVERSITY OF CHICAGO PRESS   CHICAGO AND LONDON

The University of Chicago Press, Chicago 60637
The University of Chicago Press, Ltd., London
© 2024 by Caroline Jack
All rights reserved. No part of this book may be used or reproduced in any manner
whatsoever without written permission, except in the case of brief quotations in critical
articles and reviews. For more information, contact the University of Chicago Press,
1427 E. 60th St., Chicago, IL 60637.
Published 2024
Printed in the United States of America

33 32 31 30 29 28 27 26 25 24   1 2 3 4 5

ISBN-13: 978-0-226-83512-9 (cloth)
ISBN-13: 978-0-226-83514-3 (paper)
ISBN-13: 978-0-226-83513-6 (e-book)
DOI: https://doi.org/10.7208/chicago/9780226835136.001.0001

Library of Congress Cataloging-in-Publication Data

Names: Jack, Caroline, author.
Title: Business as usual : how sponsored media sold American capitalism in
    the twentieth century / Caroline Jack.
Description: Chicago : The University of Chicago Press, 2024. | Includes bibliographical
    references and index.
Identifiers: LCCN 2024007577 | ISBN 9780226835129 (cloth) | ISBN 9780226835143
    (paperback) | ISBN 9780226835136 (ebook)
Subjects: lcsh: Capitalism — United States. | Mass media — Political aspects —
    United States. | United States — Economic conditions.
Classification: LCC HB501 .J25 2024 | ddc 330.973/091 — dc23/eng/20240316
LC record available at https://lccn.loc.gov/2024007577

♾ This paper meets the requirements of ANSI/NISO Z39.48-1992 (Permanence of Paper).

Contents

INTRODUCTION. Left to Perish in Debris 1

CHAPTER 1. The Contradictions of Economic Education 15

CHAPTER 2. Selling America to Americans 28

CHAPTER 3. Expertise and Affirmation 52

CHAPTER 4. The Great Free Enterprise Campaign 77

CHAPTER 5. The New Economics 107

CHAPTER 6. From Institutions to Markets 141

CHAPTER 7. The Triumphs of Economic Education 172

CONCLUSION 181

Acknowledgments 199

Notes 203

Index 253

Introduction

Left to Perish in Debris

How did the idea that private enterprise is natural, inevitable, and deeply American come to be so prevalent in the United States? Promotional culture—which includes the ideologies, institutions, and media systems that intersected with advertising, corporate public relations, and propaganda—had an important role to play. Notions of capitalism as natural, inevitable, or patriotic had to be *sold*. This book tells how sponsored "economic education" media sold American capitalism: by using rhetorics of affirmation and neutrality. I argue that "economic education" was a genre of twentieth-century US media that has been overlooked because of its ephemerality, but whose internal contradictions reflected the uneasy coexistence of capitalism with civic life.

Throughout most of the twentieth century, corporations, professional societies, and trade groups were among those who used mass media to "sell" private enterprise to US publics. By the mid-1970s, these mass media productions—including pamphlets, public service advertisements, films, radio and television programs, and more—represented a multifaceted range of attempts by US business interests and their allies to promote the idea that private enterprise, and the market forces that gave capitalism its dynamic qualities, were deeply connected to political freedoms and therefore intrinsically American. These mass media production trends continued well into the latter half of the twentieth century, and the ideas they promoted became both institutionally formalized and culturally embedded in popular discourse.

Proponents of these media productions often used the term "economic education" to describe these media productions, and I largely adopt this label, but with some reservations. For the people who used the terminology of "economic education," this label did important rhetorical work, signaling a very specific set of ideas and assumptions about knowledge, media, and politics. Economic education media was not simply informative media about the scholarly discipline of economics. Rather, it was *persuasive* media that sought to inculcate positive attitudes about capitalism and private enterprise. Its defining claims were, first, that such positive attitudes were tightly linked to American national ideals of personal and political freedom—a claim that was, more often than not, made in an optimistic and even celebratory style—and, second, that understanding of the American economic system was equivalent to appreciation for it. Labeling such media as *educational* was itself a rhetorical sleight of hand that made the peculiar capitalisms of the twentieth-century United States out to be as natural and inevitable as the laws of science.

The twentieth-century battle for corporate power over US policy and culture—of which economic education media was a part—has been the subject of much scholarly examination. To be sure, the answer to the question of how private enterprise became seen as natural and inevitable in US culture wends through the intellectual history of neoclassical economics, corporate and institutional histories, histories of the rise and fall of organized labor power in the twentieth century, and histories of the strains of Christian fundamentalism that came to embrace ideologies of entrepreneurship and prosperity. Business historians, intellectual historians, and political historians have surveyed the ideology, imagery, and political-institutional-cultural networks that were employed in corporate efforts to maintain power and legitimacy, documenting how US corporations and their allies used techniques such as lobbying and publicity to claim and sustain the autonomy of private enterprise; limit, co-opt, or break labor organizing; defy public calls for accountability; and resist federal attempts to regulate corporate practices.[1] These works are essential in documenting what Kim Phillips-Fein aptly describes as "the businessmen's crusade"—but while these works often examine media texts and promotional campaigns as *evidence* of business interests' strategic attempts to seize power, they less often focus on such media or approach them as centrally important sites of sense-making that not only reflected but, crucially, *cocreated* cultural meaning. This book centers such meaning-making processes by focusing on sponsored economic education media, the aspirations of its proponents, the ways they imagined mass media could influence public opinion, and the sense-making required to

INTRODUCTION

present such media productions to the public not as propaganda, but as public service.

Why Sponsored Media Matter

I approach economic education media as a type of *sponsored* media. Film historian Rick Prelinger explains that sponsorship both "implies the packaging of information from a particular corporate or institutional perspective" and signals "direct institutional support" in the form of funding, services, or other direct assistance. Prelinger focuses on sponsored *film*, but his criteria can be used to understand a much broader assortment of sponsored media outputs across film, broadcast, and print media forms (including, but not limited to, informational pamphlets, advertisements, and billboards).[2]

Sponsored media were among corporations' and trade groups' favored modes of public relations communications in the middle decades of the twentieth century, especially from the 1930s through the 1970s. Such media ranged across many different forms. These included straightforward advertisements that celebrated products, companies, and industries. They also included what would likely be categorized today as *content marketing*: media productions that, despite their institutional sponsorship, primarily offer viewers information, entertainment, or something else of value in place of a sales pitch about a product's attributes—for example, a trail etiquette guide for first-time hikers produced by a hiking boot manufacturer or the travel-oriented magazines produced by some airlines for in-flight reading. Sponsored economic education media productions claimed to *inform* and *educate* their audiences—but this claim often strained reasonable belief because of the biased and selective presentations of information they contained. To be sure, the rhetorics, framings, and constructions of reality contained in sponsored economic education media were ideological, in the sense that that they expressed how supporters of economic education imagined their relationship to the real conditions of twentieth-century US life. I draw here from cultural theorist Stuart Hall, who argues that from a critical perspective, ideological expressions are necessarily both signifying and social: in his words, "the world has to be made to mean" through the ways people create significations of ideas and attach them to their lived experiences. This process expresses hegemonic power to the extent that class interests engage in what Hall calls "the shaping, the education and the tutoring of consent." As Hall explains, the category of the ideological encompasses ideas, the ways ideas are signified, and assumptions about the terms by which debate can or should proceed.[3]

Most economic education media during this time could be categorized as *sponsored* not only because they were funded by corporations, corporate-affiliated philanthropic foundations, or trade groups, but also because they depicted social and economic worlds that centered and valorized managerial capitalism. Scholars of the political economy of media have observed how the content of entertainment and news media that are funded by advertisements can be influenced in ways that favor, or at least that avoid challenging, the interests of advertisers. Economic education media, being funded largely through sponsorship in the form of donations and grants, directly expressed its benefactors' imperatives. It was not only the *production* of materials that was sponsored by private interests. Importantly, as Prelinger's definition of sponsored media alludes, the very *ideas* these materials presented were attuned to managerial concepts and worldviews. The ideas touted in sponsored economic education media were often summed up in significant phrases such as "free enterprise," which conflated civil liberties with commercial prerogatives. For this reason, I use the phrase "private enterprise" to describe the *idea* of a system in which market forces and privately owned companies, not central planning or active management by the state, are imagined to take the lead in determining the course of economic development. It must be said, though, that this phrase, too, carried an illusory impression of objectivity, because it obscured how such privately owned institutions rely on the state for the legal infrastructures, such as property rights, that allow them to operate. And, further, the meaning of enterprise or what constituted an enterprise-based system varied, depending on who wielded it: for some users, it signaled an economic system in which government and labor had legitimate, if limited, roles alongside businesses; for others, quite the opposite. Terminologies contain multitudes. Like free enterprise, economic education was a blanket term under which a range of financial interests, political imperatives, and visions of societal benefit could be gathered. Sponsored economic education media provided expressive outlets for these visions.[4]

Sponsored media have a peculiar relationship to temporality. They are designed to circulate among their chosen audiences and publics, where their intended meanings can be folded into the individual and collective ideas, logics, and styles that constitute ideology. This, at least, is what the creators and promoters of sponsored media hope will come to pass: that

INTRODUCTION 5

the ideas and narrative frames conveyed in their media texts will be taken up by audiences in ways that influence audience members' thoughts, feelings, and behaviors. Such sponsored media is often ephemeral—that is, produced for a particular historical moment, and leaving only fleeting traces once that moment has passed. Ephemeral media are defined by their impermanence and their service to a "short-lived purpose," as noted by curator Jim Burant. They are "useful" media, to borrow an adjective from film historians Charles R. Acland and Haidee Wasson, that are inextricably situated in history: they do things, or at least are part of an attempt to do things, in a particular time and place.[5]

The materiality of ephemeral media from the past includes phases of movement and rest. They moved through the world in a particular moment of the past, in service of historically specific goals. In the process, many were discarded or destroyed. Some which remain come to rest in archives or attics. If they circulate, they often do so online or in last-chance material spaces such as flea markets—twilight way stations for objects on the verge of being cast off as junk. Often, they circulate shorn of their original context. Their original meaning is fleeting, tied to a set point in time. Encounters with these ephemera often evoke a sense of decontextualization that underscores how their moment of urgency, the moment in which they were meant to intervene, has passed.

This book contends that the ephemerality of sponsored economic education media has allowed sponsored economic education media to largely escape serious examination as a coherent persuasive genre with its own distinctive ideas, logics, and styles. These materials are traces of the past, but they do not represent the past in a straightforward way. It's tempting to say that they spoke to a reality that no longer exists, but that statement doesn't capture how the reality they spoke to may not have even existed even in the past, other than in the imaginations of their proponents. As business ephemera, the persuasive media created through the sponsorship of corporations, trade associations, and their allies spanned the space between the worlds that sponsors, creators, and distributors believed they lived in and the worlds they believed to be possible.[6]

The very sponsored-ness of these corporate-sponsored media, their implication in the practice of commerce and the pursuit of profit, made them doubly ephemeral. It marked them to many observers as media with little intrinsic value: media that may have attempted to entertain, inform, or be expressive, but only toward the central goal of aligning audience thoughts, feelings, and behaviors with the imperatives of business promotion or publicity within a particular moment. Because of their instrumentality, sponsored media seemed to invite audiences not to take them entirely seriously. To be sure, sponsored media were self-serving and instrumental in ways that generated justifiable skepticism in many audiences — but they also documented the images and narratives that their creators believed would sway audiences. Ephemeral sponsored media can be taken seriously as expressions of the images and narratives that symbolized hegemonic ideas and values in their historical moment, even if some audiences at the time could and did regard them dubiously.[7]

Focusing on the ephemerality of sponsored economic education media permits a deeper understanding of how ideology, sense-making, and affect are implicated in the seemingly ordinary processes of promotional culture. Consider the example of Isadore Warshaw, a midcentury collector of business ephemera. Warshaw remarked to the *Rotarian* magazine in 1957 that his expansive collection of obsolete and discarded business artifacts, including bookkeeping records and promotional materials, preserved an important but overlooked aspect of cultural history: in his words, "People are beginning to realize that while the romance of war, fashion, and science, for instance, is well preserved in swords, wax dolls, and fascinating models . . . the romance of business in the form of ledgers, sample books, posters, and tin cans tends to perish in debris." Warshaw specialized in providing evidence from his collections for trademark dispute cases. The cultural meanings and narratives contained within these ephemera were in many ways tangential to the trademark disputes Warshaw was often employed to settle. Yet, Warshaw's insistence that there was a "romance of business" is worth considering in further depth.[8]

Warshaw's words seem to suggest that the romance of business included seeing material traces of business history as worth preserving, and recognizing business artifacts' ability to evoke wonder by offering a sense of connection to the people who used these everyday objects in another place and time. To be sure, in the time since Warshaw's comments business history and the history of capitalism have become well-established fields that emphasize the importance of understanding past business practices, corporate histories, and managerial ideologies. Yet, there is something more about Warshaw's phrasing that resonates: a certain attention to the ephemeral. A 1958 *Business Week* magazine article about Warshaw's collection described business management coming to see ephemera of the type Warshaw collected as "charming," "delightful," and "picturesque," terms that signaled an imaginative and affective experience of being plea-

INTRODUCTION

surably drawn in. Following the example of scholars of ephemeral media such as Haidee Wasson, Charles Acland, Rick Prelinger, and many others, I take Warshaw's eloquent phrasing as inspiration to critically examine media that is sponsored, useful, ephemeral—elements of consumer culture whose impermanence and instrumentality imparted rich layers of cultural meaning.[9]

The Themes and Structure of This Book

This book traces sponsored economic education media across a broad swath of the twentieth century. It is worth noting that the notion of *the economy* is itself a relatively new one, and that the terms *economy* and *economic* have been used in many different ways. As political theorist Timothy Mitchell explains, political economists started using the phrase to refer to a self-contained and all-encompassing system of national economic activity relatively recently, in the 1930s and 1940s. Mitchell notes that this new epistemological object *the economy* developed along with social scientists' new conceptualizations of the nation itself as an entity that could be known through distinctive practices and technologies of representation and analysis. At that time, some politicians, commentators and journalists used the term *economy* to denote a quality of avoiding waste, especially as pertained to government spending—a double inflection of meaning that was evidently attractive to sponsored economic education media's advocates. Others seemed to use the term *economic* to refer to behaviors that were compatible with the principle of economic competition: for example, advertising historian Inger Stole's discussion of accusations of monopoly in the advertising field examines a 1940 commentary in the advertising trade magazine *Printers' Ink* about critics who characterized advertising as monopolistic and, thus, "uneconomic."[10]

In the process of examining the history of sponsored economic education media, the book draws upon two core concepts. The first of these two concepts is *promotional nationalism*, in which businesses and their allies used patriotic or nationalist imagery and ideas to promote the commercial, publicity, and policy interests of management and capital. Communication scholar Melissa Aronczyk argues that scholars of nationalism should ask how "the material and the discursive interact to produce similar affective investments across a range of concrete cases"; Aronczyk takes influence from Canadian historian M. Brook Taylor's focus on how narratives of the nation have been produced chiefly by "*promoters*, individuals who stood to profit in some way from the account they provided." Aronczyk's approach allows for viewing sponsored economic education media as transparently self-interested accounts of nation, economy, and society—and recognizing them as being culturally consequential *in light of*, not in spite of, their biases.[11]

The second of these two concepts is what I am calling the *affirmative style* in American politics, a mode of promotional-political discourse that paired framings of celebration and certainty with a refusal to engage ideological opponents beyond the level of superficial dismissal. I take the nomenclature of *style* in American politics from Richard Hofstadter's essay "The Paranoid Style in American Politics," which approaches style as "the way in which ideas are believed." On a related and more recent note, organizational theorist Elizabeth Popp Berman argues for the increasing presence in US policymaking circles, from the 1960s onward, an "economic style of reasoning" in which efficiency was assumed to be a politically neutral and objectively beneficial quality. Berman, in turn, draws on philosopher of science Ian Hacking's description of "styles of scientific reasoning." For Hacking, a style of scientific reasoning is a way of making claims that adheres to distinctive assumptions about what counts as knowledge, what methods can be used to generate knowledge, and to what ends. Hacking contends that a style of reasoning sets out "what it is to reason rightly, to be reasonable in this or that domain." Hacking stipulates that styles of reasoning are discursive and public: they involve thinking, indeed, but also "talking and arguing and showing." And, importantly, he argues that styles of scientific reasoning are persistent because their internal logics are "self-authenticating": "the truth of a sentence (of a kind introduced by a style of reasoning) is what we find out by reasoning using that style."[12]

Style, these uses suggest, is a cultural framework—a method for framing reality—that has temporal implications: it can sustain an ideology as new events unfold. I take style to be important because it allows proponents of an ideology to engage in political discourse, interpreting new events through that ideology's central assumptions and policing the boundaries of what is imagined to be up for debate without exposing those central assumptions to close scrutiny or potential revision. Adapting Hacking's observations about style, I argue that for many proponents of private enterprise in the twentieth-century US, the affirmative style became established as the way to "reason rightly" about the roles of corporations in society.

INTRODUCTION

The affirmative style is woven into the history of the United States. M. Brook Taylor aptly observes how early narratives describing the colonies that would eventually become the United States took on an implicitly promotional cant: "anything that was not derogatory was, to some degree, promotional." The promotional imperatives of colonists, developers, and promoters inflected the social construction of colonized lands. Within the context of twentieth-century managerial capitalism, historian Lawrence Glickman notes that, as early as 1925, business writers insisted that businessmen, companies, and the business culture as a whole should be celebrated without hesitation. Proponents of private enterprise in the twentieth century embraced this tendency toward celebration, combining it with promotional nationalism. For proponents of promotional nationalism within US manufacturing and media industries, I argue that the affirmative style imparted tones of optimism to their pursuit of two important goals: aligning American identity with private enterprise and excluding critiques of managerial capitalism from the sphere of legitimate debate.[13]

Chapter 1 of this book takes a closer look at these two core concepts, examining themes in the history of sponsored economic education media that promotional nationalism and the affirmative style brought to bear. It explains how sponsored economic education media drew on an idea of freedom that linked the commercial-managerial imperatives of private business firms to personal and political liberties in ways that alluded to managerial anxieties about the political power of ordinary people. It identifies a foundational contradiction between selling and education in sponsored economic education media, examining how this contradiction allowed supporters of the genre to imagine it as a form of public service. And, finally, it reflects upon the temporality of consumer culture, examining how the imaginaries expressed in sponsored economic education media constructed the past, present, and future in ideological terms.

The ensuing chapters cover time spans of varying length, each focusing on a distinctive phase in sponsored economic education media's rhetorical, institutional, and ideological development, to tell a story in three parts. The first part of the story, in chapters 2 and 3, shows how a constellation of factors—including the rhetoric of selling America between the First and Second World Wars and the institutional transformation of public service messaging during the Second World War—made it possible for sponsored economic education to take new forms and carry new cultural meanings. The second part of the story, in chapters 4 and 5, examines what might be called a golden age of economic education from the 1940s through the late 1960s, in which both promotional nationalism and a seemingly scientific form of anticommunism played important parts in connecting private enterprise to patriotism in the popular imagination. The third part of the story, in chapters 6 and 7, examines how these golden-age discourses fared as New Deal policies and approaches faltered and gave way to neoliberalism.

Although New Deal policies are often seen as the events that provoked US corporations' campaigns to promote private enterprise, chapter 2 argues that an ideological prehistory of sponsored economic education media can be traced further back in time, in the changing uses of the slogan "selling America to Americans" from the time of the first Red Scare (immediately after World War I) to the late 1930s. Tracing the lineage of this catchphrase shows how it developed with, and responded to, the tensions of managerial capitalism in the early twentieth century—and how it came to encapsulate the idea that individual thoughts and feelings, not grassroots collective action or government policy, were the forces that could both define and efficiently enact national identity. It shows how sponsored economic education media and its predecessors were always and innately an attempt to align public opinion with corporate imperatives through rhetoric about national identity and patriotic feeling. As the chapter explains, those who adopted the rhetoric of selling America to Americans attempted to sway public opinion in ways they imagined were systematic and scientific means of fostering a stabilizing and antiradical national culture in the United States.

The logics of an affirmative style of promotional nationalism played out against the backdrops of the Great Depression and World War II, both turning points for sponsored economic education media. Chapter 3 recounts how the promotional efforts of trade organizations—the National Association of Manufacturers (NAM) and the Advertising Council, itself an offshoot of the American Association of Advertising Agencies (which I refer to here as the AAAA, but which is colloquially known as "the 4A's") and the Association of National Advertisers (ANA)—helped define economic education as a strategic promotional media genre in the 1930s and 1940s. Business managers and executives who chafed at the federal management of the economy during the 1930s helped circulate claims about the necessity and significance of economic education media. These included an emphasis on professional communicators' expertise and the positioning of corporate-sponsored economic education media

INTRODUCTION

as information in the public interest. Subsequently, the need for wartime public messaging led to the creation of an organizational and practical infrastructure of public service advertising that not only supported and reinforced prewar economic education tropes and publicity narratives about the intertwined nature of private enterprise and political freedom, but also strengthened the advertising industry's claims to expertise and public service. As this chapter shows, the Advertising Council's successes at industry-government cooperation during World War II not only strengthened the advertising industry's political and economic position in US society, as Inger Stole has observed; it also positioned them to claim professional jurisdiction over public service messaging. This confluence of factors set the conditions for the forms in which economic education flourished after the Second World War.[14]

Chapter 4 focuses on the influence of advertising trade industry groups, including the Advertising Council, in carrying out a broad program of sponsored economic education campaigns in the late 1940s and early 1950s. By the early 1950s, multiple sectors of the postwar consumer economy including manufacturers and retailers, advertisers, publishers, and broadcasters were participating in popular discourses that promoted ideologically freighted keywords such as free enterprise and the "American way of life," as historian Wendy Wall has observed. A great deal of the sponsored economic education media of that time sounded remarkably similar. This chapter shows how the direct influence of a joint committee of the AAAA and ANA facilitated consistent public messaging across many different sponsored economic education media projects. This joint committee created a strategy for promoting economic education, as embodied in its flagship study, the Smock Report. The postwar 1940s and 1950s seemed to be a golden age of sponsored economic education media. During this time, a range of sponsored economic education media were distributed to wide audiences: for instance, television stations hungry for programming broadcasted films that extolled the virtues of American capitalism, and interactive exhibits that linked private enterprise to US political traditions traveled around the country.[15]

These projects combined promotionally nationalist narratives with the managerial knowledge claims, institutional configurations, and communicative infrastructures that the Advertising Council and its allies had established during the war. For all its successes, however, the joint committee of advertising trade groups stopped short of enacting its boldest aspiration: the widespread teaching of appreciation for private enterprise in the nation's schools. The subsequent efforts of the Joint Council on Economic Education, a different style of economic education organization that aligned business leaders and educators, to facilitate the teaching of economics in the nation's schools is the focus of chapter 5.

From the late 1940s through the late 1960s, the Joint Council on Economic Education (JCEE) advanced an alternative version of economic education that favored abstract analysis as a style of intellectual and civic reasoning. This skill set, JCEE economists claimed, would lead students to rationally and objectively reach the conclusion that private enterprise was superior to socialism or communism. Chapter 5 examines how the economists, educators, and business leaders behind the JCEE developed economic education programs for schools. The approach they used, which emphasized critical thinking and careful analysis while still insisting that private enterprise was the best principle upon which to base economic practices, gained ground in the late 1950s amid the perceived educational crisis brought on by the Soviet Union's unexpected launch of the first human-made satellites. The chapter argues that the JCEE used the education crisis to raise its own profile and promote decentralized, systematic decision-making according to economic models as a fundamentally democratic means of organizing American society. Yet, its efforts to center what it presented as fair and reasoned analysis challenged managerial constituencies' expectations that economic education media would adopt an affirmative style, leading critics to see the JCEE's approach as insufficiently freedom-minded. However, the chapter argues that the scientific anticommunism of the JCEE and affiliated groups did not conflict with, and in fact *complemented*, the aims of the affirmative style of earlier sponsored economic education efforts. The chapter closes by examining a failed 1969 collaboration between the Advertising Council and the JCEE that revealed ideological differences between the two organizations and signaled that the focus of sponsored economic education was shifting from Cold War geopolitics to the domestic economy.

Chapter 6 considers the Advertising Council's mid-1970s "American Economic System" public service advertisement (PSA) campaign, a massive promotional effort that reflected the advertising industry's changing ideas about how to portray managerial capitalism as politically neutral. It argues that the seeming emergence of neoliberal ideology in the 1970s was in part an adoption, adjustment, and rearticulation of well-worn economic education tropes. The neoliberalism of the late 1970s echoed earlier economic education media's strategies of scientizing ideology and refram-

INTRODUCTION 13

ing it as knowledge, and rearticulated discourses of fairness and objectivity in a shift away from prior decades' scientific anticommunism by imagining market forces themselves as apolitical and objective. This portrayal contrasted with the vision advocates at the JCEE had promoted: that market forces would need to be harnessed through judicious use of analysis, informed by personal values. Chapter 6 focuses on how the Advertising Council reinstated the affirmative style of economic education in the context of sociocultural change—most notably, increased regulation, anticorporate activism, and growing economic disruption. Business advocates' responses to these new conditions rearticulated familiar claims that private enterprise was in itself socially responsible and inextricable from political liberty, fortifying the claim that a campaign in support of private enterprise could be an act of public service. The Advertising Council created a campaign for the US bicentennial that instantiated these ideas, calling back to the JCEE's earlier scientific anticommunism, but trading prior economic education projects' focus on institutions for a new emphasis on abstract market forces. This market-oriented narrative elided structural imbalances of power in US society, a critique that was taken up by activist media creators in the public interest advertising movement. As the chapter shows, both the Advertising Council and its progressive opponents used the infrastructures of broadcast policy to advance competing narratives about the American economy.

Finally, chapter 7 reflects upon the seeming triumph of economic education by the early 1980s, amid a general turn to the political right. It examines the widespread passage of state mandates for economic education in schools, a trend that news coverage framed as the culmination of twenty years of economic education efforts. Further, it examines the adoption of simulation games for the teaching of economics in the 1970s and early 1980s, arguing that economic educators saw simulation as a means of capturing student interest and building empathy for managerial subject positions. These educational goals belied popular imaginings of economic actors premised on rational utility maximization, instead presenting an imagined economic subject whose ability to reason was matched by their ability to understand themselves and others. This empathic economic citizen was not an anomaly, but the expression of a foundational assumption of economic education, present since the 1920s: that economic citizenship was something that had to be both known and felt.

It is my intention through these chapters to trace an arc of change over time in the imaginaries of capitalism and consumption in the United

States, as reflected in sponsored economic education media: from interwar concerns with radicalism, American identity, and the role of the state in managing economic conditions, through a postwar promotional nationalism that developed in tandem with an institutionally funded, modernist vision of a carefully administered free society, to the fractured social worlds and atomized market imaginaries of the late twentieth century.

Economic Education and the Romance of Business

Taking sponsored economic education media seriously means not just asking whether it influenced public opinion as intended—but also asking what economic education made imaginable for the people who championed or tolerated it. It also means closely examining the media texts into which the ideal of economic education was crystallized, since these media texts not only influenced perceptions of what economic education media could do, but also drew sponsored economic education media campaigns into historically specific technological affordances, distribution systems, and regulatory regimes.

In one sense, this is a story about the political economy of media as expressed in specific events and practices—for example, the granting of money and other resources that funded the creation and circulation of economic education media campaigns, and the existence or creation of rules and regulations that created both opportunities and vulnerabilities for economic education media campaigns. In another sense, it is a story about the ephemeral, the fleeting, and the intangible. It examines porous boundaries between persuasion and education, and it considers the ideological projects and understandings of self in society that such porous boundaries made possible. It is a story about how corporate actors narrated their own moral, organizational, and social locations. It takes seriously the ephemeral media of economic education, describes the imaginary worlds conjured by the texts of economic education media, and examines the ideological, political, and cultural possibilities brought forth through the production and circulation of these texts. Indeed, the romance of business should not perish in debris; yet neither should the political and cultural implications of the worlds it attempted to build go unexamined.

CHAPTER ONE

The Contradictions of Economic Education

Several themes weave throughout this book. The first is an idea about freedom: the emblematic assertion, on the part of business advocates, that private enterprise was so intertwined with political and personal liberty that a threat to one was a threat to all. Beneath this lofty claim lurked a long-standing but unresolved ambivalence about the voting power of ordinary people in a democratic society. Many business advocates feared that ordinary people, if left to their own devices, might vote for politicians or policies that limited managers' control over domains such as wages, prices, labor conditions, and production. The second is a foundational contradiction between education and selling, which was itself premised on assumptions that managers' practical experiences of business made them experts on what they called the American economic system (and additional, underlying assumptions that constructed resistant publics as uninformed). The third is the importance of individual and collective imagining in twentieth-century consumer cultures, in which experiences of longing, desire, morality, and anxiety were mapped to narrations of the imagined past, present, and future.

The Idea of Freedom

The most insistent idea in sponsored economic education media was one that attempted to link private enterprise to political, civic, or personal freedoms. Consider the John Sutherland Productions animated film *It's Everybody's Business* (1955), sponsored by E. I. Du Pont de Nemours and Company—known today simply as DuPont—and distributed by the

Chamber of Commerce of the United States (hereafter the US Chamber of Commerce), one of the nation's largest business lobbying groups. The film used animation to dramatize a version of US history centered on business, drawing a direct line from the small businesses of European colonists to the modern corporations of the mid-twentieth century. For example, one scene depicted the colonization of North America through a visual metaphor of European settlers laying foundation stones at the edge of an Atlantic harbor. Some of these stones were labeled with civil liberties ("FREEDOM OF WORSHIP," "RIGHT OF ASSEMBLY," "PRIVACY IN THE HOME"), while others enshrined industrial principles ("RIGHT TO GO INTO BUSINESS," "RIGHT TO REWARDS GAINED THROUGH COMPETITION") or ascribed limited rights to workers ("FREEDOM TO WORK IN JOB OF OWN CHOICE" was present, for example, and "RIGHT TO BARGAIN WITH EMPLOYER," but a right to unionize was not mentioned). The film didn't distinguish the civic from the industrial, however; all were simply presented as building blocks of the nation.

FIGURE 1.1 Foundation-laying scene from the animated short film *It's Everybody's Business*. Digital still from a digitized 35 mm print courtesy of the National Film Preservation Foundation, https://www.filmpreservation.org/preserved-films/screening-room/it-s-everybody-s-business-1954. *It's Everybody's Business*, directed by Carl Urbano (1955; John Sutherland Productions), 35 mm film.

FIGURE 1.2 Foundation stone from the animated short film *It's Everybody's Business*. Digital still from a digitized 35 mm print courtesy of the National Film Preservation Foundation, https://www.filmpreservation.org/preserved-films/screening-room/it-s-everybody-s-business-1954. *It's Everybody's Business*, directed by Carl Urbano (1955; John Sutherland Productions), 35 mm film.

Indeed, promotional materials for the film captioned this stone-laying scene with a statement that the nation's "forefathers constructed the foundation of this nation by interlocking, inseparably, the blocks of our personal, political, and economic freedoms." The foundation stone motif carried through the film into the midcentury era, where the same foundation stones were shown, now supporting a city of high-rise buildings, and standing strong despite being buffeted by a tidal wave colored red and labeled "WAR." The notion of the inseparability of civil liberties from market economies was not uncommon: historians of science Naomi Oreskes and Erik Conway observe that this idea, which they dub "the indivisibility thesis," developed as a political strategy among trade associations in the 1920s and 1930s, and went on to become a signature rhetorical strategy of business advocates for the rest of the twentieth century.[1]

A strikingly similar claim about a mutual dependence between freedoms and capitalism was present a few decades later in the Advertising

Council's 1976 booklet *The American Economic System . . . and Your Part in It*, which closed by arguing that "economic freedoms and personal freedoms have a way of interlocking." These claims summed up the worldview that sponsored economic education was truly selling: an understanding of capitalism as equivalent to freedom. This understanding was based on a managerial conceptualization of an American economic system in which business played a leading role. For the promoters of sponsored economic education media, assenting to this constructed vision of an American economic system based on private enterprise was Americans' civic duty—and their obligation, if they wished to live free and happy lives. These claims also alluded to managerial anxieties about democratic power that spurred the creation of sponsored economic education media: many business leaders and their allies were aware that members of the public might support, and even vote for, policies that would reign in corporate power (or leaders who would pass such policies) . . . unless they could be convinced otherwise.[2]

One might imagine *It's Everybody's Business* or *The American Economic System . . . and Your Part in It* to be tidbits of historical ephemera, too obviously self-serving to gain much of an audience. In fact, these media texts were remarkably widely distributed to American publics, even though audiences did not universally accept the messages they put forth. The Chamber of Commerce released *It's Everybody's Business* to be shown in movie theaters, at community screenings, and on local television stations—whose managers, the Chamber of Commerce advised local affiliates, would "welcome the chance to telecast a well-produced film that informs and entertains its viewers." In the eight months following its release, the Chamber of Commerce estimated that between television broadcasts and private showings in schools, businesses, and local civic organizations, *It's Everybody's Business* had reached over thirty million people. Within a few years of the film's release, the Chamber of Commerce's records estimated the audience for the cartoon on television alone to be approximately sixty million people—more than a third of the United States population at the time. The Advertising Council's 1970s efforts reached millions as well: within two years of its debut, the Advertising Council had distributed more than ten million copies of *The American Economic System . . . and Your Part in It*, with millions more exposed to public service advertising for the booklet in print, display, and broadcast media.[3]

The history of economic education media shows how powerful people in industry and government hoped mass media could efficiently bring pub-

THE CONTRADICTIONS OF ECONOMIC EDUCATION

lic opinion into alignment with managerial values—an important task in a society whose purported ideals of democratic governance had been counterposed by the presence of concentrated wealth and disproportionate economic, cultural, and political power. Indeed, sponsored economic education media often paid lip service, at least, to democratic ideals. Business leaders and their allies attempted to bring the public into ideological alignment with them: by using mass media to associate national identity with the idea of private enterprise, by insisting that managers and executives' firsthand experiences in business gave them an expert level of knowledge about what they imagined to be the American economic system and its principles, and by presenting these ideas with an air of optimistic certainty. In short, the promoters of private enterprise attempted to exploit the blurred boundaries between education, promotion, knowledge, and ideology.

Economic Education's Central Contradiction

Sponsored economic education media campaigns carried within themselves a fundamental contradiction: although economic education proponents in the promotional industries and beyond labeled their efforts as *educational*—taking on intimations of objectivity and social benefit—these same proponents' conversations with one another about influencing public opinion often relied, perhaps unsurprisingly, on metaphors of *selling*. Advocates for American industry would use persuasive expertise honed in the fields of advertising, marketing, and public relations to convince Americans that their political and personal liberties were couched in, and dependent upon, private enterprise.[4]

What can one make of such a seemingly contradictory set of claims? The observations of cultural studies scholar Raymond Williams suggest that the contradiction is exactly where one should direct their attention. As television gained popularity, Williams wrote, popular concerns proliferated about violent television programming: would representations of violence in mass media lead to violent behavior in communities? Williams argued that closer examination of the problem revealed a "contradiction within the social system itself": popular discourses claimed that the society did not condone violence, but the presence of representations of violence in popular entertainment media suggested that the society simultaneously accepted and disavowed violence. Thus, Williams argued, the primary objects of study should be the "sociology of the contradiction" and the social order that made such a contradiction possible. Williams's insights suggest that the contradictions of economic education were symptomatic of the broader social order within which they were embedded. The contradictions between selling and teaching, between promotion and education, were symptomatic of a society in which many powerful constituencies in US society insisted that the United States symbolized both capitalism and freedom. Yet for many ordinary Americans the conditions of capitalism could be cause for limitation, worry, want, and fear of the future—and for many powerful constituencies, the popular vote could seem like a source of threat. Sponsored economic education media campaigns offered narratives that, its supporters hoped, would reconcile these contradictions. Indeed, the entirety of sponsored economic education rested on paradoxical claims about what it meant to be American: business advocates declared that managerial capitalism was quintessentially American yet insisted that ordinary people in the US needed mass media campaigns that could persuade them to act and think in line with this imagined Americanness.[5]

The story of sponsored economic education media is a story about ideas, to be sure, but it is also a story about the expectations powerful people attached to mass media and the ways those people defined knowledge during a broad ideological struggle. Managerial culture's capacity to depict sponsored economic education media as *educational* required a distinctive set of assumptions: that US business practices were at the heart of a particularly *American* economic system fundamentally centered on private enterprise, and that business managers and executives, *by virtue of managing businesses*, were highly qualified experts on that system's practical workings. When business advocates and their sponsors created or supported economic education materials, they made explicit assertions about this conceptualization of an American economic system and implicit assertions about knowledge, expertise, and the public interest. Campaigns often framed knowledge about, and approval of, business operations as so-called economic understanding. Claiming the mantle of economics for what was essentially a mix of ideological promotion and business education was a way to give managers' practical knowledge a gloss of scientific objectivity and indisputability, especially in an era of increasing prestige for economists. In the chapters to come, I show how proponents of corporate-sponsored and corporate-affiliated economic education media drew on the trappings of science to garner legitimacy for their efforts. This scientization took different forms in different historical moments: leaders in the promotional industries drew on discourses of expertise, efficiency, and systemization to position themselves as expert persuaders before and after the Second World War, and economic educators in the Cold War era framed economics as a systematic style of reasoning that could create better citizens.

Further, the supporters, funders, and allies of sponsored economic education media were convinced that what they called *economic understanding* would lead to civic harmony and national prosperity by helping the public become more knowledgeable (that is, more supportive of capitalism). Accordingly, they framed the dissemination of their favored ideas as a form of public service. In doing so, they reproduced what intellectual historian Sophia Rosenfeld identifies as populist ideas of "common sense," which rest on assumptions that ordinary people have been led astray from practical, straightforward ideas and that, if enacted politically, such commonsense ideas would unify the polity by providing "good and universally applicable solutions to real political problems." Rosenfeld notes that this political mythology "became increasingly useful" from the mid-nineteenth century onward, in part because it responded to powerful constituencies' persistent anxieties that ordinary people would use their newfound enfranchisement to vote for policies that adjusted the balance of power.[6]

Such concerns were often present in supporters' justifications of the need for sponsored economic education media. Sponsored economic education media relied on the idea that ordinary people were either uninformed or had been misled and, therefore, needed economic education to lead them back to faith in US capitalism. As historian of capitalism Lawrence Glickman shows, free enterprisers often framed faith in businesses (and disdain for government) as the well-reasoned acceptance of self-evident principles; this allowed free enterprisers to portray their support for private enterprise as a simple matter of common sense. The faith in capitalism that Glickman highlights may be seen as being in tension with the scientizing strategies I highlight in this book—but I contend that these two strategies may be understood to be acting together to help make private enterprise seem inevitable and natural in US culture. Sponsored economic education media's scientizing impulses generated a sheen of impartiality that worked in concert with free enterprisers' faith to help cement the assumption that market forces and capitalist systems were commonsense ideas that sat in the realm beyond politics: natural, apolitical, and inevitable. Thus, economic education media were a way for sponsoring business executives and advocates to position themselves as knowledgeable and their own actions as socially beneficial.[7]

Audience, Affect, and Imaginaries in Economic Education Media

Even as the business managers and executives who developed and supported sponsored economic education campaigns putatively addressed general or targeted publics, they also indirectly addressed themselves and one another. Sponsored economic education media may have facilitated something similar to a third-person effect. In communication theory, the third-person effect refers not only to the expectation that mass communications will "will have a greater effect on others than on themselves," but also to the way persuasive media could be found to ultimately have influenced someone other than what theorist W. Phillips Davison called the "ostensible audience." As advertising historian Inger Stole observes, many advertising professionals in the 1920s and 1930s imagined themselves as tasked with reaching relatively "irrational and easily manipulated" audiences. I contend that business managers and executives could see their production and promotion of sponsored economic education media as a symbolic gesture toward public service, one that demonstrated the good citizenship of companies and their leaders. These narratives were then available to inform the ongoing articulation of managerial culture: stories about business managers and executives as patriotic and morally sound figures could act as a counterforce to the anxieties and frustrations managerial subjects encountered when critiques of US corporations' monopolistic, antidemocratic, and exploitative capacities periodically gained momentum in the public discourse.[8]

Here, I build on historian Benjamin Waterhouse's finding that economic education projects had both an "external audience"—the restive publics imagined to need convincing—and an "internal audience" comprised of the business leaders and trade group–affiliated allies who were already in accord with, and indeed in some cases helped to develop, the core ideas of sponsored economic education media. As Waterhouse observes, "unifying the internal audience yielded a more important legacy than persuading the external audience," because it created "common identity" across organizations. To Waterhouse's points, I add that these media also offered managerial subjects conceptualizations of self, industry, and professional expertise premised on the logics of consumer culture, especially its principles of anticipatory pleasure. For internal and external audiences alike, support for (or, indeed, opposition to) the circulation of economic education media, undergirded by an invitation to feelings of shared

THE CONTRADICTIONS OF ECONOMIC EDUCATION

purpose, could inform constructions of responsible citizenship along-side assumptions about the power of media and the role of business in society.[9]

All this is to say that the allies of sponsored economic education media were engaged in the metaphorical selling of ideas on more than one level. The leaders from the promotional industries who became involved in economic education media were indeed, as they professed, bringing techniques of advertising and promotion to bear in an effort to influence key publics' understandings of economics in a national context. Just as importantly, they were building a world and selling it to themselves, each other, and the nation. In this world, the figure of the businessman and the abstraction of private or "free" enterprise could be seen as symbols of American ingenuity, political liberty, and moral virtue rather than symbols of greed, exploitation, and moral decay. This world had, in addition, a distinctive affective tenor: one that replaced anger, fear, and conflict with optimism, confidence, and patriotic pride.

Sponsored economic education media portrayed private enterprise, American identity, and what managerial culture imagined to be a distinctively American economic system and way of life—and did so in ways that expressed affective postures of optimism, confidence, and patriotism. In this sense, sponsored economic education media attempted to perform affective alchemy: they promised to transform workers' and consumers' dissatisfactions with the system—and, by extension, managerial anxieties about the ways these sentiments could influence public opinion—into optimism, certainty, and confidence.

Sponsored economic education media promised to sell America, or to sell the American way of life: this description was oft-repeated by creators, sponsors, and allies of economic education campaigns. In the face of complaints about exploitative and predatory business practices from organized labor, consumer groups, and progressive political coalitions, sponsored economic education media framed managerial prerogatives as the American way, implicitly categorizing critiques of those prerogatives as anti-American.

These media campaigns seemed to serve both cynical and earnest purposes. Sponsored economic education media portrayed the world in ways that fit comfortably with the accumulation of corporate profits; in this sense, they may be seen as merely self-interested or promotional. However, even as critics saw the narratives that informed and emerged from sponsored economic education media as self-serving or socially harmful, sponsored economic education media crystallized a *moral* rationale for the practices of managerial capitalism and, subsequently, market fundamentalism. Sponsored economic education media can be interpreted as evidence that the creators, funders, and distributors of these materials not only wanted a public atmosphere friendly to the creation of profits, they wanted to understand themselves as proponents of social good in the process. This strategic self-narration included expressions of optimism and confidence.

It bears considering that sponsored economic education media flourished in the same historical period as the culture of mass consumer goods, and that this culture of consumption had its own distinctive logics. US consumer society in the twentieth century placed great importance on pleasure: it invited ordinary people to imagine the possible future in ways that allowed them to connect consumer goods to emotional experiences of longing, delayed gratification, and explained-away disappointment that could inform their own identities. Part of what made this consumer culture so compelling, sociologist Colin Campbell argues, is that it offered consumers the pleasure of imagining that the act of consuming might lead to an enjoyable or satisfying future. "Deferred gratification," Campbell notes, is not the opposite of pleasure-seeking, "but its basic ally."[10]

The makers and allies of sponsored economic education media attempted to manage the affective tenor of the moment by creating and circulating a particular set of ideas about how the world worked. The media artifacts of the past can only give a partial approximation of what it felt like to be in a historical moment: while the media artifacts of a moment persist into the future, the "structure of feeling" that "operates in the most delicate and least tangible parts" of culture in Raymond Williams's words, that inflected that moment can't be recaptured. However, it is possible to discern the *imaginaries*—ideas about how the world works or about how it *could* work—that were associated with economic education media. These imaginaries reflected and incorporated the consumerist modes of imagining that informed American politics and culture in the postwar period and beyond, in which affect played a central role.[11]

Imagining is not a strictly personal process. Beyond personal experience, imagining is a means of drawing upon shared social ideals of what a person can be and incorporating them into one's image of the possible self—of creating, in other words, a certain type of subjectivity. If pleasure is to be had in imagining a materially comfortable future, it is not only pleasure in imagining material comfort. It is also pleasure in imagining

THE CONTRADICTIONS OF ECONOMIC EDUCATION

the self, in turn, as a particular kind of person *embedded* in conditions of material comfort and networks of social relationships. In the context of how capitalism was practiced in the twentieth-century US, such imagined figures could help to hail individuals into understandings of personal goodness that resonated with long-standing mythic ideals of meritocracy.

The history of sponsored economic education media in the twentieth century incorporates crosscurrents of positive and negative affect. These include the frustrations of ordinary people subject to inequitable and often harsh institutional and economic logics; the same ordinary peoples' hopes for a better future; the fear and contempt with which some business leaders regarded restive public opinion, labor power, and government oversight; and the declarations of self-assured optimism and national pride that the creators, sponsors, and allies of sponsored economic education offered in hopes of countering these perceived threats.

The chapters that follow show how affect inflected ideological struggles in the twentieth century. The practices and projects of the managerial class in the 1910 and 1920s established a role for affect in a variety of persuasion contexts: these include the so-called scientific advertising techniques that defined emotional sales appeals as efficient and therefore scientific (with all the allusions to objectivity entailed in the imagery of science) and the 1920s Americanization movements that celebrated patriotic loyalty and passion as correctives to radical politics. The anti–New Deal public relations campaigns mounted by corporations and business advocacy groups in the 1930s reworked these tendencies, crystallizing an affirmative style that focused on celebrating capitalism as a means of raising public morale. This affirmative style endured into the early 1950s, encompassing both the Second World War and the economic and labor upheaval of its aftermath. In the 1950s and 1960s a second affective posture came to be associated with a different vision of economic education, moving away from aggressively sunny patriotism and toward a projected sense of calm and certainty amid the national anxiety of the nation's space-race setbacks. These affective postures continued to develop into the 1970s, as sponsored economic education offered placid assurances about the predictability of economic forces as a counter to economic shocks, public attitudes critical of the business establishment, and managerial feelings of besiegement.

Media texts helped to inform these imaginative processes, in both obvious and subtle ways. In the most direct sense, media offer representations that can inform who audiences imagine themselves to be. The depictions of subject positions in media (whether the media in question are advertisements, entertainment, or news and nonfiction narratives that use framing devices to transfigure events into stories) are memorable examples of what one can imagine oneself someday having or being. This is not to say that audiences uncritically accept the depictions offered in media, or that all audiences perceive media in the same light: as Stuart Hall observed, audience members may accept the hoped-for interpretation of what is offered in whole, in part, or not at all. Yet, even if an audience member rejects a media text's intended meaning, they remain aware of the narrative on offer, and aware of how that narrative frames what it means to be the right kind of self. Even an oppositional reading of the text acknowledges the preferred (that is, hegemonic) reading as a frame for reality.[12]

Further, when media texts circulate, they themselves can become gathering points for "affective publics" in which, as media theorist Zizi Papacharissi argues, feeling becomes the common ground from which politics can take shape. In addition to strengthening political positions and the networks necessary to promote them, sponsored economic education media can be understood as contributing to the creation of moral and cultural collectivities through which market-oriented politics could be elaborated. Papacharissi argues that interactive digital media, in their urgent temporality, allow people to "feel their way into politics" by enabling connection and belonging. The materiality and affordances of the twenty-first century digital media Papacharissi examines are, to be sure, quite different from those of midcentury pamphlets, PSAs, and filmstrips. Yet, the ephemerality of sponsored economic education materials gave them a degree of temporal immediacy that invites comparisons to the interactivity of digital media. This immediacy, in turn, leads me to ask how sponsored economic education media intersected with the affective worlds of business leaders and their intended publics, and to ask how such media texts reflected or attempted to cultivate feelings of optimism and certainty as they made claims about national identity, belonging, and moral legitimacy.[13]

Media-informed imagining is a crucial part of the creation of social meaning, including the development and maintenance of one's sense of society, self, and of one's place in the world. People draw upon media to inform their imaginings in ways that constantly create, refine, and adjust structures of social meaning. For example, as Benedict Anderson has argued, the very existence of mass media designed for a particular audience fosters the coherence of large-scale social constructs such as the nation, because such media makes it possible to imagine a community of like-minded others far beyond the limits of our own "face-to-face contact."[14]

The construct of imaginaries introduces an element of temporality by emphasizing that people imagine into the past and into the future. Social imaginaries construct and coordinate meaning through narratives that justify and explain the present by recounting the past and envisioning the future. For example, historian of technology David Nye argues that white immigrants to the US in the early twentieth century developed a racialized folklore of the nation's past that, for those who believed in it, "conferred entitlement to the continent to white immigrants." Imaginaries portray the future in terms of what is possible—they are "visions of desirable futures," science and technology scholar Sheila Jasanoff observes, that contain normative claims about what *should* be created (and, conversely, what should be prevented). As this example makes clear, imaginaries' temporal reach into the past and the future is normative and can act to justify, excuse, or conceal the workings of power.[15]

Sponsored economic education media made a distinctive set of images, vocabularies, and narrative patterns available for imaginative adoption and rearticulation. These included patriotic and scientific imagery; rhetorics of motivational optimism; specialist analytical jargon; and narratives of unity, triumph, and progress. They also contributed to the construction of social imaginaries by suggesting the presence of an audience of peers—an imagined community, as Anderson phrased it—with a particular past, present, and future. An imaginary expresses a vision of human lives embedded in a community that lays claim to the future, based on what are imagined to be its traditional practices and ideals. Supporters of sponsored economic education media purported to be teaching an understanding of economics, but in fact conveyed a set of political assumptions and normative frames about what defined economic knowledge or thinking. These imaginaries helped to make sponsored economic education media meaningful and give it a sense of legitimacy.[16]

CHAPTER TWO

Selling America to Americans

In February of 1948, *Business Screen* magazine featured an essay by Henry Link, vice president of the polling company the Psychological Corporation, titled "How to Sell America to the Americans." Its essential argument was that corporate communicators not only could, but *must* use their persuasive skills to create mass media that would lead the public to an appreciation of private enterprise. Link's essay was part of a larger strand of late 1940s popular business discourse that touted the importance of "selling America to Americans" in the emergent postwar social order. Such discourses tended not to state directly what it meant, exactly, to sell America to Americans, but contextual cues suggested that when such discourses mentioned selling America, they often meant selling an appreciation for American capitalism, both in theory and in practice.

Link asserted that people in the US, despite enjoying the nation's economic prosperity, were either misinformed or misled about the American capitalist system. Link's essay conveyed an idea that was prevalent in popular business discourse by the late 1940s: "American industry has not been nearly so successful in selling the principles of free enterprise as it has been in selling its products." For those interested in this sales job, Link offered strategies that his company's audience testing of corporate messaging had found effective. First, companies should write promotional materials using simple vocabulary, so that ordinary people could understand executives' meaning. Next, Link suggested, use "emotional appeals" that readers could "interpret ... in terms of their own emotional attitudes and moral standards." Finally, Link advised executives to feature stories of "individuals or families who have made use of the opportunities provided by our system." This last element, Link cautioned, should be framed in terms of US "*spiritual* heritage": new appliances and automobiles, in this formulation, could be imagined not as showy wealth, but as an expression of a system that preserved individual "dignity." For business advocates like Link, the way to defend the nation against communism or socialism was to *sell* the desired public opinion positions to the public through the creation and distribution of engaging and imaginative media materials that would inspire confidence in, and loyalty to, US corporate business practices and worldviews.[1]

Link's directives signaled an implicit model of persuasion: to "sell" the idea that US managerial capitalism itself was synonymous with democracy, freedom, and patriotic tradition, corporate communicators should use mass media to deploy facts in concert with emotional and moral appeals. Such ideas were foundational to postwar sponsored economic education media, but they did not fully originate there. Rather, postwar sponsored economic education media drew upon an established corporate-managerial tradition of public relations communications that had become gathered under the umbrella phrase of "selling America to Americans." This chapter examines how, from the late 1910s through the late 1930s, the idea of selling America brought together notions of corporate public relations, national identity, and affective lived experience in ways that shaped sponsored economic education media in the 1930s and beyond.

Historians note that at midcentury, US corporations and trade groups described their campaigns for private enterprise as "selling America to Americans," "sell[ing] Americans on the benefits of capitalism," or "sell[ing] 'free enterprise' to the American people." For example, historian of advertising Inger Stole has observed that executives in advertising were using the catchphrase "selling America to Americans" in 1941 to frame how they could foster positive attitudes toward advertising during the war without being "seen as taking advantage of the situation." Historian Lizabeth Cohen observes that the 1930s had brought about a new ideal of the "purchaser consumer," whose "aggregate purchasing power" would, it was hoped, lead to economic growth and stability. The catchphrase of selling America indicates an additional configuration of consumption in the same time period: alongside the push to increase consumption of goods, business leaders by the late 1930s and early 1940s imagined political and economic ideologies as, themselves, commodities to be sold.[2]

However, historians have not explored in detail what selling America would have *meant* to the historical actors who used it to describe economic education media from the late 1930s onward. The use of this catchphrase by historical actors and historians alike invites closer examination: what did it mean to sell America, and how did selling America seem to become synonymous with selling private enterprise? Answering this question requires looking back to the period between the First and Second World Wars. The impetus for a wide-ranging campaign to promote corporate interests is often traced to the 1930s, when many business leaders responded with horror to New Deal expansions of the state's role in national life. Indeed, the New Deal's overhauls of labor law, tax policy, and economic policy mobilized business interests, inspiring corporate leaders and their allies to frame corporate accountability to labor and the state as a betrayal of principles of free enterprise. Yet, as the critical historian of public relations Alex Carey pointed out, a repeated pattern of modern, mass-mediated "popular economic proselytizing" in US culture can be traced further back in time to the immigrant-focused Americanization movement of the 1910s. Further, focusing on the terminologies that came to symbolize advocacy for private enterprise, Lawrence Glickman argues that the idea of so-called free enterprise as a symbol of business opposition to government intervention—and the accompanying assumption, among business advocates, of an existential threat that besieged American businesses—preceded the New Deal, having developed over the 1920s and 1930s. Carey's and Glickman's insights highlight how the era preceding the New Deal was the seedtime of later popular discourses.[3]

Building on that insight, this chapter shows how the use of the catchphrase "selling America to Americans" developed from the late 1910s until the late 1930s, coming to signal a constellation of meanings—including antiradical politics, managerial ideals of efficiency, and an affirmative style of promotional nationalism—that laid the groundwork for the sponsored economic education media projects of the postwar era. More specifically, this chapter examines how the rhetoric of selling America to Americans moved through distinctive phases in the 1920s and 1930s. First, it explores how ideas of selling America could be seen in public discourse in the late 1910s through patriotic projects that attempted to use the evocative and persuasive qualities of film to address tensions about immigrant workers, national identity, and ideology. Next, it shows how, in the 1920s, selling America stood for the propagation of national identity in state and national politics as well as in two promotional contexts: the motion picture industry, which partnered with state officials to advance political antiradicalism, and the domestic travel industry, for whom the notion of selling America positioned domestic locales as desirable alternatives to overseas travel. Then, the chapter examines how these attempts to instrumentalize American political identity were subsequently adapted in the 1930s to express distinctive logics of sponsored economic education. These included not only opposition to New Deal policies, but also corporate leaders' and prominent political commentators' hopes that a national mythology of resilience and optimism could forestall political and economic change ... or, at least, channel it in alignment with their own interests.

Examining the slogan of selling America to Americans in public discourse raises two points that extend the historiographical narrative about twentieth-century business conservatism. First, the idea of selling America is prominent in postwar sponsored economic education rhetorics, but midcentury free enterprisers did not invent the idea. The rhetorical lineage of selling America embeds the rhetoric of midcentury economic education media in a longer timeline of US corporate efforts to instrumentalize nationalism and acculturate key publics to the power of managerial capitalism. Second, it shows how the persuasive selling power of feelings was a persistently *scientized* theme in the rhetoric of selling America to Americans. The slogan of selling America to Americans was informed by a fascination with efficiency and systemization that enabled many managerial practices, including advertising and public relations, to be seen as rational, scientific, and efficient. The motto of selling America to Americans was a way for the allies of US corporations to use those intimations of modern efficiency in a political project designed to fortify and entrench corporate power.

The implications of reframing political conflict as something that could be addressed with a sales pitch were far-reaching. By the late 1930s, the catchphrase was being used in ways that strategically left little room for political debate, compromise, or opposition to be recognized as legitimate. From this perspective, being sold on America required people to not only internalize hegemonic understandings of the nation's language, history, and civics, but also to experience feelings of patriotic pride and optimism. Far from being a mere catchphrase, the motto of selling America to Americans drew upon managerial ideals of efficient persuasion to crystallize an affirmative style of political discourse in which positive affect was both the promise of a bright future and the means to reaching it.

A "Mighty Project" to Reconcile the Conditions of Managerial Capitalism

Between the First and Second World Wars, the slogan of selling America to Americans conveyed a hope that promotional techniques could systematically and efficiently create an environment of public opinion friendly to the interests of industrial management—a hope that sponsored economic education media would also come to express. The ideas that undergirded such projects were evident in promotional discourses of the moment, such as in advertising trade journal cartoons from 1919 that depicted employee education as a bulwark against violent radicalism (figures 2.1 and 2.2): in these images, a wild-eyed agitator serves as the foil to a manager whose clean-cut and tranquil employees receive instruction in "reason" and "American ideals" amid a stack of "educational literature" topped with American flags and a portrait of President Lincoln. Editorial copy on the facing page urged advertising professionals to support a congressional bill promoting English literacy, warning that illiteracy was "the basis of mob violence, and what is worse than that, the seed of Bolshevism." Through such measures, the commentary added with approval, "we improve the reading public to the purpose of being more responsive to advertising." Alex Carey argues that the rhetoric of American identity in the 1910s was linked to industrial conditions, especially the rising public profile of the Industrial Workers of the World (IWW), which, Carey argues, provoked an Americanization movement that stirred fears of "an alien workforce captured by a radical union movement." Film historian Cristina Stanciu documents how corporations used sponsored "educational" films that "served the gospel of Americanism but also advertised the company's (and capitalism's) humane side": as she notes, 1913's *An American in the Making*, an Americanization film sponsored by US Steel, enjoyed broad distribution through the National Association of Manufacturers.[4]

The project of assimilating immigrants took on increased urgency, and garnered more public attention, during and after World War I. The tone of these projects was inflected by the first Red Scare. Historian Erica J. Ryan describes how, in 1919, anxieties over radicalism, feminism, and immigration ballooned into a struggle of "constructed . . . ideologies" in which "Bolshevism in America came to embody all that was threatening to the American status quo." An example of the ideas that would be summed up in the catchphrase of selling America to Americans, and its links to the popular discourses of Americanism, appeared in a collaborative project between the US Department of the Interior and the motion picture industry in 1919. Officials had seen patriotic messaging via mass media as remarkably useful to the war effort, and they hoped film could be used in similar ways to manage peacetime industrial and ideological conflicts. For members of the presiding Wilson administration, partnership with the

FIGURES 2.1 AND 2.2. Cartoons appearing in the trade journal *Associated Advertising*, a publication of the Associated Advertising Clubs of the World, that were published alongside endorsements of "Americanism" campaigns. The cartoon (figure 2.1, *top*) imagined a wild-eyed agitator wielding a red flag and cartoon bomb, touting ideas described as "wrong" and "radical"; management's sponsored patriotic programs (figure 2.2, *bottom*), conversely, were depicted as an education in "American ideals" and "reason" that would foster a clean-cut, agreeable, and mannerly employee pool. Digital images courtesy of Hathi Trust. "Are you leaving your employees to this—? [cartoon]" and "Or are you giving them this? [cartoon]," Thomas Dreier Service, published in *Associated Advertising* 10, no. 3 (March 1919): 11, accessed June 28, 2023, https://babel.hathitrust.org/cgi/pt?id=iau.31858034256317.

motion picture industry promised a means of steering public opinion as the nation returned to peacetime footing after the war.[5]

In June of 1919 the Famous Players–Lasky Motion Picture Company announced the production of *Your America*, a series of short films made in partnership with the Department of the Interior and approved by its secretary, Franklin Knight Lane. Publicity materials announcing the film series touted "Mr. Lane's mighty project of selling America to Americans," noting that films would focus on such topics as labor relations, natural resources, and assimilation of immigrants. At a subsequent meeting with film industry executives in December of 1919 that the *Indianapolis Star* described as a "fight for Americanism," officials drew comparisons between wartime propaganda and peacetime patriotic messaging. Lane framed national identity as part of a battle of ideas, declaring that in the aftermath of the war, leaders would need to inspire the populace to "a patriotism of peace as intense as the patriotism of war." Vice President Thomas Marshall indicated the role the film industry could play in this movement, asserting that the motion picture industry had done more than any other to "arouse the zeal, the fervor and the patriotism of the country" during the war, and going on to suggest that movies could play a similar role of "winning . . . America for Americans" in peacetime. As Stanciu documents, the meeting would spur the formation of the Americanism Committee of the Motion Picture Industry, which facilitated US motion picture companies' production of short features on Americanization themes. Subsequent meetings made clear what Lane had in mind: films designed to "combat Bolshevism and ultra-radical tendencies" by portraying themes of cooperation between labor and management against a backdrop of patriotism. Film historian Larry Ceplair observes that Lane's exhortations to the motion picture industry resulted in relatively few film productions. However, Lane's Americanization drive and its fascination with the uses of motion pictures illustrated how the catchphrase of selling America to Americans encapsulated a promise to resolve managerial capitalism's cultural contradictions, while incorporating its promotional logics to encourage patriotic sentiments and deflect conflict or critique.[6]

Managerial capitalism—in which the owners of large business enterprises turned the day-to-day operations of the firm over to a hierarchical system of "salaried managers who had little or no equity ownership in the enterprises they operated," in the words of business historian Alfred D. Chandler Jr.—had developed in the late nineteenth and early twentieth centuries, facilitating a US management culture that Chandler notes was oriented toward efficiency and marketing. Labor historian Stephen Meyer describes how changes to the techniques of manufacturing ramped up production capacity dramatically and opened up employment opportunities for workers with little prior training, many of them European immigrants. Further, as historian James R. Barrett describes, the so-called new immigration wave of the 1890s to 1910s included many southern and eastern Europeans, as compared to the western and northern Europeans of prior immigration waves. The Americanization movement had aimed to cultivate such immigrants' compatibility with the infrastructures of managerial capitalism. As historian Gary Gerstle notes, Americanization became embedded in community and educational institutions through requirements to teach "citizenship." Americanization was about more than one's place of birth: it was, as communication theorist Jennifer Daryl Slack observes, a process of "becoming socialized into the industrial culture" of the United States. The Americanism touted by Lane and others during the Red Scare built on these earlier Americanization efforts, combining cultural assimilation with aggressively antiradical politics.[7]

Meanwhile, in the field of advertising, ideas about how to efficiently persuade mass audiences were circulating—and these ideas bore similarities to Interior Secretary Lane and Vice President Marshall's hopes of using mass media to fight political radicalism by arousing patriotic feelings. As branded goods had become more prevalent in the early twentieth century, the promotional industries had both expanded and became more professionalized. As business historian Walter A. Friedman describes, corporations and entrepreneurs had adapted traveling salesmen's earlier methods for selling and sales management to create systematized, scalable, and reproducible practices while retaining much of the optimistic and confident affect of salesmanship. In advertising copy, too, an attention to feelings and the ineffable was part of the systematization of the field. For example, psychologist Walter Dill Scott touted what he called "scientific advertising," arguing that advertisements that linked sensory, emotional appeals to product attributes would be more efficient than the advertising strategy of conveying concrete information about product attributes and benefits in a straightforward, evidence-based manner. Advertising historian Peggy Kreshel observes that Scott's approach framed advertising "not as education, but as persuasion."[8]

The most scientifically advanced advertisements, Scott argued in a 1904 essay in the *Atlantic* magazine, would use words and illustrations with such nuance and grace that the reader could imagine the *feeling* of using the product. If advertising was done correctly, the reader would be able to vividly imagine the experience of product use, including the senses it would stimulate and the social situations it would facilitate. Scott's perspective gained popularity over the course of the 1910s, resulting in magazine advertisements that increasingly highlighted pathos alongside product attributes. Scott's personal involvement in the First World War was focused on personnel classification and other management tasks, as business historian Edmund C. Lynch has documented. Yet, the effectiveness of his persuasive techniques was seemingly borne out by the United States' propaganda arm, the Committee on Public Information (CPI), which had used the techniques of advertising—emotive imagery, memorable slogans, and stirring copywriting—to convey persuasive messages of public importance via familiar media formats. Indeed, advertising historians Robert Jackall and Janice M. Hirota document how the CPI tapped the presidents of the AAAA and the Associated Advertising Clubs of the World for leadership positions in the CPI's Division of Advertising. The CPI's chairman, George Creel, would later characterize the organization's work across its many divisions as advertising: Creel's memoir of his time leading the CPI was titled *How We Advertised America: The First Telling of the Amazing Story of the Committee on Public Information That Carried the Gospel of Americanism to Every Corner of the Globe.*[9]

A similar attention to the power of stirring words and images characterized mass-mediated Americanization efforts. The widespread use of film by the Americanization movement, Cristina Stanciu has shown, was premised on assumptions that silent film could transcend language barriers. Film could also communicate across language divides by offering powerful images with affective punch, a capacity that may have inspired some of Franklin K. Lane's interest. The importance of feelings in Interior Secretary Lane's imagining of Americanism can be better understood by examining his speech "The Living Flame of Americanism," which was published posthumously in the New York Times Company's magazine *Current History* in 1921 and circulated further through its inclusion in numerous readers for schoolchildren or general audiences. The speech reflected a conviction that it was not enough for immigrants to adopt the English language or take on everyday practices common in the United States: they also, Lane argued, had to experience an inner transformation that developed a depth of personal feeling. Lane declared, "the process is not one of science; the process is one of humanity": being an American meant being inspired by American ideals, he asserted, and this inspiration could only be conveyed by those who were, themselves, "aglow with the sacred fire" as shown by "our kindness, our courage, our generosity, our fairness." Lane was suggesting that American identity, to borrow Papacharissi's description of affective attunement, was something that immigrants had to "feel their way into."[10]

Considering these conditions, the slogan of selling America to Americans could carry considerable symbolic weight: its metaphor of selling gestured to how emotive appeals were thought to be powerfully efficient at influencing the attitudes and behaviors of mass media audiences, and its invocations of the nation and its people captured the tensions between a xenophobic Anglo-American establishment and its demand for immigrant labor. Lane's "mighty project of selling America to Americans" combined business-friendly notions of immigrants' cultural assimilation with a growing sense of mass media's capacities to deliver persuasively efficient appeals to emotion and sensation. Many of the anticommunist currents that developed during the Red Scare continued to find expression over the course of the 1920s. For supporters of the industrial status quo, the slogan of selling America would often be marshaled to impart a sunny tone to a promotional nationalism that imagined capitalism and patriotism to be cut from the same cloth.[11]

Place-Making and Antiradicalism: Selling America to Americans in the 1920s

Into the 1920s, the motto of "selling America to Americans" was used by the press, businesses, and activist groups in the context of projects that used patriotic or nationalist imagery to advance the nation's commercial interests and define its national culture as antiradical—strategies that would come to find fuller expression in sponsored economic education media. First, the catchphrase of selling America surfaced in coverage of multimedia citizenship projects that aimed to influence public attitudes and behaviors by stirring audiences' patriotic feelings toward antiradicalism, as demonstrated by Lane's "mighty project." Like Scott's scientific advertising, such media-rich Americanism programs aimed to influence public attitudes by engaging the senses and emotions. Second, the slogan was also used in place-promoting efforts that attempted to tie commercially developing regions of the Midwest and West to centers of commerce in the eastern United States, responding to ongoing questions about national identity. There was some overlap between these two elements of the catchphrase's use, and they enacted a consistent set of concerns: talk about the selling of America functioned as a way of constructing the United States as a unified nation that stood apart from Europe and of invoking an ineffable sense of spirit.

Marketers invoked the slogan of selling America to Americans to justify and contextualize economic regional and international competition between the developed east and developing west of the nation, and between the US and Europe. These place-based invocations of selling America followed a tradition of place promotion in which the promoters of locations in the US Midwest and West competed for "potential settlers and investors," as planning historian Stephen V. Ward notes. Business-friendly organizations oriented toward tourism and commercial development—especially in relation to western US states and cities—used the idea of selling America to position developing cities and regions in the Midwest and West as commercially promising. These rhetorics of place promotion benefited from implicit racial exclusion and nationalism. Further, the business orientation of place promotion implicitly rejected any politics critical of enterprise, and some place promoters expressed anti-immigration sentiments.[12]

For example, a rash of publicity for the National Association of Real Estate Boards' annual meeting in 1921 highlighted a keynote speech titled "Selling America to Americans" by Frank Branch Riley, an Oregonian realtor whose lectures focused on travel and promoted the landscapes of the American West—with a dose of politics. Riley's speech to the National Association of Real Estate Boards (an organization that then actively supported exclusionary policies that created barriers to homeownership for people of color, as urban historian Paige Glotzer documents) included calls for a slow pace of immigration until, as a reporter for the trade journal *Commerce and Finance* put it, the "aliens now in the Melting Pot" could be Americanized. Riley's speaking engagements reflected commercial aspirations for Oregon's postwar economy, touting the state's capacities for domestic trade and its ocean linkages to trading partners in Canada and Asia. Similarly, in 1923, the *San Francisco Examiner* reported on the founding of an American Travel Bureau by the American Hotel Association, with strong support from California hoteliers. The new bureau, the *Examiner* reported, was expected to "develop the 'See America First' spirit by 'selling' America to Americans"—which, in this case, meant urging travelers from eastern cities to choose travel in the western United States instead of travel overseas in Europe, as well as promoting travel to North America from other parts of the globe. The motto of selling America rhetorically connected the western regions of the United States to the commercial activity and tourism dollars concentrated in the eastern part of the country.[13]

The language of selling the western United States in domestic markets developed in the 1920s alongside the promotion of a rapidly popularizing consumer technology: the automobile. Newspaper advertisements featured sales pitches for automobiles that drew upon the imagery of the western United States, celebrating the beauty of its landscapes. Cars could be used to travel on to areas unreachable by train. To this end, in mid-May of 1924 Congress passed an unprecedented $7.5 million in federal funding to build roads within national parks—otherwise protected lands that the *Austin Statesman* characterized as "great examples of the true America." The president of the American Automobile Association praised the bill's passage, commenting that congressional support for the bill highlighted the work of automobile clubs "at this time when the automobile is becoming more and more important as an agency in selling America to Americans." By 1927, leaders in the US travel and tourism industries were urging Congress to apportion millions of dollars to publicizing US national parks and forests domestically in the name of selling America.[14]

In the context of place promotion, the rhetoric of selling America alluded to the construction of a American identity that was separate from Europe, yet still sometimes carried intimations of whiteness. For example, a 1927 story in the *Los Angeles Times* covered a meeting of the American Travel Development Association, whose secretary C. F. Hatfield lamented the finding that Americans spent more money on travel to Europe than on travel within the United States. Hatfield explained that his organization had "adopted the slogan of selling America to Americans," expressing hopes that the US's "natural scenic marvels and community wonders" could be as captivating to tourists as the "ancient ruins and statues" of Europe. Just as Lane's vision of Americanism had characterized the ideological influence of European immigrant workers as an outside pressure, place promotion constructed Europe as a foreign other that Americans could avoid by vacationing domestically. Further, the rhetoric of selling was associated with the ineffable and felt experience, through rhetoric that portrayed the West as a site of scenic beauty. As late as 1930, the travel industry continued to use selling America as a catchphrase for promoting travel in the US to both domestic and overseas audiences, whom they urged to "see America first." Such phrasing would have struck a familiar chord for Americans who had seen the phrase "America first" used to denote isolationism, nativism, and white supremacy; historian Sarah Churchwell observes that the many associations articulated to this parallel catchphrase of "America first" were difficult to disentangle in ways that potentially benefited at least some of the people who used them by "creat[ing] plausible deniability": as she writes, such coded language could "muddy the waters, to keep people from seeing their own faces in the pool."[15]

By the late 1920s, selling America to Americans was taken up in more explicitly exclusionary rhetorics of mass-mediated nationalism that expressed what I am calling an affirmative style. Take, for example, the American Hour Broadcasting Committee, a coalition of veterans' groups, anti-immigration groups, and antiradical organizations whose membership ranks combined nationalism with a burgeoning big-business constituency. Starting in January of 1928, the American Hour Broadcasting Committee announced a fifteen-minute radio address series that was to run weekly for nearly nine months on major radio stations. The American Hour Broadcasting Committee's organizer, Fred R. Marvin, was a former journalist and newspaper editor who claimed that would-be immigrants were socialists and communists who could provoke another war. In relation to the launch of the radio series, Marvin declared that it was "about time some one [sic] took an advanced step to 'Sell America to Americans'" because an influx of "foreign lecturers and propagandists" had influenced public opinion and profited from criticizing the United States. Marvin further framed the committee's founding as a revival of patriotism and a commitment to promoting the committee's understanding of "our form of government, our institutions, ideals, traditions, and culture." Marvin's rhetoric expressed a movement toward an affirmative style by arguing for the need to *celebrate* a patriotic vision of the country, which Marvin suggested would offset the supposed threat posed by criticisms of the nation.[16]

Newspaper coverage of the American Hour broadcasts indicated an ideological portfolio that included antiradicalism, militarism, and scapegoating. In the thirty-seven cities reached by the program, individuals affiliated with Marvin's organization, Key Men of America, served as local chairpersons, identifying "prominent" local figures to read weekly addresses organized around the theme of selling America. For example, a speech in favor of funding military technologies, written by the secretary of the navy, was read by Lieutenant-Colonel Leroy F. Smith on KFWB, a leading Los Angeles radio station affiliated with the Warner Brothers motion picture studio. Smith was identified as a member of the Better America Federation, a business conservative organization that used rhetorics of antiradicalism to advance its antilabor and antiregulation policy positions. Later that same month, the station hosted Mary Logan Tucker, an antiradical activist and president of Dames of the Loyal Legion. Tucker reportedly read a resolution over the KFWB airwaves that demanded the investigation of schools and advocated for laws that compelled teachers to take a loyalty oath to the nation. The American Hour Broadcasting Committee's offerings were poorly received by some, including a columnist for the *Cincinnati Enquirer* who criticized the militaristic tone of an April 1928 broadcast as "Flag waving—Fourth of July stuff—pure propaganda. Bunk." Nonetheless, Marvin's framing of the American Hour Broadcasting Committee as selling America to Americans showed how the slogan could be deployed to promote anti-immigrant and antiradical sentiments as quintessentially American, and to associate them with a militaristic nationalism that demanded displays of loyalty.[17]

Projects like the American Hour Broadcasting Committee's radio programs built on the associations of meaning that Lane and his collaborators in the film industry had promoted, in which the catchphrase of selling America was articulated to patriotic mass media projects that framed nationalist and antiradical messages as patriotic and civically responsible. The two senses of selling America that developed in the 1920s—knitting together disparate regions and holding them in contrast to Europe and promoting an ideological vision that excluded leftism from public life— would find new context in the Great Depression, during which the catchphrase would link national identity more directly to the celebration of capitalism and the power of private enterprise.

The Politics of Morale

The New Deal created new context for the idea of selling America. As this section details, some Depression-era speakers drew upon antiradical meanings of selling America to express resistance to social welfare policies and anxiety about industrial nationalization, while others foregrounded the optimism of selling to promise that better national morale would be good for business. These uses of selling America drew together ideas, logics, and styles that would find expression in sponsored economic education media. The economic prosperity and unprecedented stock market participation of the 1920s ended with the market crash of 1929, setting in motion an economic depression that dominated the 1930s. Meanwhile, a grassroots consumer activist movement, driven both by notions of individual rights and a vision of the collective good, pressed for better safety standards and more reliable product information from manufacturers and retailers. President Franklin D. Roosevelt took office in 1933, enacting New Deal policy interventions designed to salvage and stabilize the economy. These interventions, in turn, prompted the strengthening of oppositional narratives among the owners and managers of major manufacturing concerns, who framed their own resistance to New Deal policies as the defense of national ideals. Under these conditions, antiradical activists, corporate public relations departments, and media personalities alike adapted the catchphrase of selling America to Americans both to express opposition to the New Deal and to argue that businesses could end the Depression by instilling hope.[18]

These commerce-oriented sentiments reflected a growing trend: historians of capitalism have chronicled how, by the mid-1930s, the rhetorics that are now-familiar elements of free enterprise ideology were beginning to crystallize. As Glickman notes, business advocates had started to use "free enterprise" as "a synonym for the business community" in the mid-1920s, and this terminology became more popular as business interests organized in opposition to the New Deal. Further, historian Wendy Wall observes that conflicts emerged in the 1930s over what values would define the nation: a vision of labor power and "activist government" that sat to the left of the New Deal, on one hand, or a vision of individual rights that conservatives and advocates for business interests framed in terms of freedom and liberty, on the other. Accordingly, this was the time period in which business firms and business interest groups such as the National Association of Manufacturers (NAM) mounted sweeping multimedia campaigns to promote business ideologies about private enterprise—as chapter 3 explores. Examining rhetorics of selling America during this time highlights how the slogan of selling America took on new affirmative dimensions. Antiradical and morale-boosting calls to sell America to Americans in the 1930s articulated American identity to the conviction that private enterprise—with minimal concessions of power to the state or labor—was a consensus-based, democratic organizing principle for US society that would render labor resistance and, for that matter, all forms of socialism and radicalism, unnecessary. In other words, selling America became a frame for denying critiques of US capitalism's exploitative attributes and excluding such analyses from the public discourse.[19]

In response to the New Deal and other plans for social reform, conservative public figures used the slogan of selling America to Americans to express outright antiradical sentiments and, subsequently, to signal anticommunism obliquely through a rhetorical strategy of focusing on the perceived virtues of American private enterprise. This shift can be observed in the ways the motto of selling America was used from the mid-1930s to the late 1930s. The use of the motto to signal explicit anticommunism was exemplified by the rhetoric of the Crusaders, a group initially founded to oppose Prohibition, but whose attention had turned after the repeal of the Eighteenth Amendment in 1933 to opposing the New Deal—with financial backing from members of the Du Pont family and executives from high-profile corporations including Sun Oil and General Motors. The California chapter of the Crusaders, helmed by Hollywood director W. S. Van Dyke, led a high-profile campaign against the gubernatorial candidacy of leftist candidate Upton Sinclair: in an echo of prior antiradical rhetorics, the California Crusaders had positioned themselves as watchdogs of the New Deal, ready to resist moves "toward Fascism, Communism or Socialism" and "pledged to fight for the advancement of Americanism." This positioning could be seen in newspaper advertisements that exhorted candidates to heed a broadcasted "warning" about the Crusaders' purported intentions to hold lawmakers accountable for their campaign promises; meanwhile, campaign cartoon advertisements portrayed "Sinclairism" as a communist threat. Speaking in 1934 after Sinclair's electoral defeat, Van Dyke declared to reporters that the Crusaders had ten thousand members in California and would "sell America to Americans and California to Californians" through a political agenda that included holding elected officials accountable for campaign promises and what Van Dyke called "a systematic barrage of civic enlightenment" focused on educators and public officials. Van Dyke's claims that his organization was selling America suggested that, for the Crusaders, vocal anticommunism was an intrinsic part of American identity.[20]

The xenophobia and anticommunism of the Crusaders' politics reiterated prior decades' antiradicalism in clear terms. By summer of 1935, the California Crusaders was describing itself grandly as an enemy of "demagogues, mountebanks and malcontents, alien and un-American groups," further dedicated to resisting governmental regulation of business practices. Further, it argued for common interests among business, industry, and farmers, arguing that failure to act together against "left wing forces" would lead inevitably to "the socialization of business and industry from the top to the bottom." National Crusaders founder Fred G. Clark would go on in 1939 to found the American Economic Foundation, a business conservative economic education organization; in an illustration of how the rhetoric of selling America functioned as a throughline for the economic education organizations that would flourish in the 1940s and beyond, Clark would declare in later years that "economic morality can be sold as surely as soap chips and television sets."[21]

The Crusaders' use of selling America to denote antiradical politics obscured the phrase's lingering ties to place promotion. However, the place-promoting sense of selling America resurfaced in reference to another major public project: the 1939 Golden Gate International Exposition (also known as the World's Fair). In the nineteenth and twentieth centuries, World's Fairs offered corporations, industries, and nations opportunities to symbolically and discursively construct their public images, and in the process to respond to concerns about the social implications of technological and commercial development with spectacular displays of progress and public order. George Creel—who had risen to prominence for his work as the US propaganda chief at the Committee on Public Information during the First World War and had served as National Recovery Administration chief for California before resigning to oppose Upton Sinclair in the primary for the 1934 California gubernatorial race—served as the federal commissioner of the exhibition. In 1937, Creel published an essay for the *Pacific Coast Review* titled "Selling America to Americans." In it, he described US federal government funding for the development of the Treasure Island fairgrounds and plans to celebrate westward expansion in terms that emphasized Creel's nation-making goals and his aspirations to spectacle. Just as promoters of the US West in the 1920s had proclaimed that the scenic beauty of the West could rival the antiquities of Europe as a tourist attraction, Creel touted "great murals celebrating the history of the West" that were to be "the work of American artists, who have developed a technique and standing in the last few years which competes with that of the best European muralists." Creel's rhetoric echoed the place promoters, too, in its understanding of federal funding as a crucial support to the project of selling the nation.[22]

Creel's sense of selling America was also oriented toward the imagination. It rejected models of persuasion based on calculative assessment of maps, charts, and statistics, favoring instead a spectacular presentation that would capture the imaginations of fairgoers. Creel framed the entire project in terms of entertainment, characterizing "Uncle Sam" as recently having taken up the role of "one of the world's most adroit showmen." Here, indigenous people were taken as sources of entertainment value: federally funded exhibits would use "dramatic and instructive interpretation" to promote narratives about the West with displays of traditional indigenous games and ceremonies that would bring "color, beauty, and dramatic interest, as well as a tremendous social significance" to the fair. This focus on spectacle would characterize the US government's own exhibit as well, which Creel promised would be "the last word in color and drama. No graphs and no statistics. No matter how important the work of a department may be, if it can't be told dramatically and entertainingly, then it's out." This approach echoed Scott's 1910s framing of emotionally evocative advertising as scientifically efficient. Creel's use of the slogan of selling America to Americans demonstrated two points: first, that the motto was not yet entirely identified with the ideology of free enterprise; and second, that even when selling America to Americans wasn't explicitly linked to an imagined American heritage of individualism and enterprise, it still brought with it accreted meanings that braided together nationalism and racial hierarchy with appeals to the senses and emotions.[23]

By 1938, expressions of promotional nationalism seemed to have taken up something akin to an affirmative style. Both national advertisers and high-profile columnists made use of the motto of selling America to Americans to suggest that the best way to promote American capitalism was not only to focus on the benefits of American capitalism, but to exclude discussion of the system's shortcomings altogether. For example, in response to the ongoing Depression, Anheuser-Busch Brewing Company launched a morale-boosting institutional advertising campaign on behalf of its Budweiser beer brand in October of 1938, with brewery president and scion Adolphus Busch III proclaiming that Americans were suffering from "a feeling of lack of security" that led them to be anxious about the future of the country. Business's role, Busch insisted, was "to sell a calm assurance of the future of America and its generous offer of rewards to each and every American who has confidence in himself; to sell confidence in the foundation laid down by our pioneer forefathers; to realize that we have comforts and conveniences beyond the reach of peoples in other nations; to sell America to Americans." As had been the case with Franklin Lane's Americanization campaigns, Busch used the catchphrase of selling America to construct an American identity that had to be experienced at the level of feelings, brought about by stirring patriotic imagery.[24]

In order to "sell America to Americans," the Anheuser-Busch campaign celebrated inspirational moments in US history and derided the doomsaying "prophets" of the past (see, for example, figure 2.3), promising "ample rewards to Americans with faith in themselves." The campaign also included a film, *Reflecting Our Confidence in the Future of America*, of

FIGURE 2.3. A morale-boosting advertisement expressing Anheuser-Busch president Adolphus Busch III's ambitions to build up ordinary peoples' faith in the future of the nation. "Doomsday was a fizzle" Budweiser advertisement, *Morning Examiner* (Bartlesville, OK), October 12, 1938, 3; accessed June 28, 2023, from https://www.newspapers.com/image/715802032/.

which more than two hundred prints were made for no-cost public showings that, the brewery claimed, attracted "millions of viewers" as well as "letters of praise and gratitude from industrialists, bankers, business men and public officials" (figure 2.4). Busch suggested that patriotic sentiment would lead to business profits: patriotic spirit could spur consumer spending, allowing an economic recovery in which businesses could find "find a normal and enduring market for our products." Busch's claims envisioned a future in which extensive state management of the economy would be unnecessary: one in which optimistic faith in the power of American individualism would boost faltering product sales, and by extension, set the manufacturing industries back on track to stable profits. Such a narrative would not have been totally unfamiliar to advocates of private enterprise: as historian of religion Dawn L. Hutchinson points out, the New Thought spiritual tradition, which prioritized the power of positive thinking, influenced business motivational literature in the early to mid-twentieth century through sentiments that "one needed to think one's way to wealth through the power of the mind."[25]

Newspaper columnists, too, adopted the slogan of selling America to Americans in the late 1930s to suggest that praise of private enterprise would assure the nation's success. Syndicated columnists were influential presences in 1930s newspapers, winning high circulation numbers as readers relied on them to "explain the truth behind the facts," as journalism

FIGURE 2.4. "Help Sell America to Americans" advertisement promoting a film sponsored by Anheuser-Busch. "Help Sell America to Americans" Anheuser-Busch advertisement, *Minneapolis Star*, December 16, 1939, 34; accessed June 28, 2023, from https://www.newspapers.com/image/179010845/.

historian Philip M. Glende explains. Consider the example of Boake Carter, a newspaper columnist and radio personality whose commentary aired five nights a week on eighty-five CBS radio stations across the country between 1933 and 1938. Media historian David Culbert documents how Carter won the highest ratings of any commentator on the air in 1936, but his sustained attacks on organized labor led to boycotts, sponsorship withdrawals, and finally the cancellation of his radio program. In the winter following his removal from the airwaves, Carter published multiple columns touting the slogan of selling America, exhorting readers to play up the positive aspects of US managerial capitalism—which Carter (and many others) referred to as the American system—instead of focusing on criticizing other ideologies.[26]

In one 1938 column, Carter lamented that "the emotionalists and ideologists go around telling us what terrorists and barbarians are the Nazis and the Fascists and the Communists—all of which are self-evident claims. But mighty few people go around selling America to American citizens" (later in the same column, Carter praised British diplomats for pursuing trade deals with Germany and Italy, declaring that he favored British "self-preservationism" to American boycotts and diplomatic objections, which, Carter declared, "draw closer to involvement in war, not on practical issues, but on ideological emotions"). Carter expanded his calls to sell America in a subsequent column, claiming that "continually howling about . . . alien isms" was effectively "handing a million dollars' worth of advertising to all the isms we do not want in this country," yet "no where [*sic*] can one find a good, bang-up sales talk on the merits of the system of popular government" that bestowed freedom and abundance through "competition and free enterprise." Carter's comments represented a shift from the sentiments of the California Crusaders. Both used the language of sales and a vaguely defined notion of Americanism to claim opposition to communism, fascism, and Nazism, but the California Crusaders' Van Dyke had imagined that anticommunism itself was a de facto endorsement of US capitalism; by contrast, Carter's commentary drew on the image of the salesman to demand positive talk about capitalism—and *only* positive talk about capitalism, which he characterized as practical, realistic, and commonsense.[27]

Carter's words, then, expressed fully an affirmative style in which celebration of private enterprise ideology was paired with marking other ideologies as off-limits for discussion. His columns promoted a regime of speech and silence in which celebrating free enterprise was coterminous

SELLING AMERICA TO AMERICANS 49

with refusing to acknowledge other ideologies, even to criticize them. Inger Stole observes that around this time, the US Chamber of Commerce positioned itself as opposed to both communism and fascism but was "far more worried" about communism. Carter's affirmative rhetoric would have been convenient for US business interests taking such a position: it allowed for promotion of capitalism while eliding potentially embarrassing discussions of how supporters of private enterprise may have been more tolerant of some political ideologies than they were of others.[28]

Another syndicated columnist of the late 1930s adopted the motto of selling America to celebrate a fundamentally affective sense of individualism. A November 1939 installment of the poet and author Benjamin De Casseres's syndicated column *The March of Events* prescribed selling America as the "job to be done by real Americans" to fight what he saw as a foreign threat from within. The column opened with a declaration: "I am an advertiser—I am a salesman. I advertise America." Taking up the rivalry with Europe that inflected prior place-promoting uses of the motto and combining it with the ideological anxieties of antiradicalism, De Casseres declared that "millions of Americans don't know it, but they are alien-minded. They vote, sometimes wave a flag in a parade, but they are, many of them, Communists, Fascists, and Nazis because they have never felt America." Most people in the United States, De Casseres argued, were "dead Americans . . . machine Americans, collectivist Americans, robotized Americans—that must be stung back to life" by a "flag-waver" who could "advertise and sell America." For De Casseres, the job of selling America had to be accomplished in the realm of feeling.[29]

De Casseres drew a line between what he took to be genuine Americans—who felt and experienced individual liberty—and those Americans who could go through the motions of citizenship without truly *feeling* in ways that would allow them to come to an interior realization about the United States' exceptionalism. From a perspective that recognizes systemic racism, sexism, income inequality, and other persistent inequalities in twentieth-century US society, De Casseres's column reads as a tragic near miss of understanding; De Casseres seemed to come close to discerning that, for many, the nation's promise of civil liberties had been unfulfilled. Yet De Casseres seemed unconcerned as to what forces might have prevented so many Americans from affectively experiencing a profound freedom that was supposedly already theirs. At the time of De Casseres's writing, people to whom the full rights of citizenship were systematically denied—including on the basis of race and gender, for example—could seemingly only be expected to somehow learn to *feel* free on the basis of the *promise* of civil liberties rather than their actualization, and all else could be dismissed as foreign subversion or undermining from within. De Casseres's essay refused to take seriously any other ideological or political positions, treating them as conditions that could not be discussed, but had to be shock-treated through displays of patriotic promotional fervor. In this sense, De Casseres's formulation of advertising as a political strategy harkened back to Walter Dill Scott's insistence, in the face of copywriters' reasons-why advertising, that systematic influence would be most efficiently accomplished by including appeals to the senses and the emotions.

Antiradicalism, National Identity, and Felt Experience

Tracing the arc of selling America to Americans underscores how the phrase was interlinked with the interests of capital from the start—and not simply as a rhetorical flourish justifying the use of promotional techniques. Managerial capitalism's transformations of social life in the United States included both an assumption that efficient selling would involve appeals to the senses and emotions and a burgeoning anxiety about immigrant workers' power to shift the culture and politics of the nation. These notions would inform how selling America developed as a catchphrase in the 1920s. An important articulation of meaning came from notions of Americanism, whose antiradical politics filtered prior Americanization efforts through the paranoid lens of the Red Scare. Further, the use of the catchphrase in place promotion showed how the idea of selling America functioned as a flexible form of nation building, sometimes tinged with anxieties about ethnic, racial, and political others.

By the close of the 1930s, the slogan of selling America tangled together prior strands of rhetoric about antiradicalism, national identity, and felt experience. Talk of selling America to Americans suggested that people and places were crucial to the process of nation-making, whether through assimilating new immigrants into middle-class Anglo-American practices, attitudes, and behaviors; through interlinking developing cities and regions of the Midwest and West with the developed commercial and transportation networks of the East; or through appropriating the histories and cultures of indigenous nations to create a sense of an ancient, mythical past. Talk of selling America also drew from ideas about the scientific efficiency of managerial communication techniques, particularly to the extent that it imagined facts and emotions less as opposing forces than complementary forces that, together, could exert considerable persuasive force. And finally, the motto of selling America was useful to those whose goals were bluntly ideological: it drew upon an imagined, managerially compatible version of US traditions to conjure an ideological counterforce to popular support for radicalism, labor organizing, and reform.

To be sure, selling America to Americans would have been a metaphor that came easily to the advertising sales executives who were often involved in economic education campaigns. However, this chapter has shown that it was much more than only that. Selling America to Americans was a fundamental assertion of how the representatives of capital could address public opinion. Under the banner of selling America, allies of the US business establishment developed an affirmative style of promotional nationalism that functioned as a rationale for excluding oppositional positions, especially the positions of labor radicals and American leftists, from the sphere of legitimate politics. The motto of selling America incorporated managerial notions that public opinion could be efficiently managed through appeals to ideas, senses, and feelings — and, in doing so, claimed to represent tradition while policing the boundaries of democratic deliberation.

CHAPTER THREE

Expertise and Affirmation

The meanings of selling America developed across many different communities of practice including politics, journalism, and promotions, from the early interwar years through the late 1930s. In the late 1930s and beyond, those in the promotional industries of advertising, marketing, and related fields were among those to make deliberate use of the promotional nationalism that "selling America" had come to signify. People in leadership positions in the industries of advertising, publishing, and manufacturing took up the rhetoric of selling America that had developed into the 1930s, elaborating upon its assumptions and intimations. In doing so, they attempted to justify and elevate their opposition to what they saw as restrictive policies, burnish the reputations of the promotional industries, and frame their own interests as coterminous with the national interest. These trade organizations and business advocacy groups developed a narrative of promotional nationalism, delivered in a distinctively affirmative style.

This chapter argues that members of the promotional industries—taken here to include advertising, marketing, and its allies in manufacturing and publishing—took up rhetorical strategies that originated in opposition to the New Deal, developed them in harmony with what I am calling the affirmative style of promotional nationalism, and used them to win influence over the apparatuses of public service messaging during the Second World War. First, the chapter considers how the National Association of Manufacturers' 1930s publicity campaigns crystallized what would come to be tropes of economic education media, including claims that private enterprise was inseparable from political freedom and claims about the legitimacy of such campaigns that rested on the expertise of media professionals. The National Association of Manufacturers (NAM) advanced claims about selling and expertise that linked the imperatives of businesses to ideals of patriotism and public service. In the process, the NAM's approach centered mass media expertise as a crucial force for fostering what they called public understanding of private enterprise (by which they meant public consent to, and appreciation of, industry pursuing its own interests).

Next, the chapter examines how, in the wake of the NAM's pervasive multimedia publicity campaigns, leaders of advertising trade associations elaborated upon the NAM's rhetorics to imagine advertising as the protector of American freedoms. The American Association of Advertising Agencies (AAAA) and the Association of National Advertisers (ANA) facilitated public messaging campaigns premised on similar promises to increase understanding and similar claims to expertise in communicating with the public. These representatives of the advertising industry, because of their skill at publicity and their managerial folk understandings of economics, would come to deem themselves experts in economic education. Then, the chapter examines tensions over the best approach to public messaging during the Second World War—a conflict in which the AAAA and the ANA, through the vehicle of the Advertising Council, claimed jurisdiction over public service messaging for the advertising industry (*jurisdiction* referring here to the prestige and power of a profession that is expressed, in part, by its ability to claim control over an area of work—as theorized by sociologist Andrew Abbott). Ultimately, the chapter shows how advertising industry leaders built the infrastructures and practices necessary for the promotional industries to control much of public service messaging in the postwar years.[1]

This chapter examines how the interwar and wartime public relations projects of the NAM, the AAAA and ANA, and the Advertising Council expressed what I am calling the affirmative style of promotional nationalism—both rhetorically and institutionally. The chapter draws upon, and contributes to, an existing body of scholarship documenting the history of these organizations' attempts to influence public opinion. For example, business historians and media theorists such as Alex Carey and Richard Tedlow examine the NAM's activity during the New Deal period, concluding that the NAM's use of public relations improved the standing of the field and led to other organizations' uptake of its methods. Historian Wendy L. Wall situates the NAM's anti–New Deal campaigns as part of an ideological struggle to define the American Way. Business historian Jennifer Delton traces the NAM's influence through the twentieth century, contrasting the NAM's conservative public messaging with the moderate policy positions taken within the NAM on topics like on international trade.[2]

Similarly, many historians have examined the role of the advertising industry and the Advertising Council in midcentury American political and cultural life. Frank W. Fox surveys the US advertising industry's influence on popular understandings of the Second World War. Elizabeth Fones-Wolf chronicles how both the NAM and the Advertising Council used public relations campaigns to undermine powerful labor unions in the postwar period. Robert Griffith documents the Advertising Council's first twenty-eight years, arguing that the council took business-moderate positions that helped to construct a vision of the US as a dynamic and egalitarian society. Crucially, communication historian Inger Stole's in-depth examinations of the AAAA and the ANA prior to the Second World War and the Advertising Council during and after the war illustrate how the advertising industry secured its prominent place in US society through a wide-ranging series of economic, political, and cultural strategies.[3]

This chapter argues that the AAAA, ANA, and Advertising Council adapted and developed an affirmative style of promotional nationalism while mobilizing notions of expertise and public service to advance their own interests in ways that would become emblematic of postwar sponsored economic education media. I make three main points about how claims of expertise and public service informed the NAM's and the Advertising Council's strategic use of promotional nationalism during the 1930s and World War II. First, the NAM's sweeping public relations program in the 1930s was characterized not only by narratives about the inseparability of private enterprise and freedom, but also by a rhetoric of media production expertise and a growing managerial fascination with the persuasive power of mass media. These NAM public relations strategies would be taken up by advertising industry trade groups such as the AAAA and the ANA. Second, I argue that advertising industry leaders' claims to expertise were supported by a body of managerial folk knowledge, in which advertising industry leaders extrapolated from their firsthand workplace experiences to assumptions about the economy and society. This managerial folk knowledge informed how business advocates came to imagine that their own visions of how business should sit in society exemplified what they called the US economic system. Third, I add to the findings of scholars such as Stole and Frank Fox, who both document the Advertising Council's consolidation of power and legitimacy during the Second World War, by arguing that these forms of folk knowledge and claims to expertise helped leaders in the advertising industry to claim professional jurisdiction over public service messaging in the US.

Overall, the chapter contributes to scholarly literature on the establishment of the Advertising Council by showing how advertising executives imagined themselves having uncommon expertise in, and a unique ability to promote, political and economic freedoms. This set of expertise claims metonymically reworked the NAM's late 1930s claims about the effectiveness of its expert-produced publicity campaigns. I am influenced here by Stuart Hall, who comments that discourses are subject to processes of articulation within different "chain[s] of connotation" in which ideologically adjacent parties can repurpose language by "sliding . . . meaning along a chain of connotative signifiers." I see this sliding of meaning in how the Advertising Council adopted and reworked earlier notions of expertise and American freedom. In addition, I contend that during and after the war, the Advertising Council's involvement in public service messaging helped establish the public service advertisement as a distinctive form of public communication that tended to reflect hegemonic politics while claiming political neutrality. This observation situates the Advertising Council's wartime activities and subsequent transition to peacetime as part of a broader strategic managerial imagining of public service that would reverberate for decades to come.[4]

Experts All: The NAM and Mass Media in the New Deal Period

The political and industrial circumstances of the 1930s led corporations and trade groups to put more money and effort into public relations than they had in the past. The embrace of public relations was both practical and political. On a practical level, public relations represented an alternative means of advancing corporate interests. Corporations had used private security firms to spy on, infiltrate, disrupt, and intimidate labor organizers for decades, but these practices generated bad press and unwanted regulatory scrutiny. Cultivating positive public opinion promised to advance the interests of big business in ways that were less self-evidently objectionable than intimidating or attacking workers. At the level of policy, a series of high-profile financial scandals in the aftermath of the 1929 market crash, along with the economic wreckage of the Great Depression itself, had led business leaders and government leaders alike to question how society should be organized and administered, with many assuming that closer controls on business would be necessary to prevent future collapses. Roosevelt's legislative agenda included social welfare and public works programs, tighter regulation of business, and worker protections—all signaling an expanded role for the state in managing US society. Corporate leaders responded to the federal economic management implicit in New Deal policies with stances ranging from tentative cooperation to outright opposition. For its part, the Roosevelt administration established a Business Advisory and Planning Council in 1933 that included leadership from many of the nation's largest manufacturing companies; some moderate members of the business community—many of whom supported social security programs and some degree of economic planning—stayed on through the early years of World War II. Others, however, organized to oppose New Deal policies and the worldview instantiated by those policies.[5]

Advertising historian Roland Marchand has documented how, in the mid-1930s, advertising executives and trade associations alike embraced what he calls a "wondrously self-vindicating stance": that in their "single-minded" dedication to producing goods for the nation, companies had neglected to keep the public informed about the workings and motives of companies, the system, and business executives. This reasoning suggested that Roosevelt, a masterful user of mass media forms such as radio, had succeeded in selling the New Deal to ordinary people through popular media—and therefore, to fight back against the New Deal, businesses would need to use their skills at salesmanship to sell capitalism itself. Indeed, Marchand argues, years of experience in studying consumer attitudes had led business leaders to see the public as "emotional, irrational, and fickle"—which could explain how the public had been persuaded by Roosevelt, but also made space for the possibility that economic education media could change their minds.[6]

Many business advocates in the New Deal era used the patriotic trappings of promotional nationalism to oppose the new policies, with varying success. Consider, for example, the American Liberty League, a group of industrialists and executives that was established in 1934. It presented itself as a defender of property rights and the US Constitution, but was ultimately unsuccessful in capturing public support, with critics scorning its seeming attempts to defend the fortunes of the rich amid an economic depression. Other groups, notably the NAM, equated opposition to New Deal policies with patriotism more deftly: business historian Richard Tedlow traces what would come to be high-profile and groundbreaking NAM publicity campaigns to a 1933 memo calling to aggressively promote a business-friendly perspective: industry needed to "tell its story" through a "campaign of education." As Jennifer Delton notes, NAM had run such putatively educational campaigns to some degree since the turn of the century. The NAM had conducted wide-ranging public opinion and lobbying campaigns, prompting lawmakers to be wary of its influence on politics as far back as 1913. In the 1930s, however, new labor laws and public support for the New Deal prompted the NAM to mount an unprecedented effort that came to consume more than half of its yearly budget. To be sure, proponents of corporate power had good reasons to want to improve the public image of corporations after a spate of legislative efforts to protect workers culminated in the 1935 passage of the Wagner Act. The act, which protected workers' rights to unionize and strike, shifted the balance of power: after its passage, senate members investigated corporations' use of private detectives for union espionage, strikebreaking, and violent reprisals. The NAM itself was directly implicated in these practices, and in the use of public relations techniques to soften their perception in the public eye. The labor press at the time noted how industrial trade groups had distributed NAM-sponsored materials (such as leaflets and radio programs) and, further, consulted with the NAM's legal advisers in their efforts to disrupt labor organizing. Mass media was central to NAM's publicity strategies.[7]

In the latter half of the 1930s, the NAM's publicity specialists designed a sweeping campaign to influence public opinion. This program set many of the standards that would be elaborated by advertising industry leaders and carried forward into postwar economic education. NAM campaigns didn't claim to be impartial about the interests of business, as postwar economic education campaigns would do, but the NAM's strategies for touting the interdependence of capitalism and freedom would have staying power. Their promotional campaigns combined multimedia messaging with a rhetoric that attempted to counter suspicion of corporate power by linking private enterprise to broadly held civic ideals (a rhetorical strategy that Oreskes and Conway trace to the National Electric Light Association in the 1920s). As historian Wendy L. Wall observes, this rhetoric had the strategic advantage of framing the NAM and other allies of corporate interests as comporting with the consensus-seeking politics of the time, deflecting the accusations of self-interest that had hampered the property-rights rhetoric of the American Liberty League.[8]

The NAM was one of many industry-affiliated groups to claim, in the late 1930s, that there was a uniquely American way of life, and that its most important components—as Wall observes—were private enterprise and civil liberties (such as freedoms of speech and of the press). These claims echoed prior decades' rhetoric about selling as a form of patriotic persuasion, along with its underlying assumption that ordinary people in the US weren't truly American unless they supported private enterprise with both their minds and their hearts. The NAM's rhetoric positioned the organization as an intermediary that could help ordinary people become more American: it described itself as "interpreting industry and the American system to Americans," reflecting a slippage between knowledge-of and appreciation-for US manufacturers' business practices. Indeed, the goal of the NAM's publicity campaigning, the organization insisted, was to correct what it called "misunderstandings" by providing information. The NAM Committee on Public Relations described its work as "the industry's greatest public information program." Yet, some labor organizations were skeptical of such claims, with labor-aligned critics calling it a "high-powered nation-wide propaganda campaign against bona fide unionism."[9]

By 1939, the NAM's publicity efforts spanned a staggering range of mass media outputs. A collaboration with the advertising agency Campbell-Ewald and the Outdoor Advertising Association of America resulted in forty-five thousand billboards that celebrated NAM's vision of promotional nationalism with billboards proclaiming the unique advantages of "the American Way" (see, for example, photographer Dorothea Lange's iconic depiction of a NAM poster on the side of a hardware store, figure 3.1). NAM celebrated itself for creating "industry's first national advertising campaign" of newspaper advertisements for private enterprise, many of which bore the slogan "There's no way like the American Way." NAM's *You and Industry Library*, a series of pocket-sized booklets, celebrated industry's role in creating better standards of living. The NAM's press service sent news releases to a reported six thousand newspapers per week; over two thousand newspapers subscribed to syndicated NAM columns and cartoons. Similarly, NAM staff writers produced newsletters for middle management (under the title *Industrial Facts*) and prewritten features for plant publications. *American Family Robinson*, a NAM-sponsored afternoon radio soap opera designed to run twice weekly, failed to appeal to the major networks but was distributed in print syndication to be read over the air at 273 stations. The NAM filmstrip *Men and Machines* (a series of projected still images with a recorded soundtrack) debuted in

FIGURE 3.1. A 1937 billboard sponsored by the National Association of Manufacturers touting conditions for workers in the US as the "American Way." Digital image courtesy of the Library of Congress, https://www.loc.gov/item/2017769742/. Dorothea Lange, photographer, *Billboard on U.S. Highway 99 in California: National Advertising Campaign Sponsored by National Association of Manufacturers*. United States (California), 1937. Photograph.

1936 to a ballyhooed gathering of "industrial, scientific, and engineering experts" at the New York Museum of Science and Industry before being distributed for local public showings. A series of NAM-affiliated "screen editorial" motion picture films—including *Let's Go America! A Screen Editorial* (1936), *Frontiers of the Future* (1937), and *America Marching On!* (1937)—were shown in movie theaters to audiences that NAM estimated totaling fifteen million. NAM's telling of industry's "story," in short, was well funded and relentless.[10]

The NAM's campaigns used tactics that would come to be hallmarks of sponsored economic education, including the use of mass media undergirded by claims of expertise. NAM literature emphasized that its public information programs were driven by the expertise of media professionals: in a promotional booklet about the campaigns, *Experts All*, the NAM declared those involved with its publicity campaigns to be "experienced craftsmen in their fields" whose expertise spanned radio entertainment and commentary, advertising, copywriting and design, public speaking, cartooning, news reporting, and informational film; this emphasis on communicative expertise would carry through to later economic education efforts. The NAM's focus on expert production of multiple forms of mass media, and on the persuasive potential of sound and vision, recalled Walter Dill Scott's earlier precepts of scientific advertising, focusing on the capacity of film and other visual media to make an impression by engaging the senses.[11]

Others involved in business communication in the mid-1930s also adapted ideas from the field of psychology to support the growth of industrial media production. Take, for example, the analysis of "the business screen" put forth in 1936 by W. F. Kruse, an educational specialist for camera manufacturer Bell and Howell. Kruse commented that advertisers "were among the first to recognize how 'eye-minded' is the human race," arguing that "the advertising man is a keen student of psychology" who could exploit the attention-grabbing qualities of motion pictures. After all, Kruse reasoned, even infants would be drawn to light, color, and sound. By 1938, business films had their own trade journal, *Business Screen*. A two-page advertising spread in *Business Screen* from Modern Talking Picture Service, an industrial film production studio, exemplified discourses around the use of films for promotion (figure 3.2). The advertisement extolled film's power to tell what it called industry's "tried, tested and most successful sales story" through the medium's "changeless perfection of detail" and "the direct, positive personality of its delivery to the onlooking audience." In this sense, industrial films were an easy fit with prior ideas about selling America through media spectacle and optimistic sales patter.[12]

Packed with advertisements for projectors, screens, and industrial film production houses, *Business Screen* promoted managerial discourses about film's superior power to persuade and the possibilities of displaying commercial or advertising films as complements to full-length feature films in motion picture theaters. A letter from NAM director of public relations James Selvage in *Business Screen*'s first issue was candid about the purpose of NAM motion picture films: deviating from prior NAM claims that films were designed to correct misunderstandings or interpret the American business system, Selvage affirmed that the films were, in his words, "designed to recreate in the minds of the mass audience a respect for the American Industrial System with its rewards and opportunities." An editorial comment following Selvage's letter praised the NAM film *Frontiers*

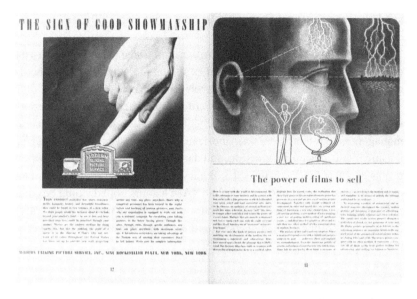

FIGURE 3.2. A 1938 advertisement for industrial film projection service company Modern Talking Picture Service, exemplifying discourses around the persuasive power of promotional film. Digital image courtesy of archive.org. Modern Talking Picture Service, "The Sign of Good Showmanship: Power of Films to Sell [advertisement]," *Business Screen* 1, no. 1 (January 1938): 12–13, https://archive.org/details/1938business1939screenmagv1rich/page/12/.

of the Future, declaring that such films did much to create sympathetic audiences.[13]

The use of motion pictures and other multimedia formats to promote managerial perspectives enacted a tension that often accompanied the production of public information campaigns: that the public was expected to be generally ignorant of expert knowledge and uninterested in dry or academic presentations of facts and figures, yet sponsored economic education media projects were premised on the idea that promotional mass media messages could change audiences' minds. This tension was present, meanwhile, in other contexts—recall, for example, George Creel's 1937 essay promoting the San Francisco International Exposition, in which Creel imagined the nation as a showman who would need to sell America through "dramatic and instructive interpretation." Engaging the sentiments and the senses through multimedia spectacle, in other words, was seen in the late 1930s as a promising way to bring together the nation, building national identity in alignment with patriotic and managerial ideals. Institutional resources could be used to interpret information, leavening data into nation-making.[14]

Examining the NAM's comprehensive promotional projects in the 1930s offers insights into the development of economic education as a media genre. The NAM articulated a public relations narrative based in national identity—one that imagined notions of political and personal freedom to be inseparably linked to private enterprise—to suggest that labor-management conflicts were un-American. It employed experts in advertising and media design, production, and distribution, presenting their expertise as proof of the campaigns' legitimacy. It made full use of the popular media forms of its time to create what NAM leaders hoped would be compelling and persuasive appeals to public opinion. These factors would carry forward into other campaigns designed to foster consent for managerial capitalism.

Managerial Folk Knowledge

The NAM was one of the best-known trade organizations to mobilize against New Deal policies, but it was far from the only one. Two trade associations linked to the advertising industry would play an especially consequential role in the shift from the anti–New Deal managerial politics of the 1930s to the economic education projects of the postwar period: the American Association of Advertising Agencies (AAAA), a trade group for advertising agencies, and the Association of National Advertisers (ANA), a counterpart organization that represented consumer goods manufacturing companies.

In the 1930s, leaders in advertising and its related industries needed to mend a poor public image: consumer activist groups had condemned advertising claims as sensationalistic, pseudoscientific, strategically vague, and generally misleading. Inger Stole documents how the advertising industry in the 1930s responded to increasing public consternation and the threat of federal regulation with a variety of public relations strategies including public-facing messaging gambits and deliberately weak self-regulation. As Stole observes, the wrangling over the acceptable limits of advertising would continue for most of the 1930s, leading to the passage of the Wheeler-Lea Act in 1938, which "extended the FTC's jurisdiction to protect consumers," in part by enabling FTC action against false claims, but incentivized advertisers to create copy and illustrations that misled by implication.[15]

EXPERTISE AND AFFIRMATION 63

Indeed, popular complaints about the industry were sufficiently widespread even after the passage of Wheeler-Lea that one member of the ANA compiled them into a list. These charges against advertising pointed to the breadth of public concerns about its potential ethical, practical, and economic harms. These complaints suggested that advertising unfairly exploited consumers' emotions and used brand names to distract from shoddy products; that advertising drove up the price of goods; and that advertising dollars gave advertisers "a stranglehold on the press" that risked undue influence over public opinion and threatened to keep competitors out of the field.[16]

In response to these perceived critiques, advertising agency executives and their clients in manufacturing came to see the nation's economic and political configurations as metonyms for their own industries' interests. This framing was similar to the NAM's earlier claim that private enterprise and civil liberties were mutually interdependent—but the logic by which advertising industry leaders made this metonymic leap was informed by their professional positioning. In early September 1941, members of the AAAA and the ANA—including representatives of major manufacturers such as Bristol-Myers and General Foods, along with delegates from leading advertising agencies—planned a larger gathering of the two organizations. The meeting would aim to address what they saw as the latest in a line of "attacks on advertising" that included possible new taxes and regulatory limitations on advertising and proposals to mandate grade labeling of consumer goods that would allow consumers to easily compare product quality across brands.[17]

Advertising industry leaders leaned heavily on ideas about advertising's civic importance that cast these possibilities as serious threats. For example, Congressman Bruce Barton (who had been one of the founders of leading advertising agency Batten, Barton, Durstine and Osborn [BBDO]) had reportedly declared in a 1940 speech that advertising was essential for the free and independent operation of both newspapers and radio, characterizing Federal Communications Commission (FCC) calls for investigation of advertising practices as a dangerous bureaucratic overreach. In 1941, ANA president Paul B. West wrote a memo along similar themes. He warned that the danger to the industry came not from "extremists" but from "those moderate elements among those in charge of the nation's economic machinery and in Congress, simply do not understand . . . what advertising is and how it functions." He urged that the possibility of new limitations and regulations not only threatened the commercial interests of national advertisers and advertising agencies, but it also posed a threat to "the national media whose very freedom depends on a large and continuous flow of national advertising revenue." Barton's and West's arguments suggested that advertising was the keystone of US political liberties. By this line of reasoning, without a system of consumer goods that competed on the basis of brand names, advertising in newspapers, magazines, and radio would be less abundant; and without the revenues from advertisers, a free press would be unable to fund itself, raising the specters of state-funded media and political censorship. A draft prospectus West prepared for the proposed meeting put the situation in grave terms, claiming that if a proposed consumer goods grading system succeeded, it could replace the branding system for differentiating goods—at which point, the prospectus warned, "advertising and the whole distributive system as we now know it virtually disappears."[18]

This line of reasoning expressed what economic sociologist Richard Swedberg calls folk economics: "how everyday people think about the economy and how it works; and what consequences this has for the economy as well as society at large." Swedberg categorizes this economic folk knowledge as a form of *doxa*: everyday, commonsense knowledge. Where expert knowledge results from standardized procedures of observation and analysis, doxa is based on practical experience—and includes normative commitments and sentiments. Swedberg posits that there are two kinds of economic doxa. Primary economic doxa is "direct" or "personal" economic sensemaking: "the kind of thick everyday knowledge of economic affairs that is based on experiencing things yourself, in the household or at work." Secondary economic doxa, by contrast, is indirect knowledge "that is often based on imagined knowledge or knowledge that comes from others": in Swedberg's words, "what people think of Wall Street, financial meltdowns, and economic institutions such as big banks and corporations" are examples of secondary doxa.[19]

The concept of economic doxa, Swedberg argues, facilitates the analysis of everyday, nonexpert ideas about economics as "units of meaning" and categories into which those units of meaning can fall. Swedberg's discussion of doxa in the abstract centers "ordinary people," a term that often alludes to nonelites and people in relatively disempowered positions. However, Swedberg's analysis focuses on the economic doxa of US president Donald Trump, making clear that the "ordinary" nonexperts whose knowledge is categorized as doxa can be people of considerable wealth and/or power. In other words, the important distinction here is between

EXPERTISE AND AFFIRMATION

those who are trained in the specialized field of economics, and those who are not: even the rich and powerful can be categorized as ordinary or everyday to the extent that they are nonexperts.[20]

The corporate executives and industry leaders of the AAAA and ANA occupied a paradoxical position with regard to economic expertise: they were not trained in the discipline of economics, yet their rhetoric about their relationship to people outside their doxic community closely mirrored the rhetoric of insiders and outsiders that Swedberg has observed among experts in the field of economics. Swedberg notes that trained economists have developed a "well-established empirical tradition" of using survey research "to establish peoples' knowledge of the economy, compared to that of economists," noting that this research (carried out, naturally, by experts), tends to find that nonexperts are "deeply ignorant about the economy." In this sense, studies of those outside the expert group serve to inscribe boundaries between an ingroup, which has specialized knowledge, and an outgroup, which lacks it. Similarly, the proponents of sponsored economic education within the advertising industry premised their messaging strategies on market research and pollster studies that interpreted survey data to conclude that the US populace was uninformed about the US economic system. This rhetorical theme of an ignorant public had been circulating in business advocacy as far back as the mid-1930s; its prominence in the rhetoric of sponsored economic education illustrates how advertising industry messaging positioned its own insiders not only as experts in selling, but as economic experts.[21]

In other words, the advertising industry leaders who developed economic education projects co-constructed a reality with their own expertise at its heart. The executives who strategized economic education campaigns held primary economic doxa drawn from their firsthand experiences in business operations but made claims that equated this knowledge with economic understanding. Implicit in such claims was a subtle movement between primary and secondary economic doxa. This metonymic slippage could also facilitate impressions of expertise: if advertising was the keystone that held the US economic and political systems together, as West had suggested, then advertising professionals' expertise could be seen as crucial to the continued functioning of those systems. Advertising industry leaders imagined that economic understanding eluded not only those they saw as radicals, but also more moderate figures—including lawmakers, midlevel executives, rank-and-file workers, and homemakers. In the process, they imagined themselves as having expertise, but in fact

66 CHAPTER THREE

displayed what we might call folk expertness: an enactment of the socio-cultural and institutional dynamics of scientific expertise, based on a body of folk knowledge.[22]

This sense of expertness informed advertising industry leaders' designs for campaigns to shift public opinion. The organizers of the joint meeting of the AAAA and the ANA in Hot Springs, Virginia, in November of 1941 hoped the gathering would spread this vision to a broader managerial cohort. The meeting included representatives of advertising agencies, consumer goods manufacturers, and publishers and broadcasters, with a formalized agenda that covered four broad topics: the vulnerabilities of the advertising and branded consumer goods industries to limitations and regulations, framed as "attacks"; the centrality of advertising to the US economic system; the "disastrous consequences" that could befall all of industry if advertising were to be limited; and, finally, how these threats could be addressed. The outcome of this meeting was a plan to reshape public opinion about advertising: not only by promoting the supposed economic and civic benefits of consumer product advertising, but also by using advertising techniques to promote public interest projects. This agreed-upon strategy was consequential in two senses. First, the United States' entry to World War II would present opportunities for the advertising industry to experiment with public service advertising techniques and formats. Second, the rhetorical frames developed at the Hot Springs meeting would inform the AAAA and ANA's joint strategies during and after the war. The narrative promoted by advertising industry leaders in the autumn of 1941 may have been hyperbolic in its predictions of a collapsing system, but it bestowed a sense of urgency upon the proposed projects. Overall, the Hot Springs meeting crystallized the managerial folk economics that would come to inform the advertising industry's wartime and postwar public service projects, including economic education campaigns.[23]

"The Publicity Boys": Home-Front Messaging in Wartime

The US's entry into World War II, only a month after the Hot Springs meeting, created "an uncontested public interest," as advertising historian Roland Marchand observes: manufacturers seized upon narratives of patriotic sacrifice in their advertising and public relations. As for the leaders of the AAAA and ANA, their public service strategy found expression in the Advertising Council, a private, volunteer association of advertising agencies and major advertisers that worked initially with the Advertising Division of the Federal Office of Facts and Figures and subsequently with the Office of War Information's Bureau of Campaigns to promote a range of home-front war efforts. Over the course of the war, the Advertising Council (known as the War Advertising Council for part of the conflict) coordinated war-supportive messaging in advertisements. In the process, it laid claim to jurisdiction over the style and form of public service announcement media in the United States.[24]

A variety of agencies had been responsible for managing official information in the lead-up to the United States' entry to the war, including the Office of Emergency Management's Division of Information, the Office of Government Reports, and the Office of Civil Defense, all of which had faced some degree of criticism for partisanship. In October 1941, President Roosevelt established a federal Office of Facts and Figures (OFF), a "central information clearinghouse" for national defense issues that would "conduct psychological warfare on the 'battleground of public opinion,'" as one press account put it—measuring and monitoring public opinion, both through the use of public opinion polling and by surveying the content of a wide range of news and entertainment media including broadcast, print, and motion pictures. Under director Archibald MacLeish (a former lawyer turned Pulitzer Prize–winning poet, editor, and Librarian of Congress), the OFF aimed to present reliable and accurate information that could inform citizens' opinions. Despite its high regard for the public's democratic reasoning, however, the OFF was less than a rousing success: critics perceived its publications as uninteresting and the organization itself as weak and ineffective. A prior head of the ANA, Ken Dyke, was appointed to lead OFF's Advertising Division. When the Office of War Information (OWI) was founded in June of 1942 with control over "virtually all the government publicity and foreign propaganda work," as reported in the *New York Times*, the OFF was folded into its domestic branch.[25]

OWI was established with the goal of creating a stronger and more coordinated program for official information. Led by journalist and radio commentator Elmer Davis, OWI had almost four thousand employees within a few months of its founding. OWI's domestic branch consisted of several suboffices, or bureaus, focused on different media forms, as OWI general counsel Abraham Feller explained in an essay published in *Public Opinion Quarterly*: these included a News Bureau that distributed government press releases and responded to press queries; a Bureau of

Publication and Graphics whose writers and artists created "pamphlets and posters on war topics"; a Radio Bureau that administered an allocation plan for radio messaging and vetted the content of that messaging (this airtime was given without cost to the government by the radio industry at an estimated value exceeding $100 million in 1942 alone); a Bureau of Motion Pictures that produced short information films, cleared films created by other parts of the government, and supported the motion picture industry's contributions to wartime messaging; a Bureau of Special Operations to liaison with the foreign press, community groups, and schools and colleges and "direct inquiries" from the public; a Field Service to adapt materials for regional needs; a Bureau of Intelligence that tracked public opinion; and, finally, a Bureau of Campaigns that coordinated messaging in advertising and retail stores through the Advertising Council and the National Retail Association.[26]

Media coverage of OWI's founding was mixed. Some publications, such as the *Chicago Daily Tribune*, focused on what were implied to be high salaries for the work of shaping public opinion, while others at the *New York Times* and the *Wall Street Journal* praised OWI for bringing more order to the presentation of war content over the radio waves. Yet, even this praise contained hints of conflicts to come. Describing the state of war information under MacLeish, columnist and New Deal critic Frank Kent positioned Davis's OWI as a much-needed solution: despite MacLeish's best efforts, Kent opined, "newspapers and correspondents, unable to get accurate information, have been flooded with vast quantities of boobish propaganda, turned out by unqualified amateurs, the effect of which was irritating and the cost appalling." Kent declared that Davis and OWI would need to not only be more informative and consistent—but, Kent cautioned, do so without engaging in meaningless hype. To support his case, Kent gestured to an Office of Emergency Management, Division of Information newsletter for graphic artists that celebrated honeybees' contributions to domestic sugar production. Kent cautioned that Davis should not allow coverage of such trivial matters to continue at OWI simply because "the publicity boys are now all calling themselves 'information specialists.'" Kent's comments telegraphed how the professionalization of public communication was up for grabs in this moment—and that for at least some commentators, affirmative promotion seemed a poor excuse for expertise in public communication.[27]

As historian Allan M. Winkler observes, OWI had considerable jurisdiction over news media, but had been "only marginally successful in freeing the flow of news, hardly able to coordinate the wartime stories that so often seemed to conflict" and thus turned its focus to "generating support for the war"—just the type of ballyhoo Kent had seemed to oppose. Kent's complaints about "publicity boys" pointed to a broader tension over how to go about messaging in the public interest during wartime, a question in which the Advertising Council would come to play a considerable role.[28]

"The Voice of Affirmation": The Advertising Council and the Office of War Information[29]

During the Second World War the promotional industries solidified their control over public service messaging and gained institutional legitimacy for their affirmative style of promotional-political communication—primarily through the works of the Advertising Council. The Advertising Council was established in spring of 1942, with members representing national advertisers (typically major manufacturers), advertising agencies, and the publishing, broadcasting, and display advertisement industries. Its organizers, many drawn from the ranks of the AAAA and the ANA, imagined the council to be an essential part of home-front war efforts from the time of its inception. Advertising was an especially important part of public communication, they reasoned, because unlike military personnel who could be given orders, civilians had to be "persuaded and inspired." Further, they reasoned, the advertising-funded systems of broadcast and print media in the US had already established methods for directing messages to "the right spot at the right time" and, crucially, advertising's short and easily reproduced messages had "insistent and repetitive force." Advertisers, in short, imagined themselves to be experts: both in using established techniques to craft persuasive messages and in delivering those messages through a specialized network of efficient content distribution channels. The Advertising Council's ascendancy was aided by a Treasury ruling in 1942 that advertising—including institutional and goodwill advertising—could continue to be treated as a tax-deductible expense, which, as Stole observes, "meant that the government sponsored advertising at an effective rate of 80 percent."[30]

Thus, the Advertising Council set out to use the already-established infrastructures and practices of the advertising industry to promote home-front war efforts. The council received requests for assistance from government agencies and assigned requests to volunteer advertising agencies, who in turn made advertisements, copy, taglines, and other promotional elements available for use by national advertisers in purchased advertising space. The council also developed a range of techniques for national advertisers who wished to combine product advertising with war-effort messaging, ranging from "all-out" advertising campaigns that focused almost completely on promoting civilian war efforts to product promotion advertisements that appeared to be mostly ordinary, save for a small snippet of war-related art or copy. Advertisements that intermixed product or brand information with information about war efforts were especially useful to companies that, for supply chain reasons related to the war, had little or no product to offer on the market: instead, they could use advertising to try to keep their companies prominent in consumers' minds.[31]

The advertising industry's investment in public service messaging was premised on its claims to both expertise and public service, which were strengthened by the Advertising Council's framing of its purpose and capacities. The Advertising Council's system of privately coordinated and industry-sponsored messaging, created by the advertising industry in harmony with its existing practices, fit neatly with the advertising industry trade groups' interwar free enterprise politics. Direct, paid advertising by the federal government itself was limited; proponents of the Advertising Council suggested that private industry could do most of the job, providing government with what its organizers called "an expert and disinterested service." Moreover, organizers stated, the war was an opportunity for the advertising industry to present itself to both government and the public as not only as a symbol of the "'good citizenship' of American business" but a much-needed element of society: "the real arsenal of democracy"— echoing President Roosevelt's rhetoric about the United States' role in the war amid the threat of dictatorships. Such rhetoric recalled advertising industry leaders' framing of advertising as the keystone of a free press and, by extension, a protector of civil liberties.[32]

A portent of how the Advertising Council would come to occupy a central position in direct public messaging during the war lay in OWI head Elmer Davis's decision to appoint magazine and newspaper publisher Gardner Cowles Jr. to lead the OWI's domestic office. Historian Sydney Weinberg observes that Cowles faced political pressures, chiefly a newly conservative Congress that suspected the OWI's domestic branch of partisan propagandizing for the Roosevelt administration. By early 1943, OWI was taking criticism from the press: for example, a *New York Times* reporter needled the agency for its "huge costs and multiple vehicles of propaganda widely held to be unskilled and politically partisan." Cowles overhauled the

EXPERTISE AND AFFIRMATION

Bureau of Publication and Graphics, replacing its existing leadership from the journalism and publishing fields with executives from the broadcasting and consumer goods industries. Although the OFF, the OWI's predecessor organization, had favored a data-laden style of in-house media production, Cowles showed little interest in continuing this approach. Cowles expressed doubt that audiences would read "long columns of type," suggesting a preference for the shorter and more direct forms of communication exemplified by the Advertising Council's offerings.[33]

The OWI Domestic Branch's preference for advertising-inflected approaches came into sharp focus in April of 1943, when several prominent writers resigned from OWI's Writers' Division over the change in division leadership, as Weinberg documents. When contacted by the press for comment, Cowles initially suggested that the resignations were due to "difference of opinion": the writers wanted "an extensive pamphlet and booklet program," Cowles stated, but declared himself "confident that OWI can get out all the information it needs to get out" through existing media channels such as newspapers, magazines, and radio. The resigning writers challenged Cowles's framing of the conflict as a disagreement about in-house publishing, insisting that their resignations had been brought on by the hiring of advertising executives at OWI and the adoption of sugarcoated approaches to public information. Cowles dismissed these concerns as "laughable," emphasizing how cooperation with private industry helped to underwrite publicity for home-front war efforts and using food industries' participation in advertising messages about point rationing as an example of the innocuousness of such collaborations.[34]

However, the resigning writers countered that the issue was truth, not format. Use of the "advertising technique" in place of pamphlets was not the issue at all, they wrote, acknowledging that advertising had a rightful place in building backing for domestic war support activities. Rather, the writers insisted, the resignations were the result of internal disagreements about a report on domestic food supplies deemed "too gloomy" by domestic branch leadership. This conflict led the writers to charge that domestic OWI activities had become "dominated by high pressure promoters who prefer slick salesmanship to honest information."[35]

The disagreement, then, was not so much about making pamphlets in-house versus using existing media channels, but rather about the underlying philosophies about what style of information would count within OWI as serving the public interest—with what I am calling an affirmative style of optimistic rhetoric winning out. Weinberg notes that both Cowles and members of the Advertising Council "tended to discourage material emphasizing the grimmer side of the war," producing instead materials that Wall calls "sentimental, patriotic, and upbeat." These materials avoided the solemn imagery and rhetorical tones that could be found in the output of writers and artists at the OWI, some of whom had worked previously for New Deal agencies or programs. Indeed, cultural studies scholar Christof Decker documents how muralist and former Farm Security Administration photographer Ben Shahn, whose unsettling posters for OWI's Bureau of Publications and Graphics won later recognition for how they portrayed the violence of wartime, left the OWI in 1943—but not before designing a satirical poster that sardonically imagined Roosevelt's Four Freedoms as products to be sold like Coca-Cola.[36]

The advertising industry's liaisons with OWI, especially through the now-renamed War Advertising Council, allowed the advertising industry to emerge from the war with a better public image and more political power, as historians have noted. Wall concludes that the resignations, along with congressional defunding, "silenced the staunchest and best-positioned advocates of a progressive, anti-fascist consensus within the federal government," which in turn "effectively amplified the voice of the business community." Similarly, Stole observes that the partnership with the US government that took shape during World War II positioned the advertising industry for success and political power in the postwar era. In addition, I argue that belief in their own expertise in the use of advertising—both its practical infrastructures and the unique rhetorical qualities of advertising as a media form—helped advertising industry leaders assert jurisdiction over public messaging and strengthened their own narratives about their industry's capacity to protect Americans' political liberties. Advertising Council leaders imagined the attention span of audiences to be suited to brief, memorable works of persuasion that employed advertising techniques such as "emotionalizing facts" and repetition. By the end of the war, public service *advertising*—with its characteristic focus on brief, often upbeat messages that, it was hoped, could both inform individual members of the public and inspire their attitudes and actions—was an established mode of public communication in the United States.[37]

The Advertising Council's Postwar Jurisdictional Claims

As the Second World War ended, participants in the War Advertising Council planned for the transition to peacetime. Council leadership envi-

EXPERTISE AND AFFIRMATION

sioned a period of economic crisis and upheaval as soldiers returned from the front and manufacturing transitioned away from wartime production, a period in which they assumed that "the forces of information and persuasion will be needed as perhaps never before." Members of the council's board of directors reasoned that the organization should continue to operate after the end of the war, to improve the image of business. They imagined that the council could use advertising to promote the collective interest, to demonstrate the social power of advertising, and to signal the industry's continued interest in cooperating with the state. Further, they imagined that doing so would allow them to create good public relations for not only the advertising industry, but for all private industries—and do so with impeccable morality. The War Advertising Council's leaders reorganized as the Advertising Council, a nonprofit organization through which US advertising agencies volunteered to create public service advertising on issues of national interest.[38]

The Advertising Council's wartime service, paired with the policy environment after the war, established its considerable influence over public service messaging. With the ceasing of hostilities in September of 1945, OWI's Radio Bureau was disbanded, and the Advertising Council took over administration of the OWI's radio allocation plan. This administrative role was at first on an emergency basis, to support the completion of the Victory Loan program in December of 1945, but subsequently continued as an ongoing reconversion program of coordinated advertiser participation in public service messaging. The release in March 1946 of the Federal Communications Commission's "Blue Book" report, in which the FCC laid out the operating rules for US broadcasters, specified that airing PSAs could help fulfill broadcasters' newly codified public service obligations. Broadcasters could either create their own PSAs or air spots that were ready-made by a third party such as the Advertising Council. The Office of War Mobilization and Reconversion collated requests from government bodies and prioritized them for coverage in Advertising Council allocation plans. The council also began accepting requests for campaigns from nonprofit organizations, a shift from its exclusive service to the government during the war. With its continuing radio activities, the Advertising Council promised to furnish radio audiences with information about matters important to business or the general welfare, under the rationale that "public service advertising is good business."[39]

The Advertising Council made another promise that suggested a strategy for strengthening their jurisdictional control: voluntary limitation (portrayed as a step to "eliminate the chaos" the council claimed had been caused by a lack of centralized clearinghouse for public service messaging). Nonprofit and governmental organizations who took part in the plan were asked to "pledge . . . not to approach national radio advertisers individually for radio coverage except as allocated by the Council." In other words, government agencies and nonprofit groups alike could enjoy the Advertising Council's services, in exchange for granting it exclusivity. The framing of this offer in terms of eliminating chaos suggested Advertising Council leadership's assumptions: that consumer opinion research could do better than the political apparatus at assessing public opinion, and that "advertising techniques" of repetition and "making facts simple, understandable and interesting" could influence public attitudes more effectively than official news releases. After the war, then, Advertising Council leadership extended and entrenched the claims of expertise that had helped them win jurisdiction over wartime direct-to-public messaging.[40]

Yet, some leaders in the advertising industry questioned whether the Advertising Council should continue to operate at all in peacetime. Advertising executive and former congressman Bruce Barton of BBDO argued in September of 1946 that "the War Advertising Council should have put an honorable end to its activities with the ending of the war." He wrote, "the Advertising Council was established to help win the war. The first casualties in every war are truth and morality. . . . We sacrificed 'truth in advertising' and did it cheerfully in order to adhere to the party line." BBDO had created advertisements about fighting inflation during the war, Barton confessed, for the sake of unity and morale: "we did not tell the truth, of course. We simply set forth . . . the Administration's argument" in a way that would raise awareness and make consumers feel good about taking small, individual-level actions that the administration had claimed would help keep the wartime economy strong. However, Barton confided to Young that in his view, inflation was in fact mainly influenced by government policy. It had been "patriotic and moral" during wartime to tell citizens that their everyday actions could stop inflation, Barton argued, but without the exigencies of war, such claims would be a misuse of advertising's influence.[41]

Council chairman James Webb Young seemed to disagree that the Advertising Council's power could be so easily misused, insisting that causes the council served had to have congressional support as well as administration support—and that at any rate, the council could refuse any request that it deemed counter to the public interest. In fact, Young explained, the council's policy was to identify issues in the public interest either

EXPERTISE AND AFFIRMATION

by acts of Congress or by the approval of the council's Public Advisory Committee.[42]

Ultimately, despite Barton's objections, the postwar Advertising Council was established as a nonprofit organization and was able to receive tax-deductible donations by September of 1946. This favorable tax status positioned the council to benefit from the considerable growth of philanthropic foundations and charitable giving over the next two decades. Nonprofit or government agencies in search of coordinated messaging could work with the Advertising Council, whose volunteer agencies would create multimedia campaigns. As Advertising Council president Ted Repplier told the trade magazine *Advertising & Selling* in late 1946, council-affiliated agencies would develop kits for advertisers and publishers:

> Our kit contains ready-built ads, "drop-in" units,[43] car cards [for display inside public transportation], window posters, commercial radio spots and regional programs, with a regular schedule of public service messages. We also furnish complete, concise information for advertisers who like to roll their own.

Advertising Council campaigns in the coming years would include matters of public health, resource conservation, international relations, and, in Young's words, "campaigns for economic and political education." These campaigns showed that, as the nation transitioned back to peacetime, the advertising industry established organizational networks that allowed its public communications work to continue, supported by a narrative about advertisers' communicative expertise and orientation toward the common good.[44]

In sum, the narratives, practices, and institutional configurations of interwar and wartime public information campaigns helped members of the advertising industry affiliated with the AAAA and the ANA to see themselves as the right people to provide economic education in the years following World War II. The NAM's 1930s public information campaigns had advanced a narrative that both framed managerial capitalism as inseparable from freedom and emphasized the expertise of media production specialists. The leadership of the AAAA and the ANA subsequently elaborated on similar themes, coming to see the advertising industry as a protector of democracy and employing economic folk knowledge to support their own claims of expertise. The circumstances of wartime bureaucracy—most notably the OWI's eventual focus on public messaging and its employment of media executives—gave leaders in the advertising industry opportunities to exercise their strategic imperatives through the War Advertising Council. This combination of promotional nationalist narratives, a business-friendly affirmative style of discourse, and institutionally endorsed expertise claims allowed the advertising industry to emerge from the war with a strong sense of legitimacy and faith in advertising's contributions to the common good, operationalized through the Advertising Council's established jurisdiction over public service messaging.

In addition to these practical effects, the Advertising Council's actions during the Second World War set the terms by which the advertising industry would make continued claims to professional jurisdiction over public service messaging in the postwar period. The advertising industry would use its newfound license to advance private enterprise ideology but would frame these efforts as public service campaigns to increase knowledge of the US economic system. The framing of industrial public relations as public service enfolded managerial folk ideas about advertising's power to defend a free press. This secondary economic doxa originated with advertising industry leaders and circulated through discourse to comprise a doxic community of supporters within industry. It informed a broader managerial ideology that incorporated prior sentiments about selling America, including nationalistic idealism, positive affect, and an affinity for mixing upbeat facts with vivid imagery in place of detailed statistics and exhaustive information. In the years after World War II, the advertising industry's jurisdiction over public service media would shape practices and norms around both public service media and the role of advertising in the US economy.

CHAPTER FOUR

The Great Free Enterprise Campaign

In 1952, the respected American business magazine *Forbes* sent its new subscribers an unusual thank-you gift: a paperback book that lampooned corporate-sponsored public relations efforts to bolster public support for private enterprise. *Is Anybody Listening? How and Why U.S. Business Fumbles When It Talks with Human Beings* opened with an examination of industry's efforts to sell private enterprise, asserting that the "great free enterprise campaign," despite eating up at least $100 million of company expenditures, was "not worth a damn." The book's author, *Fortune* staff writer William H. Whyte, heaped scorn on "free enterprise" publicity campaigns for purporting to "sell America" to the masses. Whyte framed this trend of campaigns to effectively "sell" free enterprise as a new development: in the course of reporting, Whyte commented, he had noticed that "selling [...] was taking on some interesting connotations; the kind that business was becoming most concerned about was the selling of itself." In fact, Whyte was critiquing a set of cultural practices that had developed over the previous thirty years—practices centered on the idea that business selling its own interests in the name of freedom was, in fact, the same thing as selling America to Americans.[1]

Many supporters of sponsored economic education media in the postwar period saw such economic education campaigns as public service projects that would enable ordinary people to make personal and political choices that would preserve democracy and protect individual freedoms. Critics, however, saw self-serving public relations at best, and outright propaganda at worst. In the pages of *Is Anybody Listening?*, Whyte warned that by attempting to "sell America to Americans" as one might sell dish soap, sponsored economic education media made an audacious error: they presumed to *tell* Americans what it meant to *be* American—as if businesspeople had exclusive insight into the meaning of national identity. To hear Whyte tell it, these attempts to sell America had "debauched and exploited" the symbols of the nation with cloying optimism: "There is a time for reaffirmation," Whyte declared, but "all of the time is not it." Whyte argued that the comic books, slide shows, short films, cartoons, speeches, and pamphlets churned out by business advocacy organizations, corporations, and trade groups in the name of selling private enterprise were not just self-serving kitsch. They were downright insulting to ordinary people in the US whose lived experiences had undoubtedly informed their own ideas about what an American way of life might entail—and, indeed, their own opinions about the American economic system's shortcomings. Ultimately, Whyte argued, economic education was a misnomer; what economic education media had to offer was often not "the facts," but political conclusions preposterously masquerading as facts.[2]

This chapter examines how members of the promotional industries designed and carried out one part of what Whyte called the "great free enterprise campaign." It focuses on advertising trade associations and their allies' roles in this campaign, and their ambitious plans to change public opinion about business and capitalism in the United States. As the chapter shows, members of the American Association of Advertising Agencies (AAAA) and the Association of National Advertisers (ANA) embraced the ideas that skeptical public opinion about private enterprise was a serious social problem—and that the advertising industry itself was uniquely able to solve this problem through a program of persuasion at every possible level of American society including schools, workplaces, and the mass media. This, they hoped, would create an optimistic sense of ideological unity in the American populace. The chapter situates the Advertising Council, the leading public service advertising clearinghouse in the US, as one of many organizations that carried out advertising industry leaders' plans to use rhetorics of education, public service, and democracy to neutralize what it perceived as threats to private enterprise.

The chapter first examines the ANA and AAAA's institutional visions of economic education, explaining how members of these trade organizations deployed managerial folk knowledge to position the advertising industry as the right experts for the job. Then, the chapter examines the Freedom Train, a traveling exhibit of historical documents that ran from 1947 to 1949, arguing that the Advertising Council's involvement in promoting the exhibit was an important proof-of-concept for its subsequent economic education campaigns—and that, despite organizers' suggestions

THE GREAT FREE ENTERPRISE CAMPAIGN   79

otherwise, the Freedom Train was received in managerial circles as a tacit celebration of private enterprise. The chapter then turns to the Advertising Council's "American Economic System" campaign, launched in 1948—detailing how the campaign carried out the ANA and AAAA's vision of economic education in an expression of what I call the affirmative style of economic education. Finally, the chapter examines the organizational partnership the ANA and AAAA cultivated with George S. Benson, the president of Harding College, a small, far-right Bible college located in Searcy, Arkansas. Benson's collaboration with the advertising industry, albeit brief, demonstrated that the industry's claims of political neutrality permitted tolerance of far-right political activity.

Sponsored economic education programs flourished in the immediate postwar period, and much of the economic education output in the United States from the mid-1940s into the early 1950s sounded remarkably similar. As this chapter demonstrates, those similarities came not sheerly from coincidence or consensus, but from the direct influence of the advertising trade associations and their plan for widespread economic education campaigns in the postwar United States. This plan came to partial fruition through such programs as the Advertising Council's "American Economic System" campaign and the launch of the "Freedom Forum" executive education program of Harding College's National Education Program. What might have appeared from the outside to be broad (if mistaken, in Whyte's estimation) consensus among a range of industry-aligned and politically conservative organizations was in part a coordinated effort to remake postwar public opinion toward what business advocates had developed over the past two decades: a promotional nationalism that prioritized corporate power in the name of freedom.[3]

To be sure, this great campaign had many parts and players: for example, historian William Bird tracks how organizations such as the NAM, along with individual companies such as General Motors, Goodyear Tire, and the Chrysler Corporation responded to labor-management conflicts by bankrolling sponsored films that dramatized managerial perspectives on American industry in the years after the Second World War. Yet, the Advertising Council's dominance of the public service advertising form gave it a unique role in this collaborative effort. Histories of the Advertising Council and its role in public life—including works by historians Robert Griffith, Stuart J. Little, Inger Stole, and Wendy Wall, among others—have documented the Advertising Council's postwar ideological campaigns and recorded the "American Economic System" campaign's link to a joint committee of the AAAA and ANA. However, there is much more that can be said about the influence of the joint committee and its role in coordinating multiple economic education projects. This chapter documents both the extent of the committee's planning and the breadth of its partnerships across a gamut of sponsored economic education media. Ultimately, it shows how advertising trade organizations, under the influence of managerial folk knowledge, set out to sell American exceptionalism and hope in a bright, unified future under the banner of a so-called American economic system.[4]

The Smock Report: Constructing Postwar Economic Education

In September of 1946—about the same time as the founding of the postwar Advertising Council—members of the ANA and AAAA formed a new joint committee, initially called the "Joint ANA-AAAA Committee to Improve Understanding of Business through Advertising." This committee, which came to be known as the "Joint ANA-AAAA Committee on Improvement of Public Understanding of Our Economic System," would come to plan and facilitate programs designed to promote and instill appreciation for managerial capitalism across many sectors of US society in the late 1940s and early 1950s.[5]

One of the committee's first actions in 1946 was to form Research and Creative Committees of advertising executives from leading firms including Benton and Bowles, Young and Rubicam, BBDO, and Foote, Cone, and Belding, tasked with creating a report on how the advertising industry could make public attitudes more favorable toward business. The Research Committee worked in consultation with the nation's top pollsters and market researchers, producing a report that set out findings and strategic plans. The report proposed a civic framing for what had initially been conceived as a public relations project. In this civic framing, I argue that the abstraction of "the American economic system" functioned as a rhetorical stand-in for the interests of the advertising industry. The creative professionals involved with the report suggested that any public messaging should be framed as being "in the interests of the American *people*" (emphasis in original) rather than business or management: this was a moral imperative, the report suggested, but also a strategic framing that would make the program "less vulnerable to attack if it could be sponsored by labor unions, educational groups, and anyone else who was interested."

The Boards of Directors of the ANA and AAAA officially approved the report in December of 1946; correspondingly, the "Joint ANA-AAAA Committee to Improve Understanding of Business through Advertising" was renamed in January of 1947 as the "Joint ANA-AAAA Committee on Improvement of Public Understanding of Our Economic System" (I refer to it hereafter as the Joint Committee on Improvement). The report came to be known colloquially as the Smock Report after Jack Smock (of Los Angeles advertising firm Foote, Cone, and Belding), a member of the Creative Committee who presented the results formally at the AAAA's annual convention in April of 1947. The creation of the Joint Committee on Improvement was an institutional formalization of ANA and AAAA efforts to intervene in public opinion: by January of 1948 the Joint Committee on Improvement had its own office space in Manhattan, a powerful chairman in Don Belding of Foote, Cone, and Belding, and a full-time director, Kenneth Wells, who was supported with a secretary funded by J. Walter Thompson Company.[6]

The Smock Report informed a wide-ranging set of efforts by US corporations, trade groups, business advocates, and conservative allies that used managerial folk knowledge to assert that the interests of ordinary people were the same as the interests of businesses large and small, and that the practices of midcentury US managerial capitalism were in fact a timeless system of managing society, using the imagery of patriotism and democracy to present managerial capitalism as an individualistic foil to the centralized state power of socialist economic systems. The previous chapter argued, drawing from the theories of Richard Swedberg, that that these managerial beliefs were a form of folk economics based on doxa, or commonsense everyday knowledge. Swedberg argues that understanding doxa means analyzing the units of meaning and categories into which those units fall. In the case of postwar economic education, one of the important units of meaning was *the system*. Economic education proponents often referred to the American system of business, the American economic system, or the American way of life interchangeably. The term *system* as used in these formulations was ambiguous enough to permit slippage between a managerial perspective on US business practices, on one hand, and a more abstract sense of a political-economic whole that included managerial capitalism, representative democracy, and civil liberties, on the other.[7]

The Smock Report was not only a research report, but a strategic blueprint. It presented a comprehensive vision of American private enterprise as an economic system, defined the perceived threats to that system, and prescribed actions designed to address those threats. The Joint Committee on Improvement's findings, representing the collaborative efforts of executives from several high-profile advertising firms including Benton and Bowles, BBDO, and Young and Rubicam, were first presented on April 17, 1947, at the AAAA's twenty-ninth annual convention. The presentation included a discussion of the defining principles of the US economy, as the committee saw them; an enumeration of the reasons why, in the Joint Committee on Improvement's view, ordinary Americans' thinking about the economy failed to align with these defining principles; and a three-part strategic plan for changing public opinion. This strategic plan was designed to promote the Joint Committee on Improvement's vision to a wide range of key publics—from leaders in the political, labor, and industrial spheres to ordinary workers, stay-at-home parents, and students—through a variety of project proposals that could be carried out by affiliated nonprofit organizations. A closer examination of the rhetoric and reasoning presented in the report shows how managerial folk knowledge informed its assumptions and conclusions.

Like the sponsored economic education projects that had come before it, the committee's research had concluded that the US public was uninformed about what it saw as the virtues of the country's economic system. After interviewing "the country's top research men" to get a sense of the public opinion landscape, the committee had concluded that two things were needed: a definition of the American economic system and a plan for explaining it to the public. The report started by defining economic systems broadly as the ways a given society coordinated labor, production, and distribution of goods and services. Curiously, though, the report characterized the United States' economic system based on how economic activity had been coordinated during "the years between the passage of the Sherman Anti-Trust Act and 1929": the years from the 1890s into the 1920s in which corporations had flourished, but years in which labor protections and other state regulations of business had been limited. During these years, the report asserted, the US economy had been defined by "private property, a free market, profit and wage incentives, competition, [and] government regulation—but not government control." Rhetorically, this move was significant: without making direct reference to the New Deal reforms of the 1930s, the Smock Report portrayed the conditions prior to the New Deal as the baseline of an established and uniquely American economic system.[8]

THE GREAT FREE ENTERPRISE CAMPAIGN 83

It also downplayed lingering issues of monopoly, framing a market economy—one in which production was imagined to be determined by demand-based pricing—as a foundationally democratic and voluntary system in which the government would be limited to acting as a "referee" of economic life. This ideological emphasis on voluntarism as a defining principle extended to the committee's proposed strategies for economic education. The committee insisted that the American people supported the "American system of free enterprise" yet still condoned individual policies that the committee imagined could detrimentally impact economic conditions. The reason for this state of affairs, the report asserted, was a lack of understanding of economic principles that left the public vulnerable to political rhetoric. The report did not seem to see the irony of advertisers, whose branded-goods campaigns often relied upon its own repertoire of rhetorical appeals, fretting over the power of rhetoric. Economic education, the committee promised, would create political, economic, and commercial harmony by inducing ordinary people to voluntarily act in ways that would reinforce the American economic system's efficient manifestations of democratic, decentralized economic power.[9]

Bearing all this in mind, the report proposed a three-part strategy to both inspire faith in the system and position support for private enterprise as something that transcended political or class conflicts, registering instead as a seemingly indisputable kind of common sense. Program One would focus on what were called plant programs: workplace information programs for ordinary workers, including persuading top management to institute such programs. The report imagined that these plant programs could not only "correct economic misinformation and lack of information that exists in the worker's mind" about economic concepts and principles, but also have second-order morale benefits of helping workers feel a renewed sense of pride and belonging in their workplaces and a stronger appreciation of the system overall. Program Two would entail an advertising campaign with the American economic system as its product. The report expressed hopes that such a campaign would "re-awaken the public" emotionally, making them eager to defend the system—a turn of phrase that echoed columnist Benjamin De Casseres's 1939 call to "advertise and sell America" to citizens who could be "stung back to life." This campaign, the report claimed, would "counteract subversive propaganda" and refute "collectivist" narratives of conflict between labor and capital. Program Three would encompass a sweeping educational curriculum using every type of available media including "advertisements, booklets, motion pictures, [and] radio." Crucially, the report urged, the second and third programs would need to be "completely fair and unbiased," acknowledging the shortfalls of both labor and management. Taken together, the three programs reflected an understanding of economic education as a way to capture both the hearts and the minds of ordinary people.[10]

From a perspective that recognizes economic education as a project of managerial folk knowledge, the work of defining the economic system and devising ways to influence public opinion about it were ways of asserting expertise and authority. The Smock Report, and the many economic education projects it inspired, expressed the primary and secondary economic doxa that had surfaced at the joint meeting of the ANA and the AAAA in Hot Springs, Virginia, in 1941. Through the lens of folk economics, the midcentury US industrial push for economic education was a conflict over knowledge claims. The proponents of sponsored economic education adopted rationalizing rhetorics that categorized their own economic doxa as expert knowledge while disregarding the conflicting economic doxa of the audiences they imagined to be ignorant or misled. The advertising industry's claims that they were protecting the US economy and polity hinged on economic folk knowledge that was in fact a constellation of secondary economic doxa, crystallized in sponsored economic education projects.

Proponents of economic education had hoped their campaigns would impact public opinion like "the constant dripping of water that wears away a stone," as NAM chairman Robert Lund had phrased it in a 1935 speech, and advertising industry leaders imagined their field to be especially well suited to the task at hand. Indeed, the Advertising Council's James Webb Young claimed that advertising's ability to "repeat . . . facts until they stuck had a power which made news releases seem like a puff of wind." Such constant repetition, advocates for private enterprise hoped, could slowly but surely wear down perceptions of the political feasibility of consumer movements, popular reform, and other impediments to corporate power. In the process, their organizers hoped, these campaigns would reduce support for policies designed to limit and regulate corporate autonomy.[11]

Supporters of sponsored economic education media described these projects in trade publications and at trade association conferences as efforts to *sell* ideas and attitudes—and often, described economic education as selling America (or free enterprise, or the American economic system) to Americans in ways that drew equivalence between private enterprise and the nation itself. The sponsors, creators, and allies of these campaigns typically justified their use of mass media in terms of *education*: they claimed that ordinary people had been misinformed or underinformed about the role of business in society, so the public needed media that could help increase their understanding. From this perspective, businesses and trade groups were offering a valuable public service by explaining the business system and increasing the public's understanding of it. Yet, these corporate-sponsored campaigns were also shaping public opinion as the means to a profitable end.

To borrow a phrase from historian of science Bruce Lewenstein's writing on postwar science, those "who used the term 'understanding' were in fact seeking public *appreciation*" of American managerial practices and ideologies. The frames of education and understanding were strategically valuable, and not only because they positioned what were essentially public relations projects as public service. Framing public relations campaigns as educational or informative could present a superficial sheen of harmony while implicitly contesting and undermining regulators, unions, and any others who critiqued corporate abuses of power. And as Richard Tedlow observes, framing public relations as education also had "the obvious advantage of not requiring businessmen to change their actions."[12]

In sum, the processes by which the Smock Report gathered knowledge about the public, the ways it presented its conclusions to other insiders, and the ways it proposed that knowledge about the economic system be disseminated to outsiders all expressed knowledge claims based on advertising industry leaders' primary and secondary economic doxa: their firsthand understandings of how business worked, coupled with their received knowledge of how national economic dynamics worked. These economic doxa, combined with the legitimacy the Advertising Council had garnered for the advertising industry during World War II, helped provide the justification for the committee's assumptions that advertisers were experts who were uniquely qualified to create economic education media. Yet, this claim to expertise was metonymically slippery: although the Joint Committee on Improvement and its allies (and the NAM before them) had expertise in publicity, advertising, and media production, the rhetorics of expertise conceived by the NAM and adopted by the AAAA and ANA before the war blurred the distinction between primary and secondary doxa, and between promotional and economic knowledge. If advertisers' primary doxa positioned advertising as the foundation of the country's democratic traditions, their secondary doxa about an American

86   CHAPTER FOUR

economic system could help them see promotional expertise as the crucial skill for shifting public opinion in defense of freedom.

Freedom Train: The Advertising Council and American Heritage Foundation's "Our American Heritage" Campaign

The Advertising Council quickly became involved in the promotional industries' efforts to shape postwar culture, as its promotions for the Freedom Train demonstrated. Launched just a few months after the debut presentation of the Smock Report, the Freedom Train was a museum-style exhibit that traveled across the United States displaying important documents from American history, including original copies of the Constitution, the Bill of Rights, and the Gettysburg Address, in a custom-built Pennsylvania Railroad exhibit car. The sponsoring institution, the American Heritage Foundation, had been created especially for this cause—and had been founded by Joint Committee on Improvement member and advertising executive Thomas D'Arcy Brophy. Event organizers created dense layers of publicity around the Freedom Train exhibit, including a pop song written for the occasion by Irving Berlin and recorded by Bing Crosby and the Andrews Sisters, with all royalties donated to support the project; multimedia "Rededication Weeks" to be held in each city prior to the exhibit's arrival that encompassed news stories, showings of a publicity film for the exhibit, and other patriotic films; advertising developed by the Advertising Council for use on billboards and in radio broadcasts; and local events programming supported by community groups such as the Rotary Club. Between fall of 1947 and spring of 1949 the Freedom Train stopped in 322 cities, hosting three and a half million visitors. Between the Freedom Train exhibit itself and the vast range of supporting publicity carried out in the name of American Heritage, the project was, in Wendy Wall's words, "one of the largest peacetime ideological campaigns ever undertaken in this country." The Freedom Train exhibit and its accompanying publicity campaigns were the site of contestation and political conflict over the nature of citizenship and questions of race and class, as Wall and Stuart J. Little have shown—and it promoted private enterprise in ways that prefigured the Advertising Council and the AAAA-ANA Joint Committee on Improvement's economic education projects of the late 1940s and early 1950s.[13]

The Advertising Council supported the Freedom Train exhibition by coordinating volunteer service for the project and collaborating with the

American Heritage Foundation on a campaign council leadership called "Our American Heritage," a year-long national "program of public education in good citizenship." In addition to coordinating local Rededication Week activities (including the creation of advertisements and news features), the Advertising Council produced a set of companion informational booklets, titled *Our American Heritage* and *Good Citizen*, prepared in cooperation with the National Education Association. Its organizers imagined that the American Heritage programs would address public disillusionment with democracy — and made clear that they imagined democracy to be under threat from "totalitarianism of the Left," in the words of American Heritage Foundation national director J. Edward Shugrue (an actor and playwright). Shugrue declared that the time had come to create "rededication to American principles and ideals"; he and his fellow organizers hoped this rededication would supplant "the inevitable economic, social, and political frictions" of demobilization with a confident and stable sense of unity that could underwrite a new global peace. The rhetoric of rededication revealed the overarching logic of the campaign: narrating the United States' past and present in terms of what the organizers saw as shared national values.[14]

Yet, Wendy Wall's analysis of the Freedom Train shows how the exhibit also downplayed (or entirely disregarded) historical conflicts over class, race, labor, and social stratification, presenting a "veneer of unity," as she puts it, that "concealed an ongoing contest over America's core values" — in which "freedom," Wall argues, came to be centrally associated with American identity, rather than "democracy." The campaign was developed in the immediate postwar period, which was a consequential moment of flux for the power balance between industry, labor, and the state. Labor unions were pressing for change, as demonstrated by the United Automobile Workers' strike against General Motors from late 1945 into early 1946. Potent symbols in US culture, including the ideas of democracy and free enterprise themselves, were open to reinterpretation, with UAW leader Walter Reuther framing the union as defending "truly-free enterprise" from business interests that would use the powerful keyword to their own ends. The version of freedom implicit in Reuther's rhetoric was countered, however, by a barrage of sponsored materials, public relations activity, and cross-institutional discourse that positioned freedom as synonymous with corporations' power to resist state regulations and controls.[15]

The idea for the Freedom Train exhibit had passed through several institutional settings, demonstrating the links between government, industry, and advertising industry–affiliated nonprofit organizations. As historian Stuart J. Little recounts, it was initially developed in 1946 by officials at the Department of Justice, quickly gaining institutional support from the National Archives and funding from the entertainment industry. Thomas D'Arcy Brophy, then director of the Advertising Council in addition to his role as an advertising executive at Kenyon and Eckhardt Agency, had proposed a similarly patriotic campaign. From early 1947 onward, Brophy served as president of the American Heritage Foundation, which would officially sponsor the project and raise funds for it.[16]

The Freedom Train exhibit and its associated publicity events were publicized as a patriotic and civic campaign, rather than specifically as an economic education campaign—and scholars such as Little have previously characterized the campaign as being only "moderately pro-business." Yet, even though the Freedom Train and its associated American Heritage programs were not primarily categorized as economic education campaigns, organizers saw them as such. Placing this ideological campaign in conversation with the traditions of promotional nationalism that developed over the 1920s and 1930s shows how the American Heritage program foreshadowed the strategic approach, content, and practices of sponsored economic education campaigns that would issue from the Advertising Council and its allies in the ensuing years—and, further, how it deployed many themes and rhetorics that linked patriotism and national identity to private enterprise. For example, in October of 1947, Advertising Council chairman Charles G. Mortimer Jr. (also a vice president at General Foods), described the Advertising Council and its campaigns—including the American Heritage campaigns promoting the Freedom Train and associated efforts—as having "supplied our American democracy and our American way of life with an entirely new weapon to be used in its defense." Figure 4.1 provides an example of promotional materials developed by the Advertising Council with the approval of the American Heritage Foundation. Many advocates for private enterprise saw the project as unambiguously taking the side of business; indeed, meeting notes reported that Brophy described the American Heritage campaigns as the "track and locomotive" that would provide infrastructure and momentum for the "train and cargo" of the Joint Committee on Improvement's other economic education activities.[17]

Brophy wasn't alone in his assessment: many private enterprise advocates were eager to elaborate on how the Freedom Train promised a new model for selling the American public on private enterprise ideology. An

FIGURE 4.1. Outdoor advertising (billboard and transit card) design created by the Advertising Council to promote the Freedom Train exhibit. Image reproduced by permission of the Advertising Council; image scan provided by permission of Wisconsin Historical Society, WHI-73165416. Thomas D'Arcy Brophy, "Progress Report to the Board of Trustees of the American Heritage Foundation" (September 4, 1947), image located between 8 and 9, Thomas D'Arcy Brophy Papers, Wisconsin Historical Society: Box 17, Folder 5.

example of their perspective could be found in coverage of the Freedom Train in *Business Screen*, the national trade journal for institutional film producers and their clients. Examining the coverage of the campaign in *Business Screen* shows how business leaders and their allies saw the Freedom Train and American Heritage programs as promoting private enterprise. *Business Screen* devoted much of its February 1948 issue to covering the Freedom Train and American Heritage programs, fielding perspectives on the campaign from corporate and military leadership, campaign planners, and business consultants. For example, James Fri, past president of the American Trade Association Executives, wrote that "one of the most tangible evidences of our American heritage is demonstrated by the contributions our free competitive system has made, and will continue to make, to a domestic economy that has no peer." The "Selling America to Americans" editorial from pollster Henry C. Link of the Psychological Corporation articulated that the Freedom Train and American Heritage program were undeniably aimed at the same goals as economic education: namely, aligning public opinion with managerial perspectives on private enterprise. Accordingly, Link described the campaign using slogans often invoked for sponsored economic education, in particular the idea that publicity campaigns could "sell America." Link praised the campaign's co-optation of the US past, calling it a "searching reappraisal and examination of the concepts which have made the success of America possible." Even advertisements within the issue reflected the discourse of presumptive faith in a receptive and enthusiastic public, with film producer Wilding Picture Productions declaring, "Despite croaking prophets of impending doom, we still have unshakeable faith in the American people." These rhetorical flourishes restated prior expressions of promotional nationalism, down to the imagery—recall how Budweiser's morale campaign in the late 1930s had crowed that "Doomsday was a fizzle."[18]

Other *Business Screen* pieces underlined what was imagined to be at stake in the tour of the Freedom Train and the events of Rededication Weeks: global power. This theme emerged in *Business Screen* articles that gestured to the trauma of recent hostilities and the growing ideological clash of the Cold War. For example, American Heritage Foundation director Shugrue framed the campaign as nothing less than an existential battle against totalitarianism, luridly describing the moment as a "rendezvous with destiny" in which "the mutilated bodies of our dead soldiers" loomed in memory. Shugrue underlined the imperative of "winning the peace" just as the nation had won the war, reviving the phrasing that had been used in the 1920s to support Americanism campaigns. A contribution from Major General Charles L. Bolte also adopted a metaphor of battle, arguing that the campaign would lead ordinary Americans to not only recognize and celebrate the campaign's vision of a unifying heritage, but also to defend it—with the US economy being "one of our strongest weapons" in a "bloodless war of ideologies" because it could be used to bring "order out of economic and political chaos" overseas.[19]

The *Business Screen* editors capped off the section with a brief editorial suggesting that "industry, schools, clubs, churches, and other organized groups," now equipped with more than one hundred thousand sixteen-millimeter "sound motion picture projectors and more than that number of sound and silent slidefilm projectors," would welcome sponsored films. The editorial celebrated recently produced films with an "American theme" including *Unfinished Rainbows* (sponsored by the Aluminum Company of America) and *Our America* (sponsored by Dodge Motor Company). In a display of seeming magnanimity, the editors cautioned that both labor and industry had created films of varying quality, including some that were "*very bad*" (emphasis in original); it concluded that both "leftist propaganda" and the "insincerity" of corporate films could harm the public's reception of sponsored materials. Yet, the following page suggested the editors' sympathies lay with business: it featured a sequence of excerpts from *This Is Our Problem*, the AAAA-ANA-sponsored slidefilm (subsequently printed as an illustrated booklet by Time, Incorporated) based on the Smock Report's vision of the nation's economy. Echoing the Smock Report, *This Is Our Problem* extolled private property, a free market as the determinant of production, incentives in the form of wages and profits, interfirm competition, and regulation by a government that stayed on the sidelines as a "referee." *Business Screen*'s editors described the slideshow as "a good beginning" to fostering better "public understanding of our economic system."[20]

Business Screen's laudatory coverage of the Freedom Train and American Heritage programs showed how business advocates saw those programs as deeply supportive of their own goals. *Business Screen* framed these promotional activities not only as celebrations of American identity, but also as paeans to the strength and vitality of private enterprise. They envisioned that the audiovisual elements of the American Heritage programs would feed a newly established nationwide infrastructure for institutional media that could shape American politics and ideologies. And, finally, they imagined American Heritage activities in domestic and global contexts: as rejoinders to those who feared a domestic economic downturn amid demobilization, and as shots in an unfolding world war of ideas. The Advertising Council's role in bringing this ideological campaign to bear reflected the power it had amassed during World War II; this power would be put to more focused ends in the council's postwar sponsored economic education campaign.

The Advertising Council's American Economic System Campaign and *The Miracle of America*

In addition to its support of the Freedom Train via the American Heritage campaign, the Advertising Council developed a focused economic education project with an advertising campaign and additional supporting materials: the "American Economic System" campaign, which launched in November of 1948 (about a year after the Freedom Train's debut) and ran through the early 1950s. This campaign would be the first enactment of the Joint Committee on Improvement's plan, as laid out in the Smock Report.[21]

The need to find themes that would be acceptable to a variety of constituencies led to a messaging strategy built around productivity. The process began in January of 1947 when the Joint Committee on Improvement asked for the Advertising Council's help executing Program Two of their three-part plan. Studebaker executive and Marshall Plan administrator Paul G. Hoffmann, American Federation of Labor economist Boris Shishkin, and Hunter College president George N. Shuster formed a subcommittee to shepherd the proposal through the Advertising Council's Public Advisory Committee, which included representatives from corporate management, labor unions, universities, nonprofit organizations, and polling companies. The Public Advisory Committee's influence did seem to moderate the stances taken in the Smock Report, resulting in a program that allowed for agreement across multiple constituencies.[22]

Meeting notes from April of 1947 reported that the many constituencies on the Advertising Council's Public Advisory Committee had been most able to agree on a campaign that centered productivity—one that would exhort individuals to take "personal responsibility for making the economic system work better by expanding productivity and making sure the yield is fully shared." This focus, the meeting notes suggested, would allow for a campaign with a simple, unified, and consistent message: it would ask for "the same positive action on the part of all segments" of society, from workers and managers to farmers alike, and would emphasize to audiences that these groups, working together to create high productivity, had brought about a prosperity that was "interlocked" with "spiritual, intellectual, and religious" freedoms.[23]

Advertising Council materials showed how the organization subtly framed the campaign's business-friendly politics in terms of education and unity. For example, James Webb Young (now Advertising Council Policy Planning Committee chairman) indicated that the American Heritage projects and this new undertaking on the "American Economic System" with the Joint Committee on Improvement were aimed toward similar goals, describing the two campaigns as the council's contribution to "economic and political education." In fact, the Joint Committee on Improvement's brief to the Advertising Council for the campaign showed how the economic and the political overlapped in what these organizations had decided every American should know. The brief conceded that what it called the "American system" was a set of "complicated mechanisms of production, finance, and distribution patterns" that the campaign would *not* set out to explain. Rather, the campaign would focus on identifying what set this American system apart from other countries. This narrative of the US's exceptional nature would inform a vision for the future in which increased productivity, fostered by both labor's and management's freedoms to play their roles in the system, could mitigate destructive cycles of growth and contraction. Rather than labor and capital struggling over the distribution of earnings, the brief suggested, the campaign could lead Americans to see corporate earnings as an infinitely scalable "stream of wealth" that, if grown with productivity, would yield "more ... for capital, labor, and the public to share." The brief also acknowledged a variety of strategies for addressing unemployment, such as such as "unemployment insurance, employment services, vocational retraining, public works, community employment projects, and family welfare programs," favoring these over "compulsory assignment of laid-off workers." The implicit message was that the truly *American* way to manage the economy was by granting much of the decision-making power over production, pricing, wages, and distribution to managers, trusting that they would negotiate in good faith with labor, instead of relying on the government controls that had shaped the wartime economy.[24]

The council officially took on the campaign in April of 1947. Shortly after, the Chamber of Commerce publicized the findings of the Smock Report, a move that Joint Committee on Improvement members saw as an undesirable overstep. This unexpected publicity pushed the project forward: the Joint Committee on Improvement pressed on with developing and overseeing its strategic plans, with the ANA developing kits for use in Program One, which focused on plant education, and the Advertising Council working with Young and Rubicam to develop ideas for Program Two, a nationwide publicity campaign. Work on advertisements for the campaign was underway by summer of 1947, and a booklet explaining the advertising campaign's themes in greater depth, *The Miracle of America*, was drafted late in 1947 with the rationale that "advertising itself could not present the entire story of our system"; it would be made available to the public in February of 1949.[25]

Overlapping membership made the lines that separated the Advertising Council from the Joint Committee on Improvement hazy. Prominent Joint Committee on Improvement members such as Thomas D'Arcy Brophy, of the American Heritage Foundation and advertising firm Kenyon and Eckhardt, also sat on the Advertising Council's board of directors along with Paul B. West, of the ANA. Although Joint Committee on Improvement documents identified the committee as the official sponsor of the "American Economic System" campaign with final approval power over advertising copy, this role would go uncredited in the *Miracle of America* booklet. Instead, the booklet's copy characterized the campaign simply as "one of a number of public information programs conducted by the Advertising Council, Inc., in the interest of a better-informed America." The ambiguities about the boundaries between the two organizations did not stop there, with Advertising Council Board members weighing the idea of fundraising not only for the "American Economic System" campaign but for "the total economic education effort" set out in the Smock Report, including Programs One and Two. Subsequent efforts to clarify the relationship between the two organizations signaled the degree of crossover: the Advertising Council had not officially endorsed Program One and thus would not raise funds for it, but it would encourage the businesses it sought support from to also support plant education, and it would make the materials it developed for the "American Economic System" campaign available to the Joint Committee on Improvement for use in Program One. The Joint Committee on Improvement still positioned itself as separate from the Advertising Council, though, seeing the council as "one of several means to an end—namely, the creation of a better understanding of the economic system."[26]

The campaign's primary goal was to persuade the public to work for the "higher productivity per man-management-machine hour" that the Joint Committee on Improvement framed as the reason why Americans had "more freedoms—spiritual, intellectual and religious—than anywhere else, because these freedoms are interlocked with economic prosperity." Fones-Wolf notes that higher productivity fit neatly with a corporate-managerial ideal of society in which "corporate leaders claimed the right to control America's economic destiny without significant interference from unions or the state while acknowledging their responsibility to make the benefits of industrial capitalism available to all." Advertisements under the tagline "The better we produce—the better we live" featured ordinary folks—a bus driver, a farmer, a grocer, a power lineman—all claiming that higher productivity meant lower costs, more jobs, and material abundance for everyday people.[27] The campaign advertisements, as shown here in figures 4.2 through 4.5, reflected an institution-friendly politics: for example, Advertising Council leaders' vision of a "better" economic system qualified its designs for increased productivity by stipulating that the gains from this increased productivity should be "fully shared"—which was, in some ways, a nod to labor, but in other ways a strategic move to elide labor-management conflicts by promising a future with abundance for all.

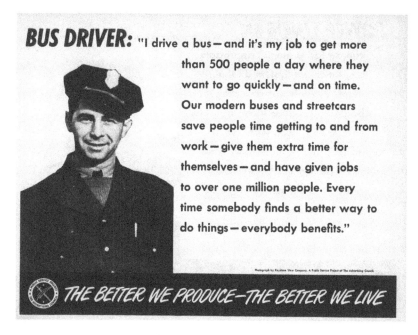

FIGURES 4.2 THROUGH 4.5 Advertisements created by the Advertising Council to support the American Economic System campaign: Figure 4.2 depicts a bus driver, using the transit system as an exemplar for the efficiency and shared benefits of finding "a better way to do things." Figure 4.3 depicts an electrical lineman, tying electrification of farms to higher productivity, from which, the ad declares, "everybody benefits." Figure 4.4 features a grocer declaring that thanks to "our American System," "Americans eat better than any other people." Figure 4.5 depicts a man in the gingham shirt and denim overalls of a worker or farmer with the copy, "Is higher production good for me? You bet it is," dramatizing the claim that higher production creates abundance for everyone. These images encapsulated the Advertising Council's efforts to create a unified message that spoke to a wide range of occupational and class positions while attempting to avoid controversy. Images reproduced with permission of the Advertising Council, image scans courtesy of the Ad Council archives at the University of Illinois. "Bus Driver [advertisement]," "Power Lineman [advertisement]," "Grocer [advertisement]," and "Is Higher Production Good for Me? [advertisement]," Advertising Council Papers, University Library at the University of Illinois, Records Group 13/2/282, Box 7, Campaign files, American Economic System.

Despite its seemingly wonkish focus on productivity, the campaign advertisements and *Miracle of America* booklet adopted the imagery of Uncle Sam, a white-bearded, flag-bedecked character best known from World War I recruiting posters. The use of Uncle Sam as the figure of authority conveyed the sensibilities with which the Joint Committee and the Advertising Council crafted its pitch: through a recourse to national mythology as a source of legitimacy.

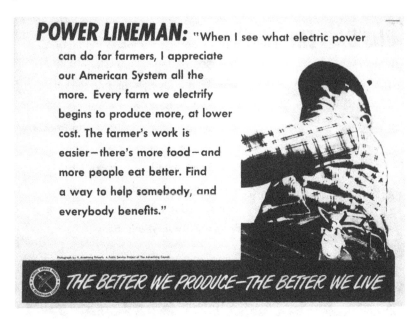

FIGURE 4.3.

The booklet presented a narrative about a family that displayed the imagery of white, middle-class norms—Mother, Dad, Sis, and Junior. The noticeable whiteness of the campaign was not unusual for the time. As advertising historian Jason Chambers observes, the staff of the major Madison Avenue advertising agencies in the 1940s was overwhelmingly white, and the executive ranks virtually entirely so: to the extent that such firms acknowledged the existence of Black Americans, they treated this segment of the population as "special markets" to be addressed separately from white audiences who, they believed, could be offended by positive representations of Black people and the challenges to the racial order such representations could imply. Showing a white family, by contrast, would have been seen as uncontroversial, even as it tacitly reinforced the country's existing racial inequalities by associating patriotism and middle-class family life with whiteness.[28]

The unreal qualities of myth seemed to suffuse the *Miracle of America* booklet itself: it opens on a domestic scene of Dad reading the paper, Mother seemingly mending a piece of clothing, and Junior at work on his homework. Junior asks:

"It says here America is great and powerful on account of the American economic system. What's our economic system, Dad?"

Dad put his paper down and appeared to be thinking hard.

"I'd like to know too," Mother put in. "I think in these times every American ought to be informed about what makes up the American way of life."

"So do I," Sis added.

"Well, I could give you all sorts of answers," Dad said. "But maybe we ought to get the story straight from the one who knows it best."[29]

The one who knows it best turns out to be Uncle Sam himself, who is illustrated only from the shoulders down with his head out of frame, almost as if to place the viewer sitting, childlike, at Uncle Sam's feet (figure 4.6). Uncle Sam declares that all Americans get "more of everything" when production is "better and faster." Support for this claim skimmed the history of the United States' colonization and westward expansion, including a supposition that homesteader families became more efficient by forming small groups that allowed labor specialization. The note of labor specialization transitions

FIGURE 4.4.

FIGURE 4.5.

the narrative into the industrial age: Uncle Sam celebrates the efficiency of production and consumption, culminating in industrial specialization, unionization, and "the greatest group of skilled workers and technicians the world has ever seen." This teleological march of progress, claims Uncle Sam, shows how productivity—brought on by new production efficiencies and economies of scale—leads to a higher living standards. Finally, Uncle Sam promises a limitless horizon of increasing wealth and well-being, "if we all understand that the social and economic system which assures individual freedom will always use its human and natural resources best."[30]

To be sure, the *Miracle of America* booklet's treatment of American history elided important elements of the US rise to national prosperity—for example, it avoided the United States' history of slavery and its influences on the development of the national economy and economic policies; labor-management conflicts, too, were downplayed. For all its claims to "sell" the American economic *system*, the booklet promoted a self-justifying managerial mythology of the American past and future, grounded in how the Smock Report had imagined the first few decades of the twentieth century to represent the entirety of US economic traditions. The *Miracle of America* booklet exemplified the paradoxical hollowness of the affirmative style, as summed up in the Joint Committee on

Junior gasped.

"Gee whiz—I know *him!*"

"Uncle Sam," Dad began,

"my boy here wants to know what makes America great. You know—our economic system and all that. Fact is, I guess we all do."

Uncle Sam smiled. "All right," he said. "Couldn't have come to a better place. Let's start at the beginning.

"How do we make a living?...

"That's what economics is, you know. The study of how men make a living. Let's go back to the early days.

"Well, like all people in a new country, we Americans needed food, clothing and shelter.

"At first, each pioneer family supplied nearly all its own needs. It was a hard life.

"As long as we lived apart, we had to work from dawn to dark to build homes, raise food and weave cloth.

"But when we began to gather in groups of several families, we found it was easier for each man to do just one thing and do it *well*. One could build houses, another could raise food, a third could weave cloth.

"Then the whole group could have more of everything because each man could produce better and faster."

FIGURE 4.6. A page from *Miracle of America* that places the reader at the feet of the mythic Uncle Sam. Images reproduced with permission of the Advertising Council, courtesy of the Ad Council archives at the University of Illinois. The Advertising Council, Inc., *The Miracle of America*, 4th ed. (New York: Advertising Council, 1950), 3.

Improvement's refusal to explain the production, finance, and distribution of what it called the American system and its efforts to instead inspire a sense of unity by focusing on American exceptionalism and visions of a productive, prosperous, and harmonious future.

The booklet also signaled a certain reluctance on the part of the advertising industry to articulate its own self-perceived importance to the public. Members of the AAAA and ANA had come to see themselves as economic authorities by virtue of their role in spurring consumption and funding a free press. Yet, the booklet suggested that economic knowledge originated elsewhere. Recall that Junior's initial query is prompted by his homework, which tells him that the nation's economic system is the source of its greatness and power; Dad leads the baffled family not to a business leader, a government official, or an expert in economics, but to a patriotic mythological figure—reinforcing the idea that private enterprise was an essential part of national identity.

In its first year, the "American Economic System" campaign racked up an estimated two billion radio impressions, six thousand outdoor advertising poster displays, received donations of advertising space from 120 magazines with a combined circulation of seventy-five million, and distributed one and a quarter million copies of *The Miracle of America*. These efforts were supported by publishers' and advertisers' sponsorship of advertisements; free promotion on billboards, on public transportation, and over the radio airwaves to "almost every home in America"; and financial support from major corporations including "General Electric, General Motors, International Business Machines, Eastman Kodak, Johnson and Johnson, Parker Pen and many others." By 1953, polling suggested that roughly fourteen million people were "familiar with" the *Miracle of America* booklet. Further, the same polling suggested that the booklet had been persuasive: when asked what accounted for the nation's high standard of living, workers and students who had read the booklet were around four times more likely to attribute the nation's economic success to the "competitive free enterprise system." These findings suggest that the campaign's affirmative style of promotion was effective.[31]

A Mighty Wave of Propaganda: Harding College's Freedom Forums

In addition to the Joint Committee on Improvement's strong affiliations with the Advertising Council, the Smock Report's three-part plan also led the Joint Committee on Improvement into partnerships with other, more partisan organizations such as the National Education Program of Harding College, a racially segregated Bible college in the small town of Searcy, Arkansas. Harding College would take part in Joint Committee on Improvement activities related to Program One, which focused on bringing sponsored economic education messages to workplaces and communities. The Joint Committee on Improvement's director of operations Kenneth Wells told the *New York Times* in mid-1949 that more than 360 US companies were sponsoring such programs in their plants and local communities. By 1950, Program One projects included a series of case history kits developed by a subcommittee of the ANA with involvement from representatives of the public relations and print publishing industries; an additional series of kits developed by the US Chamber of Commerce, with an estimated distribution of fourteen thousand; and a series of seminar retreats for executives at Harding College.[32]

Harding College first gained national notoriety in the early 1940s and would by the 1960s come to be pictured in the press as the center of ultraright anticommunist thought in the nation. Harding's president, theologian and activist George S. Benson, was a prominent political and cultural figure who, historian Robbie Maxwell argues, reconfigured Southern populism for the consumer era by asserting that "the conflict between ordinary Americans and eastern elites resided exclusively in the relationship between citizens and 'big government.'" Benson had been active as an advocate for tax "economy" (in press coverage of Benson, economy was used as a keyword for conservative reform premised on lowering taxation government spending, in a similar manner to "thrift"), first making national headlines in 1941 for his comments before the House Ways and Means Committee of the US Congress opposing federal tax-funded programs. Benson was a vocal opponent of New Deal programs such as the Civilian Conservation Corps (CCC), the National Youth Administration (NYA), and the Works Progress Administration (WPA), going so far as to claim in 1941 that the CCC ought to be eliminated entirely since his Bible college could "board and educate four boys" for the cost the government paid per enrollee in the CCC (in 1941 and 1942, Benson reused this rhetorical flourish but with wavering numbers, claiming anywhere from two to four boys could be educated at Harding College for the cost of one enrollee in CCC). Benson's name further arose in relation to a 1942 congressional spat between Democratic senator Harry F. Byrd of Virginia and NYA director Aubrey Williams, in which a group of Harding College students publicly requested that Williams remove them from the

NYA payrolls—leading Williams to describe Benson derisively as a "ringleader in the so-called economy drive." Many of the programs in Benson's crosshairs, including the CCC, the NYA, and WPA, would be shuttered or winding down by the end of 1943. Meanwhile, Benson's rhetoric shifted toward economic education.[33]

During the war years, Benson's rhetoric began to echo the promotional nationalism that had gained momentum in the New Deal era. At a Chicago Rotary Club appearance in April of 1943, for example, he called for not only for reductions in government spending, but also for "mass adult education to keep our people sold on the system of free private enterprise." Benson's phrasing of keeping people *sold* on private enterprise recalled the interwar catchphrase of selling America to Americans; in the same appearance, Benson echoed the NAM's messaging strategy with a declaration that "constitutional government and free private enterprise go hand in hand." By spring of 1946 Benson had taken up the trope of selling America wholeheartedly. For example, at a March 1946 meeting of the California Taxpayer Association, Benson declared that an economic education program was the "only hope" for the nation—and that "the American public can and must be resold on the American way of life." Benson's antitax, small-government philosophy dovetailed neatly with the ANA and AAAA's shared conviction that government should remain on the sidelines of US commerce and industry, limiting its role to that of a referee. Further, as the Advertising Council was debating the form it would take in the postwar period, Benson was developing relationships with advertising industry leaders who would later become affiliated with the Joint Committee on Improvement.[34]

In autumn of 1946, for example, Benson was involved in developing the first of a series of economic education cartoon shorts, *Make Mine Freedom*, with funding from the Alfred P. Sloan Foundation. In a thinly veiled anticommunist allegory, the film featured a traveling salesman character hawking bottles of a patent medicine called "-ISM." The film was produced by the animation studio of John Sutherland Productions, whose head, John Sutherland, was a former Disney animator (Sutherland would go on to produce *It's Everybody's Business* and many other economic education cartoons). Hoping to drum up financing for the distribution of motion picture short cartoons, Sutherland had presented an in-progress script for *Make Mine Freedom* to executives at the insulation and roofing manufacturer Johns-Manville Corporation, including a member of the Joint Committee on Improvement. Upon the release of *Make Mine Freedom* in summer of 1948, meeting minutes of the Joint Committee on Improvement would note with seeming approval that the motion picture included "many suggestions" from that committee member and "much from the Smock Report."[35]

A stronger connection between the Joint Committee on Improvement and Harding College was forged as Benson and Harding College got involved in Program One. Wells, Belding, and Benson came to an agreement that Harding College would take over Program One in January of 1949, with Benson proposing a plan for both an ongoing management seminar series at the college campus and biannual seminars in New York City. The Harding seminar series would be known as the Freedom Forum, which one *New York Times* journalist described as "intensive one-week seminar courses in the basic fundamentals of the American system particularly designed for business executives." Benson pledged to use the Smock Report as a basis for the Freedom Forum series. Harding College would promote and finance the events; Wells would be employed by Harding part-time to manage the program and the Joint Committee on Improvement would play an initial advisory role. After a visit to the campus, Wells described Harding College as "the strongest germ cell for the multiplication of freedom ideas now existing in the nation."[36]

From February 28 to March 5 of 1949, Harding College held its first Freedom Forum with seventy-eight RSVPs from fifty-five major American corporations. The agenda included seminars taught by Wells and Benson along with talks from Jack Smock, the lead author on the Smock Report; T. C. Kirkpatrick, the editor of the anticommunist newsletter *Counterattack*; John Beatty, president of the Employers' Association of Chicago; and California Institute of Technology physicist Robert A. Millikan. The Joint Committee on Improvement's official involvement would be limited. A memo from Don Belding to members of the Joint Committee on Improvement in May of 1949 noted that Benson had hoped for an ongoing partnership in which the committee could both advise Benson on issues that arose for the forums and, crucially, promote the forums to its affiliates, but members had questioned whether to do so. Despite Benson's aspirations, the partnership would be short-lived: the formal relationship between Harding College and the Joint Committee on Improvement was terminated in January of 1950, just one year after it began. Still, the Freedom Forums, given a strong start by the Joint Committee on Improvement's resources and extensive business connections, would continue through the 1960s — albeit with an increasingly pointed focus on communist subversion.[37]

The Joint Committee on Improvement's quick exit from its formal partnership with Harding College demonstrated the committee's overall reluctance to establish itself as anything other than a planning board whose designs could be implemented by others. Even before Benson's Harding College took over Program One, members of the AAAA had floated the idea that it might be better to disband than to implement programs themselves, much preferring that a third party, such as the Committee for Economic Development or the American Heritage Foundation, take over implementation. The partnership with Benson was a turning point for the Joint Committee on Improvement (whose funding from the AAAA and ANA was expiring), allowing it to shift its role to that of a "creative and plans board" and "a point of contact to channel the activities of others."[38]

The Influence of the Smock Report

By the early 1950s, it was clear that the Smock Report had been an exceedingly influential basis for sponsored economic education projects at the national level, even if financing from the ANA and AAAA had run out. It had served as the basis for a slidefilm,[39] *This Is Our Problem*, that publicized advertising industry leaders' arguments about the need for economic education at every level of US society. Program One, focused on changing workplace attitudes, encompassed both public-facing information programs such as the US Chamber of Commerce's "Explaining Your Business" program of community outreach and Harding College's executive-focused Freedom Forums; and Program Two's goal of advertising the US economic system was instantiated in the Advertising Council's "American Economic System" campaign, reaching tens of millions. Program Three's broader aims of facilitating educational outreach had some limited manifestations through *Freedom Is Indivisible*, a film featuring then general Dwight Eisenhower, and the formation of the nonprofit Freedoms Foundation, founded by Wells and Belding, whose activities included an "American Credo" republished in *Reader's Digest* and annual awards to citizens whose works—from high school graduation speeches to mass media content—enacted its take on American ideals. At its founding, the Freedoms Foundation portrayed itself as an offshoot of the Joint AAAA/ANA program to promote economic understanding whose rhetoric it echoed, stating in its charter that its purpose was to create better understanding of the United States' founding documents and "our 'bundle' of indivisible political and economic freedoms inherent in the American way of life"; press coverage of the foundation's establishment noted that the Joint Committee's projects included "an educational program yet to be fully developed." Historian Kevin Kruse identifies the Freedoms Foundation as one of several business-funded advocacy groups in the 1940s and 1950s that, he argues, emphatically linked advocacy for private enterprise to "piety and patriotism," drawing potent symbols of US culture into their efforts to oppose state power.[40]

In 1952, Joint ANA-AAAA Committee researchers surveyed the reach of the report and its affiliated projects, finding some results that seemed broad but uneven. Market research by leading firms such as Psychological Corporation and Opinion Research indicated that although the direct impact of economic education media was difficult to measure, public opinion seemed to be moving toward acceptance of the advertising industry's messages, in both indirect and direct senses. Psychological Corporation studies showed "a general favorable trend" in attitudes toward "big business" and less support for "government control of business"—although the same studies indicated that the public was still skeptical of business's profit-taking, its spending on advertising, and its stewardship of investors' money, and, moreover, that public attitudes of opposition to "socialism" did not preclude public support for such programs as public funded housing and pensions, rural electrification, and minimum wage laws. Opinion Research Corporation studies suggested that workplace-based economic education programs ranging from six-hour discussion courses to forty-week training courses resulted in improvements on a quiz designed to test "economic literacy"—although the desired results seemed more in evidence when it came to the topics of productivity, capital, competition, and regulation than to matters of profits and "how the system shares."[41]

However, the "great free enterprise campaign" did not meet with unanimous approval, as William Whyte's skewering of it demonstrated. Whyte was among many commentators in the 1950s who expressed reservations about sponsored economic education media. In 1951, the Brookings Institution, a prominent think tank for the social sciences, published an overview of economic education projects of all kinds including those created with industrial sponsorship. After administering questionnaires to more than two hundred groups involved in economic education, conducting personal interviews, and observing economic education programs in practice, its authors concluded that "organized educational institutions have not adequately met the educational requirements in this field," and that while some courses developed by "non-academic agencies" including professional groups and nonprofits had some merit, programs "for the general public" that used "the techniques and media of advertising" were "less valuable as means to genuine education." The authors asserted that "attractive pictures, catchy phrases, and reiterated listener impressions" were no "short cut to economic literacy" and that the effect of such campaigns on the people who had been exposed to them was unclear. Other critics of economic education media in the 1950s used harsher terms, describing economic education films as civically harmful materials that propagandized "through selection and omission of facts."[42]

Questions of whether the Joint Committee on Improvement should continue had been a matter of discussion since 1949. Just a few years later, internal committee documents questioned the very foundations of the project, observing that approaching public opinion as a problem of so-called understanding had only been partly effective. The Joint Committee on Improvement had assumed that the problems it sought to address were caused by misinformation, and "if we could replace this misinformation with information the job would be done"—but it had found that, especially with regard to Program Two's advertising for the American economic system, "When we encounter interested, open minds and friendly, emotional attitudes we have no problem. But when we run into the stone walls of apathy and emotional hostility our case simply doesn't get a hearing." Meanwhile, industry-led economic education efforts had proliferated, and committee members observed that the Joint Committee on Improvement no longer occupied the position of leadership it once had.[43]

By 1952, the Joint Committee on Improvement's attention seemed to be moving toward a focus on marketing. Discussions of how to get better uptake of its offerings in Program One and Program Two centered on how media and copy could be customized to different "economic, ideological, occupational" groups and other subsegments of the market. The committee also seemed to concede that it had made comparatively little leeway on its aspirations to reach the schools through Program Three, including multimedia curricular materials for use in educational settings: "Whether economic education in the schools is a responsibility that should be undertaken by advertising groups is a matter of question." As the 1950s progressed, the Joint Committee on Improvement would turn away from productivity discourses and toward a new focus on marketing. Meanwhile, a different group of experts, with a different style of economic education, was taking shape to address the question of economic education in the schools.[44]

CHAPTER FIVE

The New Economics

The question of economic education in the schools would be taken up by a different group of allies, whose distinctively scientific style of economic education would be shaped by global ideological conflict. This group, marshaled by business leaders, educators, and economists, cast itself as a rigorous and objective alternative to the perceived biases of companies' and trade groups' free enterprise promotional nationalism. Leaving aside much of the bombast of business institutions' economic education efforts, the Joint Council on Economic Education (JCEE) emphasized teacher training, coalition building, and cross-institutional consensus seeking, led by educators and supported by a board of politically moderate representatives of key constituencies including business, labor, and agriculture. It would grow to become the leading economic education organization in the United States. The JCEE advanced an imaginary of economic education based more in notions of teaching and training than notions of selling and feeling. Despite its stated commitments to objectivity and dispassionate analysis, however, the JCEE's rise to prominence in the 1950s and 1960s was nonetheless steeped in the ideological, cultural, and affective logics of the Cold War.[1]

This chapter examines how the JCEE's academics, teaching specialists, and their institutional sponsors developed and built the organizational infrastructure to support an alternative approach to economic education that emphasized academic rigor—in ways that confronted, yet ultimately harmonized with, the affirmative style of promotional nationalism that had characterized sponsored economic education in the immediate postwar period. The chapter begins by explaining how, after about a decade of steady organizational growth, late 1950s US geopolitical anxieties about the Soviet Union created an opportunity for the Joint Council on

Economic Education to present economic education as a part of the solution to a gap in scientific achievement. The chapter then examines how, in the early 1960s, the JCEE and the National Task Force on Economic Education set out a comprehensive vision for its style of economic education through a portfolio of reports, programs, and other publications. It shows how the JCEE's media outputs positioned the organization's vision of economic education as a rigorous, objective, and foundationally democratic way of thinking—but disappointed some business leaders, who saw the task force's emphasis on objectivity and critical thinking as an influence that could undermine young peoples' faith in the American system. The chapter then examines an unsuccessful collaboration between the JCEE and the Advertising Council in 1969. It argues that this campaign's failures revealed the limits of attempting to reconcile the JCEE's approach to economic education with the affirmative style of free enterprise business conservatism. Still, the story of how and why it failed shows how the two organizations incorporated changing rationales for economic education, moving in tandem from a Cold War contest of ideologies toward a focus on the domestic economy as an object of individual stewardship.

"Economic Citizenship" and the Committee for Economic Development

The JCEE was the product of a corporate-liberal arm of the US's mid-century business establishment, embodied in such organizations as its founding sponsor, the Committee for Economic Development (CED). As historian Robert M. Collins explains, the CED had been founded in 1942, describing its own goals in terms of facilitating public policy research and broadly planning for businesses' roles in the postwar economy. These goals were undergirded by a vision of the US economic system that, in contrast to the free enterprisers' rejection of government planning, saw federal management of the economy as a necessary measure to foster high employment levels and ensure the continuation of the United States' private enterprise system. The CED's moderate stance reflected its own institutional lineage: many in the CED's leadership circle had been members of the New Deal–era federal Business Advisory Council. Still others came to the CED through the University of Chicago, whose leadership included former businessmen, and whose trustees' interest in public affairs had facilitated exchanges between scholars and executives.[2]

As Elizabeth Fones-Wolf has observed, the CED's "moderate" approach, and its view "that economic stability depended upon an expanded role for the government in the economy," stood in contrast to the insistent free enterprise positioning of the NAM. The ANA, AAAA, and Advertising Council, much like the NAM and the US Chamber of Commerce, focused on an essentially antiregulatory, corporate-managerial economic doxa that rejected state management of the economy. In comparison to the free enterprisers, the conciliatory stance of the CED enfolded a broader variety of stakeholders, especially academics, and was focused less on cultivating affect around potent symbols like the flag and Uncle Sam than on enacting a technical approach to economic planning and analysis (to be sure, this approach had its own affective valence, but it tended less toward bombast than toward a placid confidence in the power of analysis). While the organization supported the idea of federal management of at least some aspects of the economy, its members nonetheless advocated for positions that benefited business and industry. For example, press coverage indicated that the CED supported pushes to cut taxes, reduce federal spending, and limit wage and price controls in the early 1950s.[3]

To say that the CED's stances were different from those espoused by the advertising industry's major professional organizations is not to suggest, however, that advertising executives were absent from the CED. Former advertising executive William Benton, who had taken a position as vice president of the University of Chicago, was a cofounder of the CED. Benton's leadership in the CED indicated that advertising executives, like business executives, were not monolithic in their political ideals and approaches to the question of how to manage the national economy. Fones-Wolf notes that the CED and the free-enterprise faction represented by the NAM both believed "individual freedom was 'the cornerstone of our economic system.'" Both camps also gestured to democracy as a rationale for economic education, claiming that the democratic decision-making public would need to be properly informed. However, as postwar economic education gathered momentum in the mid- to late 1940s, concerns about the appearance of bias appeared to prevent the CED from aligning itself too closely with corporate-funded economic education projects.[4]

Indeed, in 1948 members of the Joint ANA-AAAA Committee on Improvement of Understanding of Our Economic System (which I referred to in the prior chapter as the Joint Committee on Improvement) repeatedly approached the CED in their search for organizations who could implement their three-part program for national economic education.

CED members reportedly agreed that an economic education effort was necessary but declined to partner with the trade groups: Joint Committee on Improvement meeting minutes described CED representatives as "sensitive to accusations of 'propaganda' activity" and reluctant to take on any project that would call their impartiality into question. The CED had good reason to be wary: businesses stepped up their attempts to curry favor with educators and students in the late 1940s and early 1950s, but industry groups' prior attempts to influence school curricula had been met with public scorn. For example, Oreskes and Conway recount how the National Electric Light Association, a utilities trade group, was found to have waged massive propaganda campaigns in the 1920s that included systematic efforts to remove critiques of the utilities industry from the nation's textbooks. And historian S. Alexander Rippa documents how, as recently as 1941, the NAM had invoked a public furor after funding a team of researchers to examine commonly used textbooks for evidence of bias in their portrayals of private enterprise.[5]

In January of 1949, a few months after declining to collaborate with the ANA and AAAA, the CED provided seed funding for the JCEE to be incorporated as an officially independent, nonpartisan organization supporting secondary school education in economics. The CED's reluctance to court controversy, and the insistence that the JCEE would be politically nonpartisan, reflected political tensions in American education. As intellectual historian Ronald Lora notes, educational resources were put toward supporting the war effort during World War II, but after the war, the country's schools were subject to a "new age of suspicion" of communist influence, coupled with a deeper debate about the proper purposes of education: "is an educational system that tries to solve the problem of unemployment, or acts as an aid to agriculture, or as 'a basic resource of national defense, something different than it has been in the past?' Are the values and purposes of 'a basic resource of national defense' similar to those of an educational system that does not serve as such?"[6]

A retelling by JCEE chairman and education scholar G. Derwood Baker traced the organization's genesis to a 1948 intensive workshop series that he had organized, the New York University Workshop on Economic Education, which had brought academic faculties of education and economics and officials from school systems together with representatives from labor unions, research foundations, nonprofit organizations, and businesses to "develop a plan for a national curriculum and teacher training movement" designed to prepare young people for "economic citizenship." After three weeks of meetings, the workshop participants had concluded that an ongoing program would be needed, leading within a few months to the formal founding of the JCEE. By mid-1949, press accounts reported that JCEE-affiliated educators were meeting in New York with the support of the CED's "business-educational committee," which included administrators from Harvard Business School, Dartmouth College, University of California, Berkeley, and the University of Rochester; top-level executives from General Foods Corporation, Time Incorporated, General Electric Company, and mortgage company Continental Incorporated; and leaders of nonprofit organizations including the American Gas Association, the American Council on Education, and the CED, who also funded the new organization. The involvement of educators in the NYU workshops, and their choice of analytical techniques, alluded to how the participants—and, by extension, the academics and business leaders affiliated with the CED—approached the problem of increasing "economic understanding" in ways that differed from the affirmative style of promotional nationalism typical of the advertising industry.[7]

Instead of relying on the affective richness and persuasive power of optimistic patriotism, the JCEE developed out of an analytical approach and a correspondingly controlled affective posture. Baker noted that the organizers of the original NYU workshops designed the sessions around a focus on the new technique of national income analysis, using it as a frame for examining socioeconomic problems. The use of such aggregate statistical measures suggested that the CED approached the question of economic knowledge in an analytical manner, through calculation and planning of economic possibilities. It also showed that the CED had embraced a conceptualization of the economic system as a proxy for nationhood that had been developed not long before—and that contained its own contradictions. Political theorist Timothy Mitchell argues that anthropologists, sociologists, and economists aided "the emergence of the idea of the economy in the interwar period," but draws particular attention to econometricians' "attempt to create a mathematical representation of the entire economic process as a self-contained and dynamic mechanism." Mitchell frames the development of "systematized" methods for calculating economic statistics at the national level as part of creating the *idea* of an economy, which, in turn, "provided a new, everyday language in which the nation-state could speak of itself and imagine its existence as something natural, spatially bounded, and subject to political management." Yet, Mitchell notes, even as these quantitative methods seemed to render the world more calculable, the qualitative and affective practices of branding and promotion flourished, too, and were more resistant to quantification: the new practices of quantification and promotion, in short, "formed both the possibility of the modern economy and the increasing impossibility of its representation." These practices of image-making had been markedly prominent in free enterprisers' patriotism-based appeals to emotions and identities. In contrast, the JCEE and CED's focus on analysis and objectivity would be premised upon expressions of capitalist norms and nationalist ideologies that were comparatively understated, but with their own kind of ideological and affective gravity.[8]

The JCEE's scholarly commitments were shaped by the Cold War. Its approach to economic education paralleled CED approaches to social problems, striving to project a public image of impartiality and political moderation. Yet, in a hard limit on the CED's claims of impartiality, CED leadership was explicitly anticommunist. For example, at a 1950 board of trustees event, former CED chairman and cofounder Paul Hoffman, who was then at the end of what historian Francis X. Sutton calls "a spectacularly successful term as administrator of the Marshall Plan," reportedly referred to the Soviet Union as "a perfectly stinking system," with incoming CED chairman, Eastman Kodak treasurer and statistician Marion B. Folsom, reiterating the notion that the country would benefit from increased productivity and further stating that businessmen must "really help in developing of national policies which will preserve and strengthen our political freedom." In this regard, the CED employed what media historian Michael Curtin calls "the discourse of scientific anticommunism," a rhetorical and cultural strategy in which "the dispassionate language of scientific method was married to the political rhetoric of superpower struggle." This is not to say that the CED's approach was free of affect, but rather that it, and the JCEE, took an affective tone of confidence that systemic, rational analysis would result in good decisions.[9]

The two competing visions of economic education that crystallized in the free enterprise NAM and AAAA/ANA, on one hand, and the academic-moderate CED and JCEE, on the other, then, can be imagined as different ways of seeing and thinking that addressed different elements of a single cultural system. The superiority of private enterprise to planned economies was a foregone conclusion for both factions, establishing a set of shared beliefs. However, the two factions' approaches to how and what to tell Americans about economics and the economic system differed. The NAM, AAAA/ANA, and other industry groups championed a

THE NEW ECONOMICS   113

foundationally affirmative narrative around the meaning of private enterprise in US cultural and political systems that relied on upbeat, brief, and patriotic direct appeals to the public. In contrast, the JCEE championed teacher training as an indirect, but richer and more finely calibrated, form of public knowledge building. The JCEE imagined its approach to be objective and rational, but it nonetheless incorporated the normative appeals to decentralization and self-determination that gave the free enterprisers' insistent message some of its links to ideas of freedom. To an extent, these approaches competed with each other for public attention and funding; yet, they can be seen as complementing one another by cultivating affective, normative, and epistemic orientations toward capitalism in popular culture in the postwar era and, in the process, seeding an atmosphere of inevitability and naturalness for the anticommunist politics of the moment.[10]

Hitching Economic Education to a Rocket: The JCEE and the Ideologies of the Space Race

The JCEE's first decade was defined by growth. For the first several years of its existence, it focused on workshops for teachers that instructed them in JCEE's version of economic essentials and, further, developed classroom materials for presenting those essentials to their students. In 1950 the JCEE offered an "extensive program" of workshops at nine universities, in which seven hundred secondary school teachers met with economists, educators, and industry leaders to learn new concepts and develop teaching materials for future use. It was hoped that the workshops would enable participants to become leaders who would help improve their communities' "understanding of the forces which make our American economy function in a democratic manner," in the words of one *New York Times* reporter. In the next several years, the JCEE would offer summer workshops on an increasing number of university campuses and coordinate a growing network of local Councils for Economic Education (CEEs) that facilitated the development and distribution of educational materials. A surge of inflation in 1950 and 1951 likely helped to build interest in the expanding economic education program, which was largely supported by an ongoing grant from the Ford Foundation—of which Paul Hoffman, formerly of the CED, would be chairman from 1950 to 1952—and augmented by additional funding from the CED.[11]

The JCEE's approach to economic education reflected its role in a developing postwar social order—one in which institutions grappled with the question of how to foster a democratic culture in the aftermath of a conflict with authoritarianism. As communication historian Fred Turner points out, the Ford Foundation's 1950 annual report had defined a democratic society as one in which citizens could see themselves as free individuals: one in which "the job of government was not to control the choices of citizens, but rather to set a principled framework within which they might make their own choices" without the rigid ideological and practical hierarchies of authoritarian systems. This emphasis on empowered citizenship extended to the Ford Foundation's view of economic education: "there is a need for every citizen to have some adequate understanding of the economic institutions, problems, and issues in our industrial society. Economic questions underlie government policy, affect the daily existence of every citizen, and are world-wide in their implications." Indeed, the foundation's declaration of its priorities included "raising the level of economic understanding of the citizens of the nation": doing so, it asserted, would support individual "economic well-being" and "improve economic institutions for the better realization of democratic goals."[12]

By the mid-1950s, the JCEE's growing size and influence was reflected in press coverage of economic education as a burgeoning trend. One 1955 report in the *Wall Street Journal* profiled JCEE workshops along with many of the business-affiliated free enterprise programs to which the JCEE offered an alternative. These included the NAM's "How Our Business System Operates" teacher training and curriculum materials (adapted from a DuPont plant education program that had itself been influenced by the Smock Report); "Business-Education Day" plant-visit programs coordinated by the US Chamber of Commerce; the American Economic Foundation's films and educational materials program, *How We Live in America*; and the information packets, books, and pamphlets provided to high school educators and debate teams by the Foundation for Economic Education, an organization that would become especially well-known for its free enterprise pamphlet *I, Pencil*. The *Wall Street Journal*'s enthusiastic coverage described "the stepped up economics education campaign" as offering "more economics instruction than ever before . . . perhaps in somewhat more palatable doses than in the past," thanks to a JCEE-inflected strategy of integrating concepts from economics into courses in other social studies disciplines such as history and civics. The JCEE's leaders had consistently argued not only that economics was a necessary topic for inclusion in the secondary curriculum, but also that properly trained teachers would be able to weave economics ideas into a wide range of school subjects. In the years to come, the sense of urgency undergirding such claims would collide with a national mood of anxiety over the escalating Cold War.[13]

The geopolitical events of late 1957 drew questions of educational reform into the ideological conflict between the United States and the Soviet Union. In October and November of 1957, the Soviet Union launched the world's first artificial Earth satellites, Sputnik and Sputnik II. The launches spurred a panic over science and technology in the United States. As cultural historian Ryan Boyle observes, American scientists were "stunned" and American lawmakers "startled"; the imagery of Sputnik suffused headlines and even started a craze for space-themed toys. Concerns only intensified, Boyle notes, after the launch of the larger and heavier Sputnik II: "after all, an enemy that could fire a satellite all the way up into space, the reasoning went, could probably hit US cities here on Earth." Just a few days later, the US Office of Education released conclusions from a two-year study of Soviet schooling. The study found that more secondary students in the Soviet Union were educated on science and mathematics, and with a greater degree of sophistication, than their American counterparts.[14]

In the face of an embarrassing and undeniable achievement gap, the Office of Education report defended the US education system's administration of educational policy at the state and local levels as a stronghold of democracy, in contrast to a Soviet educational system that it characterized as overly centralized, "rigid and inflexible," and fixated on loyalty to Soviet ideology. From this perspective, seeming Soviet advantages in education and science were in fact a temporary illusion, brought about by an oppressively restrictive and totalizing political culture. If the United States seemed to be lagging behind the Soviets in technical achievement, the report implied, it was only because Americans favored a decentralized system that enacted and protected American democratic values. In other words, the report reframed the United States' struggles to keep pace with the Soviet technological advances as a consequence of the US's *political* freedoms.[15]

Nonetheless, the Sputnik launches set off a wave of public concern about the quality of the US educational system and soul-searching about American culture's failure to prioritize intellectual achievements that could translate into technological and military power. These concerns led to an influx of new funding through the National Defense Education Act of 1958 and further, as historian of education Campbell Scribner notes, to instructional mandates to teach American children about the comparative systems and societies of the United States and the Soviet Union. They also opened possibilities for the JCEE to raise its profile in the national conversation.[16]

News coverage suggested that the JCEE and CED's rhetoric shifted toward a Cold War frame during the period after the Sputnik launches. One early JCEE-affiliated commentary, in response to a *New York Times* editorial published a week after the launch of Sputnik II, echoed the sentiment that the US needed to catch up to the Soviets. The initial editorial had observed that, amid calls for increased education in science, Americans would need to understand science better, and scientists would need to build up their awareness about the economic ramifications of their findings. This last point transformed the subtext—the Cold War clash of economic systems—into an explicit call for economic concepts to be included in the expansion of science education. JCEE associate director George L. Fersh seized on this opportunity. In a letter to the editors, he praised the *Times*' editorial, declaring that not only scientists but the public at large should be trained to "appreciate the structural and financial framework of our own economy within which scientific effort must be advanced."[17]

By the following summer, CED rhetoric had become thoroughly inflected by Cold War tensions. In March of 1958 the CED published a collection of comments from a recent meeting under the title *Soviet Progress vs. American Enterprise*, which a *New York Times* book reviewer deemed to contain "humbling, but important and most necessary" evidence that Americans had underestimated the Soviet Union as an adversary. CED president Alfred C. Neal caught journalists' attention in June of 1958 by declaring that economic growth was a "major weapon in the contest which is now going on for the world," and again in August of 1958 by asserting to JCEE workshop attendees that any seeming Soviet scientific or economic progress was in fact built upon "a base provided by the free societies of Western civilization," whose standard of living, Neal suggested, the Soviets could not hope to match. Meanwhile, a Purdue Opinion Poll of thousands of high school students found that youth support for "socialistic ideas" such as nationalized medicine and low-income housing had declined as compared to five or ten years prior but, as the *Chicago Daily Tribune* put it, "surprisingly large percentages of them are ready to turn

THE NEW ECONOMICS

over important segments of our economy to government regulation." Such findings seemed to confirm economic education proponents' insistence that if not trained to think otherwise, young citizens could turn their voting power into policies that would favor state economic management over individual liberties.[18]

These anxieties led to educational reforms that, for the JCEE, offered opportunities to position economics not only as a central topic in American secondary education, but also as a method of analytical thinking that students could use in every part of their lives. The calls for educational reform prompted by the Sputnik launches were formalized in 1958's National Defense Education Act. The act, based on the recommendations of an expert committee appointed by Marion Folsom, authorized $1 billion of federal funding for programs to improve the development of young Americans' skills in science, mathematics, foreign languages, and technology. As education scholar Wayne Urban observes, "all participants in the NDEA campaigns used Sputnik to pursue educational agendas that ran far beyond the national defense scare it created." The JCEE and CED, too, seemed poised to make the most of the public's renewed interest in redesigning education.[19]

In 1960, the CED organized and funded a new project: the National Task Force on Economic Education. The American Economic Association selected five economists—George Leland ("Lee") Bach, Lester V. Chandler, Robert A. Gordon, Ben W. Lewis, and Paul A. Samuelson— who were joined by JCEE director M. L. ("Moe") Frankel and education expert Arno A. Bellack. Bach, an economist trained at the University of Chicago, was at this point the dean of Carnegie Institute of Technology's Graduate School of Industrial Administration and a leading figure in the reform of US graduate business schools in the 1950s and 1960s (a movement that was itself funded with millions of dollars of Ford Foundation grants). With the assistance of JCEE-affiliated educators, the task force would aim to "define what economics high school students can and should be taught for effective citizenship and participation in the democratic system." Task force chairman Bach played up the task force's departure from the normative and ideological emphasis of free enterprise sponsored economic education projects to a *New York Times* reporter in 1961, declaring that the top priority for reform of the teaching of economics was a fundamental change in approach that would replace "emotional 'good guys vs. bad guys' types of snap judgments" with "an orderly, objective way of thinking about economic problems." Bach's comments gestured to a sense of analytical rigor that seemed to align his vision of economics with the knowledge-creation procedures of the sciences, implying that the JCEE's style of economic education harmonized with the improvements in scientific education called for in the National Defense Education Act.[20]

Bach's comments aligning the National Task Force on Economic Education with the rigor of the sciences reflected a central theme of the JCEE's approach to economic education. From its founding in 1949 to the establishment of the National Task Force on Economic Education in 1960, educators and business leaders affiliated with the CED and the JCEE had emphasized the scholarly rigor and political moderation of their projects, insisting that their approach was more analytical and impartial than that of the NAM and other business advocacy groups. Even so, the CED and JCEE's projects were as committed to capitalism as the free enterprise campaigns they purported to replace: their seeming endorsement of scientific objectivity was undergirded by a comparatively soft-spoken but resolute anticommunism. This ideological position set up the CED, the JCEE, and their allies in the National Task Force on Economic Education to benefit from national soul-searching over American educational shortcomings in the wake of the Sputnik launches. Their declarations of commitment to capitalism could tamp down Cold War anxieties while bestowing a sheen of scientific objectivity on efforts to build American youths' understanding of, and appreciation for, private enterprise. In the years to come, the JCEE would use the educational reform spirit of the late 1950s and early 1960s to launch an ambitious new agenda.

Setting the Agenda: The National Task Force and *Economic Education in the Schools*

In the 1960s, the National Task Force on Economic Education set out a vision for the reform of economics teaching, and the JCEE developed and distributed training programs, materials, and curricula to make that vision a reality. The task force's report suggested that economic education could develop a rigorous, objective, and fundamentally democratic way of thinking that would enable youth to see the benefits and drawbacks of both capitalist and communist systems. This analytical way of knowing the world, the task force reasoned, would ultimately help young people recognize capitalist systems as more economically and politically desirable than socialist or communist systems. Yet, this approach failed to satisfy some CED members and commentators, who saw the task force's attempts at objectivity as more likely to undermine youths' faith in the American system than to bolster it.

The National Task Force on Economic Education announced its plan to reform economic education in the fall of 1961. The task force advocated for a multipronged approach, supported by a range of media materials designed to appeal to both teachers and the general public. *Economic Education in the Schools*, its comprehensive report on secondary education in economics, presented a rationale for the project and a survey of the economic concepts and ideas that, the task force argued, every student should know. Additional materials developed by special committees of the JCEE helped support this agenda: for example, a descriptive review of teaching materials based on the guidelines of the task force report, *Study Materials for Economic Education in the Schools*, was sent to twenty-five thousand high schools, along with samples of the most highly rated teaching materials. Further bolstering these efforts, *The American Economy*, a television series aimed at teacher training and spanning 160 episodes of college-level telecourse content, was broadcast on CBS in the 1962–63 school year to what later JCEE fundraising documents described as "the largest viewing audience in its first year for any course in educational television history." The Ford Foundation offered $300,000 in grants to publishers to develop new teaching materials, and the task force coordinated a national effort to train more teachers and promote secondary-level instruction in economics. Press coverage positioned the task force's project as an "overhaul" of secondary economics teaching that made "economics the first of the social sciences to follow the revolutionary reforms instituted in mathematics and the sciences."[21]

The task force's 1961 report, *Economic Education in the Schools*, made the case that national concerns could be addressed with more and better economic education. It opened with a now-familiar assertion that the American public was ignorant or misled about economics. To establish the scope of the issue, the task force presented statistics about the lack of formal economics training in US secondary education: for example, it stated that only 5 percent of high school students took an economics course (which, the report warned, were "generally descriptive and all too often dry and sterile"). The report argued that the best form of economic education would teach students "to reason clearly and objectively about economic issues," a skill that the task force imagined as an important step in students' overall "mental development." This reasoning positioned economics as a way of thinking that was both systematic—calling to mind the procedures of scientific inquiry—and useful for democratic decision-making. In this sense, the task force adapted discourses that had been articulated to the teaching of science in the 1950s: as historian Audra Wolfe observes, some science educators at the time attempted to reconcile seeming rifts between the pressure to train a new generation of scientists, on one hand, and the call to create well-rounded citizens, on the other, by arguing that instruction in science could develop not only students' technical skills but also their abilities to "think for themselves" and, by extension, their capacities to be responsible citizens.[22]

The report then turned to what economic concepts students should know, focusing on production, growth, and distribution, all taking place under assumed conditions of scarcity. It noted that most economies—Soviet and American economies included—were "mixed," with some elements of both central management and private enterprise. Throughout, the report emphasized the importance of explaining areas of controversy and the major conflicting viewpoints to which they pertained. This was especially notable in the report's treatment of communism and socialism, which focused on the effects of the Soviet Union's centralized planning and ownership in encouraging economic growth and stability. Next, the report offered recommendations for both stand-alone economics courses and the inclusion of economics in history, business, and "Problems of American Democracy" courses (Scribner comments that such "Problems" courses could be grab-bag offerings that mixed "bland civics" with such unrelated topics as driver's education and life skills). Returning to its claims about economics as a knowledge technique, the report suggested that the "prime objective" of economic education should be a "rational way of thinking"—this, the report stated, was more important even than a broad command of economic concepts. In closing, the report offered several recommendations for the improvement of economic education, including an embrace of "controversial" topics; mandated training in economics for social studies and business teachers; teacher participation in JCEE workshops and the national television course; continued development of teaching materials; and support from professional economists and members of the public.[23]

The task force's production of a public-facing and highly publicized report offers evidence of how organizations affiliated with the CED both constituted a community of practice and constructed that community's purpose. As anthropologist Matthew S. Hull argues, bureaucratic documents are artifacts that help to organize and constitute organizational networks. Further, organizational scholars JoAnne Yates and Wanda Orlikowski adapt the term *genre* to describe institutionally recognized forms of communication (such as the memo or the meeting): a "genre of organizational communication," they explain, is a "typified communicative action invoked in response to a recurrent situation." The research report can be understood as belonging to a genre of organizational communication through which a group asserted its expertise on a given topic. In response to a situation where action was perceived to be necessary, the research report organized information, represented that information as credible, and conveyed that information to a broader audience. In this light, the task force's research report can be seen as a statement about the legitimacy of the organization's interventions in the secondary curriculum—one that crystallized a shared set of ideas from which further coordinated organizational action could be generated. In other words, the task force's report served both denotative and connotative functions: it explicitly conveyed information on behalf of the task force, the JCEE, and other affiliated organizations, but it also implicitly asserted the task force's authority, knowledge, and credibility.[24]

From this perspective, *Economic Education in the Schools* may be seen as both a declaration of the task force's expertise and a statement of purpose—similar to the platform of a political party—that could guide the development of CED-affiliated media outputs such as *The American Economy* telecourse and such supporting materials as study guides. Orlikowski and Yates elsewhere observe that an organization or community will tend to use a "genre repertoire" of "multiple, different, and interacting genres" that "are habitually enacted by members of a community to realize particular social purposes." From this perspective, the National Task Force on Economic Education can be understood as being part of a community of practice that included the JCEE and economists affiliated with the American Economic Association. The task force's flagship report, *Economic Education in the Schools*, expressed that community's norms by portraying the members of the task force—primarily economists, joined by specialists in the teaching of economics—as people qualified to design an educational agenda that could train citizens to see capitalist economic systems as aligned with principles of democracy and self-determination.[25]

The task force insisted that it was nonpartisan and "completely independent" of its parent organizations, a quality that the leaders of the CED and the American Economic Association emphasized when, in their preface to task force's flagship report, it declared that the report would give "scant comfort" to special interests. For example, the report disapprovingly described the coverage of economics in American secondary textbooks as containing "superficial" reasoning and unreflective value judgments, made worse by a "flood" of "special pamphlets and materials" sponsored by business, farm, and labor organizations, many of which the report wrote off as "sheer propaganda." In contrast to these unsavory materials, the task force positioned their own work as impartial, reasoned, and fair. Indeed, the task force's focus on teaching reasoning skills may have been a way of reckoning with the complexity and contestedness of economic issues, in which clear answers seemed scarce: as a *Business Week* magazine feature on the task force put it, "one of the oldest cracks about economists is that if you laid them all end to end, they would never reach a conclusion. Economics itself is regarded, by most laymen, not as a systematic body of knowledge, but as a foggy battleground on which opponents of different ideologies or interests clash by night."[26]

However, the task force's approach ultimately found only a lukewarm audience with members of its own parent organization, the CED. A skirmish between task force leader George Bach and the press in 1961 prefigured some business conservatives' frosty reception of *Economic Education in the Schools*. A *Wall Street Journal* editorial in late 1961 dismissed the report, complaining that the task force's coverage of socialist and capitalist systems was "apologetic, if not downright critical of our alleged economic inadequacies," and likely only to impress upon students "the inadequacy of freedom." In a letter to the editors, Bach retorted that the *Journal* had misleadingly taken a brief passage out of context, going on to defend the recommendation that US youth study the Soviet system in order to rebuff it. Bach wrote:

> Communism will not go away because we pretend it's not there, or that it can't work. It is there, and it does work—not nearly as well as our system, but well enough to make it a dangerous enemy and a real alternative to the private enterprise way in the eyes of much of the world. We had better face up to its power if we want to understand it and fight it effectively.

Bach went on, chastising the *Journal* for pushing its own ideology instead of supporting students in reaching their own conclusions, and warning business leaders that "by trying to insist on nothing but their own viewpoints in the high school classroom, they risk losing the whole battle for economic literacy." *Journal* editors continued the attack, publishing Bach's letter along with a further comment that doubled down on its critiques. In doing so, they drew on NAM-style rhetorics of freedom, insisting that the report's acknowledgment of shortcomings in the private enterprise

THE NEW ECONOMICS   123

system implied that "economic freedom"—and by extension all forms of freedom—were "inadequate."[27]

The scuffle between Bach and the *Journal* presaged a public disagreement between CED members and the task force. In March of 1962 the CED's research and policy committee issued a statement reexamining the task force report and stating concerns that the report "had not sufficiently emphasized the fact that 'personal freedom and freely chosen institutions are basic to our type of society and that these are values which should be emphasized to high school students.'" To this end, the CED policy committee's statement declared,

> With reference to personal freedom, we would take a more affirmative position than the Task Force report. The Task Force report, it seems to us, regards freedom as one among competing values, of which the individual may want more or less. In the abstract, we cannot quarrel with this. But . . . other goals—rising living standards, high employment and security—have value only if individuals maintain their freedom to choose their way of living and their employment.

The CED policy committee ultimately still endorsed the task force's guidelines for educational reform, but echoed the *Journal*'s earlier critiques: it rearticulated the claim that economic and political freedoms were inextricable from one another, implying that affirming "our free enterprise economy" should be a priority of economic educators.[28]

These controversies illustrated the risks inherent in the task force's attempts to perform an objective assessment of economic systems while maintaining an underlying allegiance to the private enterprise system: to some publics, the task force's report fit with the analytical mode typical of scientific anticommunist consensus politics in the early 1960s. With business advocates invested in the affirmative style of free enterprise promotional nationalism, however, the task force found itself in a no-win situation: anything other than praise for free enterprise and condemnation of central economic planning generated accusations of socialist sympathies.

In a Free Society, We're All Economists: *The American Economy* and Cold War Media Flows

The JCEE's ideals of objectivity and systematic thinking carried over to the *American Economy* television course. The course was produced by

Learning Resources Institute, a nonprofit media production organization that specialized in educational television, with cosponsorship by the American Economic Association, the JCEE, and the National Task Force on Economic Education. The program used the broad reach of television to present both teachers and the public with economic education media that presented itself as objective and democratic. In the process, it became part of the media flow of broadcast television, reinforcing popular media narratives that counterposed freedom against communism.[29]

Media historian Anna McCarthy observes that in the Cold War era, a range of powerful sectors, including government, business, and philanthropy, attempted to use television programs to construct and convey understandings of citizenship, developing the individual into "a rational, moderate, and self-managing self, informed enough to evaluate intelligently the choices it confronted in the marketplace, in the political arena, and in the realm of arts and culture." *The American Economy* was no exception. Many of the themes that had typified the National Task Force on Economic Education's agenda for the civic applications of economic education in the 1960s were present, too, in the pitch for the television series. Promising to clarify "the difference between value judgments on one hand, and objective description and analysis on the other," planning materials positioned the program as an aid to new ways of thinking. This did not, however, mean that the series would espouse leaving aside values and emotions entirely. Rather, a brochure introducing the series candidly admitted that "facts are essential for analysis, but emotions are essential for making the policy choices that follow hard upon analysis. Rational thinking about economics separates the facts from the emotions, but keeps a role for both." Students would need to use knowledge along with their own personal judgment and principles. This emphasis on individual decision-making carried through to expectations for how teachers should use the television program. The telecourse was offered with the stipulation that teachers should have the academic freedom to teach the materials as they chose, echoing the logics of democratic decentralization that typified the US's reckoning with the US education system in the aftermath of the Sputnik launches. Overall, the course presented economics as a sophisticated mode of thinking that would create thoughtful, informed democratic citizens.[30]

Promotional materials were frank about the program's corporate sponsorship but insisted that this funding did not compromise the program's academic integrity. The official study guide for the series included a lengthy roster of seventy-five sponsors, almost all corporations and corporate philanthropic foundations, that contributed financial support for the series, imparting a gloss of managerial blessing and institutional consensus over the series. But, the guide insisted, these organizations were not in control of the series' content. Rather, the content was decided by the "National Teacher" who hosted and presented the program. Public comments from the man filling the role of National Teacher—labor economist John R. Coleman, then a professor of economics at Carnegie Institute of Technology—may not have been partial to any particular company but did echo some of the ideological tones of Sputnik-era educational discourses. Coleman suggested to a *Pittsburgh Courier* reporter that better knowledge of economics would help citizens not only to improve their personal budgets, but also to make better voting decisions about the "role of the Federal government in the economy" and the United States' "dealings with world countries, friendly and unfriendly." Coleman's justifications for the program telegraphed an understanding of economic education's stakes in the Cold War United States: Coleman declared to the *Courier*, "economics is too important to leave for economists alone. In a free society, we're all economists." In unspoken contrast to popular portrayals of the Soviet Union's educational, economic, and political systems as autocratic and rigid, Coleman's comments positioned students as politically empowered democratic participants who, with the right training, could make decisions that continued to set the nation apart from its most powerful rivals. It also reinforced long-standing rhetorics of economic education, framing freedom and capitalism as so inseparable that living in a free society made economic knowledge essential.[31]

Television, with its broad reach into postwar society, seemed to be a form of media distribution that was compatible with the JCEE's assumptions about economic education and democracy. The television course was aimed primarily at high school teachers, with intended additional audiences of the "thoughtful members of the general public" and "interested college students" that could be reached through broad distribution over the airwaves. High school was a crucial moment for educating "the citizens of tomorrow," planning documents for the series observed, but high schools rarely offered instruction in economics—and even the teachers who did offer such instruction often had little formal training to do so. By proposing the television course as a remedy for these problems, the task force positioned the television series as a mode of *training*—a different form of communication from the framings of appreciation and persuasion employed by free enterprisers. Through this training, the JCEE suggested, secondary school teachers and ordinary members of the public alike could come to appreciate freedom by learning how to think like economists. Further, supporting materials for the series highlighted the special affordances of television, such as expanded possibilities for visual aids, dramatizations, and guest lecturers.[32]

In the 1962–63 school year, *The American Economy* was broadcast over the airwaves of 182 CBS network affiliates and fifty-four educational television stations across the nation, with an estimated viewership of over a million people per episode. It covered a considerable range of concepts including methods for economic analysis, market price mechanisms, natural resources, econometrics, money supply, employment and inflation stabilization measures, monopoly, income distribution, organized labor, taxation and federal budgets, world trade, and the comparative systems of capitalism, socialism, and communism. A review of the series premiere in *Variety* magazine characterized Coleman as a host of "good grace" who promised to lead viewers to a nuanced understanding of economic life.[33]

The airing of the series over the CBS television network linked *The American Economy* to other programs in ways that complicated the task force's claims about the television series' objectivity. Michael Curtin argues that US television networks' claims to objectivity in reporting in the early 1960s must be understood as being part of a documentary television production boom that enacted the ideal of objectivity in a "historically specific" way that "was a key element in the discourse of scientific anticommunism"—and that, paradoxically, articulated "objective methodology with the hegemonic interests of transnational capital." Although *The American Economy* was not quite the same genre as the documentary news reports Curtin analyzes, CBS officials framed it as part of a nonfiction television programming portfolio that also included its news and documentary programs. Executives at CBS, including president Frank Stanton, publicized *The American Economy* alongside a weeklong prime-time special CBS News series, *Money Talks*. The latter series, cohosted by Coleman, was comparatively brief at five thirty-minute episodes that aimed to demystify economic concepts such as gross national product, inflation, and economic growth. In comments promoting the two series to network affiliate stations, Stanton presented the network's news reporting on economic matters and its educational programming as parts of a whole, declaring, "we must report now not only in depth, but we must provide the background for greater understanding—a substantial and extensive foundation of fact and detail." In other words, for the JCEE and CED,

The American Economy telecourse was part of an interorganizational genre repertoire, but for CBS, the series was part of a strategic broadcast portfolio, where it supported the network's ambitions to be seen as an authoritative source of information about the nation's place in a complicated and unstable world. Michael Curtin observes that on CBS's flagship news program *CBS Reports* in the early 1960s, "tropes of 'freedom' are woven throughout the core of these documentaries, and freedom is cast in relation to its other: the unspoken threat of Communism"—a pattern that was even more explicitly articulated elsewhere on the television dial. Curtin's findings underscore how the two programs featuring Coleman—the accessible *Money Talks* and the more detailed *The American Economy*—were part of an overall flow of programming at CBS that, like the JCEE, positioned objectivity and anticommunism as internally consistent.[34]

The cultural scholar Raymond Williams argued that television can be seen less as a series of discrete programs than as a "single irresponsible flow of images and feelings" that signals the common ideas within a culture. Keeping this in mind, the presence of *The American Economy* and *Money Talks* on the CBS airwaves signaled not only the broad reach of the JCEE and National Task Force's vision of economic education, but also the roles of the JCEE, American Economic Association, and the National Task Force on Economic Education in contributing to a flow of content that helped to construct a tacitly anticommunist ideological tone on the nation's airwaves. Indeed, discourses of freedom (and communism as its implied foil) appeared in a magazine advertisement for the series sponsored by the chemical manufacturing corporation Union Carbide. The advertisement, which ran in major news magazines in September of 1962, promised that the series would describe not only how "our economic system works" but also "how it enhances individual freedom"—once again suggesting that political freedoms and the US economic system were inseparably linked (figure 5.1).[35]

In the next few years, the JCEE would further build out the capacities envisioned in the task force report and elaborated in *The American Economy* telecourse. In June of 1964, the JCEE announced the development of a new curriculum program, the Developmental Economic Education Program (DEEP), for public school students from kindergarten to twelfth grade. Participating school systems would receive grant funding, consulting, and teaching materials from the JCEE in exchange for a commitment to devote time and personnel to the program. The program would initially be implemented in thirty school systems, with expansions planned beyond the pilot phase.[36]

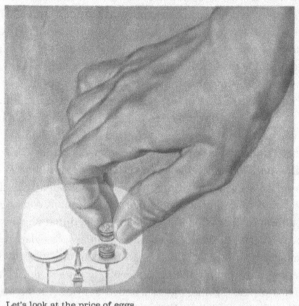

FIGURE 5.1. An advertisement for the CBS television series *The American Economy* sponsored by chemical manufacturer Union Carbide. The advertisement copy frames the workings of the nation's economic system as an enhancer of "individual freedom," echoing longstanding discourses around economic education media. Image scan provided with permission of the Hoover Institution and Library. Union Carbide Corporation, "Let's look at the price of eggs [advertisement]," Joint Council on Economic Education Records, Box 23, Folder 5, Hoover Institution Library and Archives.

By this time, the JCEE was ramping up fundraising and developing its administrative capacity—including an expanded executive committee and more staff dedicated to administrative functions such as fundraising and public communications. It was no longer receiving funds from the CED, instead raising funds from US businesses and philanthropic foundations.

THE NEW ECONOMICS

JCEE rhetoric about the program emphasized links between industry and citizenship. For example, JCEE fundraising presentation materials for prospective corporate donors in 1964 asserted that corporate sponsors had good reasons to support economic education projects: first, that the United States' private enterprise system supported the United States' global strength and its ability to fight communism; second, "economic illiteracy in the electorate results in laws that impair the effectiveness of private enterprise and creates a poor climate for business profits"; and third, that "economic illiterates don't make good citizens, good customers, good workers, good supervisors, or good executives." These justifications were seemingly tailored to appeal to business audiences and leaned rhetorically toward free enterprisers' promotional nationalism, in contrast to the rhetorics of objectivity and scientific thinking that had typified the task force's 1961 report. Nonetheless, the presentation materials emphasized how DEEP incorporated teaching materials and assessments that had been developed in tandem with the task force's *Economic Education in the Schools* report, including the telecourse *The American Economy*.[37]

These materials also emphasized how DEEP built on prior infrastructures, incorporating the JCEE's network of local Councils on Economic Education: the presentation materials, prepared by the JCEE's Executive Committee, declared that because "course-building and teacher-training are so enormously decentralized," DEEP was "a *local* program, with local commitments and local financial support." This positioning of the program as a decentralized effort recalled Sputnik-era rhetorics that had celebrated the United States' educational system and its local systems of administration as fundamentally democratic. Structurally, then, the JCEE's new program, too, could benefit from discourses that imagined decentralized educational implementation as being more democratic, more flexible, and therefore American by design, in contrast to the perceived rigidity of education under the top-down socialist system of the Soviet Union.[38]

The fundraising materials borrowed the imagery of space exploration, linking their program to the global space race that served as a proxy for ideological tensions. For example, the JCEE described their new curriculum by declaring that "we have on the launching pad—ready to go into orbit—a carefully built 'idea capsule' (the New Program), with powerful 'boosters' (prior programs) and a good 'guidance system' (management). All it needs for takeoff is 'fuel' (money)." Funding projections listed an anticipated $150,000 from the Ford Foundation, with the remaining $450,000 of the program's budget to be contributed by other foundations, businesses, and labor

130 CHAPTER FIVE

organizations. Building this base of financial support for the JCEE required a framing that could compel prospective corporate sponsors. JCEE materials, accordingly, positioned the organization as addressing a danger posed by "economic illiteracy" among citizens in a democratic society.[39]

News coverage in the ensuing years reflected a growing adoption of JCEE methods and ideas. For example, a 1965 *New York Times* feature on John Coleman noted that teaching economics had come into fashion, with teachers eager to learn how to teach "the new economics." A 1967 *Los Angeles Times* feature detailed DEEP's techniques such as teaching young children to see their own households in terms of consumers and producers, claiming that despite having been "long a stepchild in school curricula," such instructional methods were making economics "less of a wallflower." This article quoted JCEE president and director M. L. Frankel, who insisted that although there would be "no sputnik [*sic*] for the social sciences regeneration," business leaders could help support the push for more teaching of economics in schools. But Frankel's rhetorical flourish, in a sense, played down how the JCEE had mobilized the dynamics of the Sputnik launches, and the ensuing perception of educational crisis, to augment its own influence and presence in the US educational system and its connections to democracy in the public imagination.[40]

The Failed Inflation Campaign: Inflation and the Contradictions of Economic Education

Later in the 1960s, the JCEE tried other forms of public communication. Between 1965 and 1968 the consumer price inflation rate almost tripled from 1.58 to 4.27 percent, leading homemakers to mount supermarket protests against high food costs in what *Newsweek* magazine called a "consumer revolt" against "the ever-rising cost of living." The JCEE, founded in contrast to managerially oriented economic education organizations such as the Advertising Council, would attempt to address public understandings of inflation by partnering with both the Advertising Council and the US Chamber of Commerce. The failure of the collaboration between the JCEE and the Advertising Council revealed the difficulties of trying to integrate the JCEE's institutionally focused style of economic education with the Advertising Council and Chamber of Commerce's free enterprise promotional logics.[41]

The year 1969 was the first of a new five-year JCEE program designed

THE NEW ECONOMICS   131

to address public attitudes about economic instability and inflation. This
new program was initiated by the US Chamber of Commerce and funded
in part by its nonprofit arm, the National Chamber Foundation. The JCEE
Annual Report for 1969 described the program's goal: to fight inflation
"by promoting an understanding of economic stability and growth as part
of the education of every student in the United States." The anti-inflation
program followed the model that had been established with the 1961
task force report: a centerpiece platform statement—in this case a peer-
reviewed paper on policies for economic stability—that was the basis for
a variety of JCEE-affiliated outputs, which in this case included curricular materials, background guides for teachers, an educational film created
in cooperation with the American Bankers Association, and a booklet
that was promoted in Advertising Council public service advertisements.
Of course, this would not be the first time the Advertising Council had
mounted a campaign designed to shore up faith in the US economy: in
addition to the "American Economic System" campaign, prior efforts had
gone under titles like "The Future of America," launched in 1954; and
"Confidence in a Growing America," launched in 1958. Expectations were
likely high for the Advertising Council campaign's success: the council
had received a record $352 million in media contributions in 1967 and
increased circulation for fourteen of its twenty campaigns in 1968.[42]

Part of the motivation for the anti-inflation campaign was a growing
sense of worry about the public's susceptibility to so-called inflationary
psychology. As one *New York Times* feature put it, inflationary psychology
was thought to be a "serious disease" of the economic polity in which, as
inflation dragged on, "people are told that inflation destroys the value of
savings accounts and life insurance, and the clever ones try to beat it by in-
vesting in stocks and real estate" and, with "speculation feeding on itself,"
the risk of economic collapse intensified.[43] Concerns about inflationary
psychology informed a new narrative about the need for economic education: one that shifted the rationale from maintaining democracy in the face
of communist threats to actively managing the nation's future collective
wealth by making prudent individual decisions. When the joint JCEE/Ad-
vertising Council campaign debuted in 1969 with advertisements created
by advertising firm Benton and Bowles, the Advertising Council's campaign coordinator T. S. Thompson—also a senior vice president at General
Foods—pointed to inflationary psychology to make the case for why the
campaign was necessary. The rationale for the campaign, as Thompson
explained it, was that even though the government and other institutions

were taking steps to curb inflation, "All of us are making our individual decisions based on the assumption that inflation will continue and that we have to constantly hedge against it." If people could be persuaded to curb such hedging behaviors, Thompson implied, worries about further inflation would not become a self-fulfilling prophecy.[44]

In keeping with the Advertising Council's tendency to emphasize individualized and voluntary actions, Benton and Bowles developed a campaign that focused on what individuals could do in their own daily lives to address inflation as consumers, workers, or employers. The campaign dramatized the idea that everyone could consume a little less, using the motif of pigs: everyone, it claimed, could be "a little less piggy." For example, one advertisement prepared by Benton and Bowles displayed a photo lineup of five people, four of which wore cartoonish pig masks over their faces (figure 5.2). The accompanying headline read, "4 out of 5 Americans will flunk this piggy test," followed by a checklist of behaviors it described as "piggy."

The actions described as "piggy" included demanding "wages that you know are more than you're earning by the job you do," buying impulsively or running up credit card bills, raising prices to protect profits, and demanding "more government services without being willing to pay more taxes for them." "Any 'yes' answer," a *New York Times* feature on the campaign reported, "immediately marks the reader as a contributor to the problem." Other advertisements tempered their individualism with acknowledgment of the federal government's role in addressing inflation, that "government must do the big part. But, as shoppers, voters, wage earners, and businessmen, each of us can help just by being a little less piggy." The campaign advertisements publicized a free-of-charge illustrated booklet, *Inflation Can Be Stopped: Steps for a Balanced Economy*, that audiences could send away for by mail order. However, the narrative on offer in the booklet did not quite convey the notion that consumer decisions could do much to stop inflation. The booklet, prepared by the JCEE, instead suggested that ordinary people could do little to address inflation other than working hard, becoming more knowledgeable, and electing the right legislators.[45]

Inflation Can Be Stopped: Steps for a Balanced Economy was a storybook-style pamphlet whose words and pictures told the story of Jim and his wife, Sue, a couple who couldn't understand why "their money had shrunk" despite having some savings and even some investments. In the booklet, Jim and Sue find a college professor who is interested in answering their questions—a notable shift from the Advertising Council booklet *The Miracle of America* (1948), in which a similarly questioning family

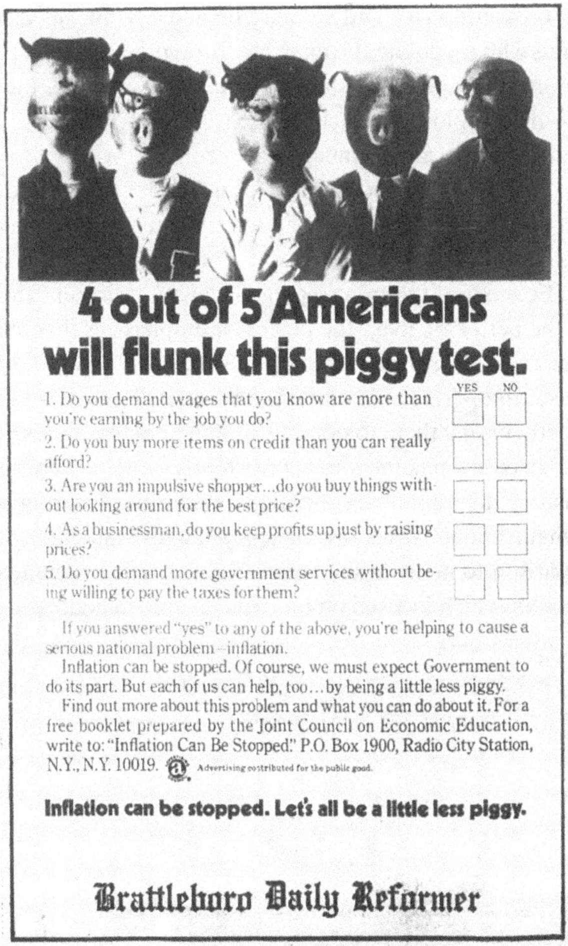

THE NEW ECONOMICS 133

FIGURE 5.2. An Advertising Council advertisement promoting the JCEE booklet *Inflation Can Be Stopped: Steps for a Balanced Economy*, depicting particular behaviors as "piggy." Image reproduced with permission of the Advertising Council. Advertising Council, "4 Out of 5 Americans Will Flunk This Piggy Test [advertisement]." As appearing in the *Brattleboro [VT] Reformer*, January 30, 1970, retrieved April 12, 2022, from https://www.newspapers.com /image/548383665/.

gained economic enlightenment from the personification of American patriotism, Uncle Sam. The professor explains to Jim and Sue that the nation has the difficult job of ensuring growth while keeping inflation and unemployment in check. The professor compares the national economy to a "a great abundance machine" that has "sometimes overheated and sometimes broken down," and so must be actively managed by government officials who modulate the machine through federal taxation, spending, and monetary supply—a state of affairs set in place, the professor explains, by the Employment Act of 1946 (figure 5.3). He further explains that the government must manage the economy while also providing training, reducing discrimination, and aiding in relocation of workers, conceding that inflation and unemployment weigh most heavily on the young, the old, migrant workers, and ethnic minorities. In an echo of the first "American Economic System" campaign's signature slogan "The better we produce—the better we live," the professor emphasizes that inflation will come under control if production outpaces incomes, underlining the need for businesses to operate efficiently. The booklet closes by addressing the reader directly, urging them to not only understand the causes of inflation, but also to elect lawmakers who "consistently work toward needed national measures" to maintain economic growth while avoiding inflation or unemployment, and to "insist on efficiency" in government.[46]

In comparison to many of the "piggy" advertisements created by Benton and Bowles, which focused on individuals' role in addressing inflation,

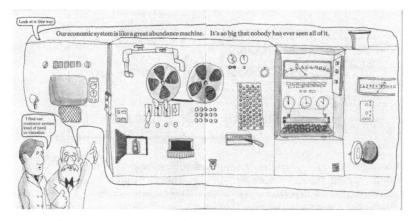

FIGURE 5.3. Images and text from the JCEE booklet *Inflation Can Be Stopped: Steps for a Balanced Economy*: Jim and the College Professor imagining the national economy as a "great abundance machine." Image provided with permission by the Hoover Institution and Library, image © 2023 by Council for Economic Education, 122 East 42nd Street, Suite 1012, New York, NY 10168. All rights reserved. Used with permission. For additional K–12 teacher resources visit econedlink.org. Joint Council on Economic Education, *Inflation Can Be Stopped: Steps for a Balanced Economy* (New York: Joint Council on Economic Education, 1969), 10–11, Box 33, Folder Advertising Council Campaign 1969—A Failure, Joint Council on Economic Education Papers, Hoover Institution Library and Archives.

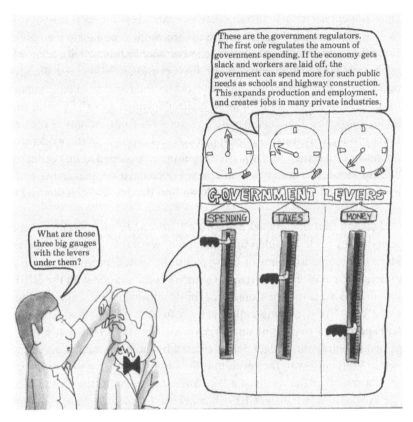

FIGURE 5.4. Images and text from the JCEE booklet *Inflation Can Be Stopped: Steps for a Balanced Economy* showing federal spending, tax collection, and money supply as controls lawmakers and federal officials can adjust to keep the machine of the national economy running properly. Image provided with permission by the Hoover Institution and Library, image © 2023 by Council for Economic Education, 122 East 42nd Street, Suite 1012, New York, NY 10168. All rights reserved. Used with permission. For additional K–12 teacher resources visit econedlink.org. Joint Council on Economic Education, *Inflation Can Be Stopped: Steps for a Balanced Economy* (New York: Joint Council on Economic Education, 1969), 13–14, Box 33, Folder Advertising Council Campaign 1969 – A Failure, Joint Council on Economic Education Papers, Hoover Institution Library and Archives.

the booklet prepared by the JCEE underscored the power of experts and the government. In addition, *Inflation Can Be Stopped: Steps for a Balanced Economy* telegraphed a model of individuals' role in the economy. It asserted that institutional decisions, and most of all the policy and regulatory decisions of the federal government and its agencies, were the primary forces affecting the national economy (see figure 5.4, depicting "government levers"). It also suggested a central role for economists, positioning academics as the right people to explain the economy to the public. It reiterated prior messages about the importance of productivity, acknowledging not only that unemployment disproportionately affected already-disadvantaged groups such as migrant workers and racial and ethnic minorities, but also that inflation hit those on fixed incomes especially hard, and finally suggesting that each American's personal contributions to the nation's productivity were "a personal, individual lever . . . on the wonderful abundance machine." Still, the booklet ultimately conceded that ordinary citizens stood at a remove from control over inflation, possessing little agency beyond being knowledgeable and productive and electing right-minded legislators.[47]

Inflation Can Be Stopped: Steps for a Balanced Economy centered the government's role in addressing inflation in ways that left the campaign more vulnerable to claims of being politically biased, partly because the announcement of the Advertising Council's collaboration with the JCEE and the US Chamber of Commerce on its anti-inflation campaign coincided with Nixon administration actions to address inflation. Congress had approved a 10 percent surcharge on income tax in 1968 that was designed to defray the budget deficit created by the ballooning costs of the war in Vietnam—with the result that the surcharge was viewed by critics as a "war tax," in the words of a *Wall Street Journal* reporter. By the time the Advertising Council/JCEE/Chamber of Commerce campaign was publicly announced in May of 1969, Nixon was pressuring Congress to approve an extension of the income tax surcharge. The seeming parallels between the Advertising Council's newly announced anti-inflation campaign and the administration's pressure on Congress to pass legislation that it characterized as anti-inflationary called into question the Advertising Council claims to be independent of any administration. Actions such as National Chamber Foundation chairman (and Wachovia Bank and Trust president) Archie K. Davis arranging a publicized White House meeting to announce the campaign, and Nixon issuing a statement welcoming it, led to concerns that the campaign's appearance of independence might be called into question.[48]

Nixon's public rhetoric suggested that his office was attuned to the JCEE's academic, institutionally oriented version of economic understanding, rather than the free enterprise promotional nationalism of the Advertising Council's prior economic education efforts. In his comments, Nixon reportedly argued, "We must curb 'inflation psychology.' When people understand

THE NEW ECONOMICS   137

what is behind the sharply rising cost of living, they see that tax measures essential for a strong budget are better than the cruel tax of inflation." Such a rhetorical appeal to economic understanding, presented as a nonpartisan issue, appeared to align the Advertising Council and the administration's legislative agenda. Nixon's invocation of public economic understanding as a *support* for a tax increase was, however, at odds with the Advertising Council's customary policy positions. The tacit support *Inflation Can Be Stopped: Steps for a Balanced Economy* seemed to provide for federal power over the economy was also at least somewhat at odds with the Advertising Council's standard techniques: instead of avoiding the appearance of partisanship by focusing solely on influencing actions and attitudes at the level of the individual, as the Benton and Bowles advertising campaign had done, the JCEE booklet emphasized "government levers" such as taxes, spending, and monetary supply.[49]

Despite these internal inconsistencies, the co-occurrence of the anti-inflation campaign and Nixon's legislative push raised concerns among legislators and labor organizations that the Advertising Council and the JCEE were engaging in partisan messaging—and these concerns led, in turn, to reduced support for the campaign. For example, congressional representative James O'Hara, a Michigan Democrat, entered a *Los Angeles Times* article promoting the campaign into the *Congressional Record*, along with remarks that denounced the National Chamber Foundation's promises to "condition the collective mind so that when something is done, they will know it will be to their best interests." O'Hara described this proposition as "frightening" and "disturbing" in its capacity to shape public opinion toward the administration's political agenda: "when something—anything, I guess—is done about inflation, the 'conditioned collective mind'—that means you and me and our constituents, Mr. Speaker— will simply warm up with delight, like one of Dr. Pavlov's conditioned dogs, drooling at the sounds of the dinner bell, whether there is any food there or not." Within JCEE circles, one JCEE committee member cautioned JCEE president Moe Frankel that the resonances between the Advertising Council campaign and the Nixon administration's economic policy seemed to skirt the edge of political bias. Meanwhile, in the wake of the White House meeting and campaign announcement, Advertising Council president Bob Keim worried that Davis's event had led people to confuse the Advertising Council with the US Chamber of Commerce and advised Frankel against any further joint media events between the Advertising Council, the JCEE, and the US Chamber of Commerce. In the end, Nixon's efforts to extend the income tax surcharge were successful but short-lived. The surcharge was reapproved at 10 percent until the end of 1969, then tapered to 5 percent for the first six months of 1970—and at its repeal, economist Milton Friedman and other detractors held up the surtax's failures as evidence for their focus on monetary policy.[50]

The tensions around publicity presaged an anticlimactic trajectory for the Advertising Council/JCEE campaign. By late 1969, it was clear that the PSA campaign had been a failure. The campaign was unsuccessful by the Advertising Council standards, with the few ads that did run prompting complaints from members of the public. One such complaint ran as a letter to the editor in the *Courier News* of Bridgewater, New Jersey, in which the writer, Mrs. Eda Finkel, reported her disgust at seeing ordinary Americans portrayed as pigs and demanded to know who was responsible for airing "such a tasteless and downright stupid piece of trash." Evidently Mrs. Finkel was not alone in her disapproval: by December 1969, only two hundred thousand of six hundred thousand copies printed of *Inflation Can Be Stopped: Steps for a Balanced Economy*, had been distributed, with demand Frankel described as "meager" at around one thousand copies per month. A few years later, Benton and Bowles president John Bowen would candidly describe the campaign to a reporter as "a stinkeroo."[51]

Leadership at the JCEE and the US Chamber of Commerce questioned whether the Benton and Bowles team's creative concept caused the campaign's lackluster performance. For example, Carl Madden, the chief economist at the US Chamber of Commerce, observed in December 1969 that newspaper and television uptake of the advertisements had been lacking, with other programs and advertisements about inflation being comparatively well received. Madden hypothesized that the "piggy" theme of the Benton and Bowles advertisements could be behind the limited uptake of the campaign, recalling having mentioned to the copywriters that they may have inadvertently chosen a word that had taken on "ominous connotations" in popular culture, including use of "pigs" as a slang term to disparagingly describe authority figures. The JCEE's Frankel also sent his concerns in a letter to Keim, emphasizing how JCEE and Chamber of Commerce representatives had wanted Benton and Bowles to concentrate on educating the public about "the aggregate steps that could be taken by the government to control inflation." Yet, the possibility of a poorly chosen theme obscured another issue with Advertising Council anti-inflation campaigns: a question about the purposes of anti-inflation PSAs that reached back to the aftermath of the Second World War.[52]

Some of the controversies around the ill-fated 1969 inflation campaign can be seen as rearticulations of debates that were almost as old as the Advertising Council itself. The advertisements focusing on individual economic behaviors as potential causes of inflation would have struck a familiar chord with advertising industry leaders who, twenty-three years earlier, had debated the wisdom of such campaigns. Recall that in 1946, Bruce Barton had privately argued that federal policy was the most effective tool for managing inflation; his company's wartime anti-inflation campaign calling for individual actions, he confided, had chiefly been useful for raising morale. Nonetheless, the Advertising Council leaders had run multiple anti-inflation campaigns between 1945 and 1959, but as with all such campaigns, direct impact was difficult to gauge; as one newspaper columnist caustically put it in 1969, "if you can't recall the results of those campaigns, don't embarrass the council by looking up the figures." Such critiques raise questions of precisely why the Advertising Council continued to execute anti-inflation campaigns despite their seeming ineffectiveness.[53]

One possible explanation is that the Advertising Council's significance was not only in its claims to influence public opinion, but also in the potential for its campaigns to serve as communicative devices in an institutional sense. The fact of the campaign's existence could be seen as making a tacit declaration about business interests' social role; in other words, creating and distributing the campaign could be consequential quite apart from its impact on public opinion. The Advertising Council's repeated anti-inflation campaigns were signals that a coalition of business organizations was doing *something* to address inflation. Even if such action was largely symbolic, it could be gestured to in annual reports and public statements as evidence of businesses' responsiveness to the social and political problems of the day. Alfred McClung Lee, a sociologist affiliated with the Institute for Propaganda Analysis, had suggested as much when he summarized the argument of *Is Anybody Listening?* in 1953: "propaganda is written chiefly for the employers of propagandists." The campaign's business-friendly organizers and promoters may have been wary of other means of addressing inflation that could have had more of a direct impact on businesses (such as price controls and/or policies limiting businesses' capacity to pass the impact of inflation on to consumers). For organizations like the JCEE and the Chamber of Commerce, their support for the campaign could be spun to prospective funders as legible proof of new projects that complemented their educational or lobbying activities elsewhere. In this sense, such campaigns would have served the original goals of the founding of the Advertising Council: to create campaigns that appeared to be in the public interest but, as importantly, imposed few limitations on management's power.[54]

The 1950s and 1960s established the JCEE as a leading economic education organization whose outputs gained wide acceptance in the nation's schools. By the twentieth anniversary of its founding in 1969, the JCEE network covered forty-two states; there were forty-five independent "statewide Affiliated Councils" and fifty-eight campus-based Centers for Economic Education, and DEEP was being implemented in 137 school systems across the country. *The American Economy* enjoyed secondary distribution on sixteen-millimeter film: condensed sixty-episode film editions of the telecourse episodes racked up over one thousand unit sales and more than ten thousand rentals in 1970, with a further fifty copies made available on loan from the JCEE to more than twenty-five thousand teachers. The JCEE's fundraising capabilities were well established as well, having gone from CED seed funding in 1949 to total donations of around half a million dollars per year from businesses, labor organizations, and foundations by the late 1960s: in the fall of 1970, for example, the JCEE received small donations from dozens of such organizations and donations of over $10,000 from organizations as varied as the AFL-CIO, the Ford Foundation, International Business Machines Corporation (IBM), the National Chamber Foundation, and US Steel. However, the shift in narratives seen in the failed inflation campaign—and the lack of a unified message during that campaign—indicated that the scientific anticommunism that had been such a major part of JCEE communications in the early 1960s landed differently by the end of the 1960s. A Cold War geopolitical framing seemed to no longer be as compelling in light of inflation at home—but the rationale that economic education could train democratic citizens to make decisions that would preserve national prosperity would find new expression in the years to come.[55]

CHAPTER SIX

From Institutions to Markets

In April 1976, the Advertising Council launched "the most massive communications effort in the 33-year history" of the nonprofit organization: a second "American Economic System" campaign, designed to coincide with the bicentennial of the nation's founding. The campaign featured a collection of public service advertisements (PSAs) promoting a twenty-four-page, full-color booklet that promised to provide citizens with foundational knowledge about economics: "the more we all know about our system," the Advertising Council promised, "the better we can handle today's challenges and decide what to preserve, what to change in the years ahead." The PSAs aimed to convince US publics that the economic uncertainties of the 1970s called for each American to develop a better understanding of economics by sending off for the free booklet by mail.[1]

The Advertising Council (now stylized as the Ad Council) offered their ready-made "American Economic System" PSAs free of charge to broadcasters, newspaper and magazine publishers, and the outdoor advertising companies that leased space on public transit and/or billboards. In radio spots, an announcer interrupted a couple's bickering about inflation to offer the booklet; television spots featured ordinary folks admitting to a man-on-the-street reporter that they couldn't explain how the economic system worked—with one passerby asking, "how do you *spell* 'economics'?" In billboard and print ads, a cluster of people stood gathered together facing the camera, their faces buried in magazine-size glossy booklets. These booklet readers represented major demographic groups: some wore the markers of occupations, such as a white man wearing a construction worker's hard hat, and a Black woman wearing a nurse's uniform; other figures keyed into age or gender demographics, such as a young white woman with fashionable sunglasses perched on her head, rings

142 CHAPTER SIX

prominently visible on the hand that held up the booklet, marking her as a wife and possibly a homemaker; and a silver-haired white man and white woman representing retirees.

Billboards paired the images of readers with the tagline, "Every American ought to know what it says. For a free copy, write: 'Economics,' Pueblo, Colo. 81009." Print ads featured questions meant to draw the viewer in:

> How much change does our American Economic System need: A lot? A Little? None?
>> Who makes our American Economic System work?
>> Does America need more government regulation? Or less?
>> Do you really know what happens when business profits go up or down?

The print ads' copy explained three points, reiterating fundamental tropes of economic education that had been circulating, at this point, for decades: first, that a recent poll had found respondents broadly disagreed about how the economy worked and how their own lives would be affected by changes in economic conditions; second, that Americans' lack of understanding of the economic system put them at a disadvantage to "make intelligent choices about it"; and third, that everyone would be better able to understand and make decisions about the country's economic system by reading the free informative booklet. One *San Francisco Examiner* columnist critical of the campaign wrote disapprovingly that the booklet associated with the PSAs was "a soft-sell pro-capitalism affair, once again suggesting to people that individuals, not big business, control the economy."[2]

The booklet itself bore the title *The American Economic System . . . and Your Part in It*, illustrated with a flowing red, white, and blue striped ribbon and a gold coin bearing the image of a colonial-era drummer (most likely a nod to the bicentennial commemorative quarter with a similar motif). Inside, an introductory blurb promised a "quick and simple description of the American economic system." Despite being conceived to appeal to voting-age adults, the booklet's brightly colored pages featured comic strip panels and illustrations of beloved characters from the *Peanuts* comic strip; in another nod to the nation's bicentennial, the introductory page featured an illustration of *Peanuts* characters Charlie Brown, Linus, and Snoopy parading with Revolutionary War–era flags and musical instruments. The booklet covered such concepts as the economic roles of producers and consumers; forces such as supply, demand, competition,

FROM INSTITUTIONS TO MARKETS

and inflation; and basic measurements of the US economy, including its gross national product. These were interspersed with *Peanuts* cartoons and simple charts and graphs.[3]

By May of 1978, more than eleven million copies of the booklet had been distributed. An initial $239,000 of seed money from the Department of Commerce was followed by over a million dollars in corporate and foundation donations and more than $25 million worth of donated advertising time and space. Both interested citizens and supportive organizations played roles in its circulation. The print, broadcast, and outdoor advertisements urged consumers to directly request the booklet by mail. Over ten thousand libraries promoted the booklet through counter displays. Many more copies were distributed by other means: an Advertising Council newsletter reported, for example, that "64 newspapers in 24 states" had included enclosures of the booklet. While the distribution through PSAs and public institutions such as libraries spoke to the putatively nonprofit nature of the Advertising Council, for-profit corporations were also instrumental in circulating *The American Economic System ... and Your Part in It*: companies such as Union Oil Company of California included information about the booklet in its mailed circulars; and 330,000 copies were included as inserts in United Airlines' *Mainliner* magazine. Corporations' enthusiasm for the booklet pointed to what made it controversial: it was perceived to have a marked pro-business slant.[4]

This chapter examines the Advertising Council's 1970s "American Economic System" campaign, arguing that it rearticulated the tropes of postwar economic education from institutions to markets, and showing how public resistance to the campaign's ideological currents played out through political culture and media policy. The chapter begins by describing the campaign itself and placing this campaign in the context of its historical moment—one in which popular business discourses responded to inflation, increased regulation, and consumer activism with a sense of besiegement. The chapter then returns to the Advertising Council, arguing that its use of survey techniques from the social sciences imagined economic subjects in terms of their supposed lack of knowledge—but constructed knowledge in ways similar to prior sponsored economic education campaigns. The chapter then recounts how, despite its supporters' insistence that the campaign was unbiased and nonpartisan, critics saw it as corporate propaganda and activists used the Fairness Doctrine to counter it. The chapter concludes by examining the ways the campaign rearticulated long-standing ideas within the tradition of sponsored economic education media for a changing social context—with a focus on how it shifted ideas about what it called the American economic system from institutions and their constituents to market forces themselves, which a developing political discourse cast as objective and apolitical.

As this chapter shows, critics challenged the "American Economic System" campaign, charging that seed money for the campaign improperly used public funds and, further, that the PSAs were biased in ways that triggered networks' Fairness Doctrine obligations to air opposing views. Nonetheless, Advertising Council leadership insisted that the campaign and its booklet were unbiased. In the ensuing controversy, the Advertising Council and its opponents used the existing structures of media policy and practice to spread their messages. The Advertising Council disavowed accusations of bias, cultivating the appearance of neutrality to secure access to media space; in opposition, public interest advertising activists used the existing policy infrastructure to either refute the campaign's messages or scare networks away from airing the Advertising Council's PSAs altogether.[5]

The "American Economic System" campaign served the purposes corporate-funded public service advertising campaigns had long served: to fulfill FCC requirements. These requirements had been in play since 1946, when the FCC issued its Blue Book, a report that laid out the standards of public service that private broadcasters would need to meet to retain their licenses. The Blue Book's initial stipulations were quickly softened to what broadcasting historian Victor Pickard calls "a postwar settlement defined by nominal public interest obligations, self-regulation and other industry-friendly terms." In the case of public interest obligations, these requirements were fairly limited, as media scholar Craig LaMay observes: broadcast licensees were expected to track programming that addressed matters of public interest, and PSAs counted as programming under this standard. Communication scholar Patricia Aufderheide notes that the Advertising Council has avoided courting controversy. Further, as journalist and strategic communication scholar Wendy Melillo observes, Advertising Council campaigns' avoidance of controversy has been a strategic choice that likely helped ensure that their PSAs would see airtime: "media companies will not run public service ads if they are concerned that the ads will offend their commercial advertisers, or if the subject matter is controversial enough that broadcast stations or publications receive complaints." The Advertising Council, Melillo notes, "manages the situation by focusing their campaigns on the individual actions a person can take to help address a larger societal problem."[6]

The "American Economic System" campaign revealed that the mid-1970s was an inflection point in the Advertising Council's narrations of capitalism in the United States. Many elements of the campaign echoed earlier decades' economic education tropes: American exceptionalism; the imagined importance of a particular kind of informed, assenting public; a persistent whiff of scientific anticommunism that framed private enterprise as objectively better than other systems; and a promotionally nationalist assertion that private enterprise was inextricably linked to freedom. However, in comparison to prior Advertising Council leaflets such as 1949's *Miracle of America* or 1969's *Inflation Can Be Stopped: Steps to a Balanced Economy*, the booklet *The American Economic System . . . and Your Part in It* described the economy less in terms of constituencies such as labor, management, or the state, and more in terms of market actors—producers, consumers, and governments—and the economic forces by which they could be understood to interact. The booklet's presentation of economic ideas was not only selective, but considerably simplified and abstracted. For example, labor unions were mentioned as "an important force in our economic system," comprising about a fifth of all workers, but labor unions, managers, investors, and entrepreneurs were all subsumed under the umbrella category of "producers." In this regard, the booklet anticipated popular discourses within neoliberalism that elided distinctions between organizations and individuals by assuming they were subject to the same market forces—as political theorist Wendy Brown observes, "both persons and states are construed on the model of the contemporary firm."[7]

Corporate Social Responsibility and Managerial Anxiety

Business interests' support for the "American Economic System" campaign, and the framing of such a campaign as a service to the public, responded to the collective tensions circulating within US cultures of business management by the mid-1970s. Persistent inflation created economic havoc and strained already-brittle corporate public relations. Consumer unrest, grassroots activism, and regulatory expansion all pushed for a reigning-in of corporate power. Preexisting corporate-managerial narrative frames of business under siege, which had crystallized in the New Deal era, made it possible to see these pressures, from inside managerial culture, as an existential threat to business itself. In light of this perceived threat, business-friendly public intellectuals and industry figureheads alike marshaled a new wave of rationales for profit-making and corporate power.

The inflation and other economic disruptions of the early 1970s enflamed tensions between manufacturers, consumers, and policymakers. Businesses large and small fretted over their dwindling purchasing power, and consumers blamed businesses for increases in the price of consumer goods. Inflation meant that money in the bank was worth less, and the impact of inflation on salaries and paychecks amounted to a de facto pay cut for the same amount of work. Inflation rates dipped below 4 percent in 1972 but bounced up to 11 percent amid recession and rising oil prices in 1975. These economic disruptions caused unpredictability that made corporate budget planning difficult. They also ratcheted up already-tense public relations with those members of the working and middle classes who suspected big business of unduly taking excessive profits and, effectively, refusing to shoulder their share of the economic pain.[8]

Many corporate executives saw themselves as squeezed by consumers' growing unrest over higher prices on one side and by tightening regulatory regimes on the other. As sociologist Patrick J. Akard observes, corporate "profit rates had declined steadily," and business discourses put the blame on high labor costs, along with social benefit programs, taxes, and regulations. Indeed, Akard and cultural historian Lizabeth Cohen document how regulatory and legislative oversight of American industry flourished in the late 1960s and early 1970s: existing regulatory agencies were reinvigorated and new ones were established. This consumer activism, and the regulatory impulses that accompanied it, was in fact more reformist than radical, as Cohen points out: consumer activists "assumed the viability and desirability of a system of capitalist private enterprise and markets." Yet, Akard describes how many business leaders by the early 1970s imagined their organizations to be facing an existential threat from the proliferation of organized advocacy groups and grassroots supporters, to say nothing of new regulatory attention to the safety of workers, consumers, and the environment.[9]

Public opinion often figured in the rationale for creating these new agencies. For example, Congressman Lloyd Meeds recounted congressional motivations for the establishment of the Occupational Safety and Health Administration in 1970. Alongside new scientific and technical conditions of exceeding complexity and a growing sense of congressional responsibility for job safety legislation, Meeds pointed to "increased . . .

public concern" about industrial pollution, and "cries for action" on the heels of high-profile industrial accidents. Similarly, William Ruckelshaus, the first administrator of the Environmental Protection Agency (EPA), looked back on his tenure at the EPA and concluded that even the popularization of color television in the mid-1960s had an impact on public calls for tighter environmental controls, since television news stories featuring "brown smog against a blue sky" had a persuasive power far beyond the same image rendered in shades of black and white.[10]

The increase in regulations and social expectations signaled to corporate managers that they would need to increase their operational scope and expenses. It also dovetailed with existing managerial narratives that framed public opinion and regulation as potentially grave threats. Corporate culture had long contained managerial impressions of besiegement. This sense of being under threat had colored the rhetoric of American business executives and the leaders of industry coalitions such as the NAM, the US Chamber of Commerce, AAAA, and ANA, which had opposed the labor power and regulatory power of the New Deal political order using rhetorics of free enterprise and an imagined American way of life that positioned US managerial capitalism as a force for liberty and progress. This narrative frame appeared to come easily to hand amid the increased pressure of the unfolding 1970s. Business leaders reported that the changing demands and expectations they faced were higher than they had been for decades. A study of business executives found them confused at having been "cast in the role of villains," characterizing the prevailing mood in terms of "a feeling of impotence" and "loss of confidence." Advertising and public relations were becoming increasingly contentious presences in the public discourse. For example, journalism historians Vanessa Murphree and James Aucoin document how Mobil Oil invested in "antagonistic" public relations designed to influence public opinion about the highly profitable oil company. Across the corporate leadership ranks, executives and their allies retorted to perceived criticisms by insisting that the practices of American corporations were not only economically necessary, but also carried intrinsic and unique benefits to society. These assertions picked up on and reexpressed prior decades' economic education rhetorics.[11]

For example, in September of 1970, the *New York Times*' Sunday magazine published an essay by economist and public intellectual Milton Friedman, titled "The Social Responsibility of Business Is to Increase Its Profits." The page layout telegraphed the narrative frame of corporations under siege: *Times* editors evoked the moment's tensions over corporate social responsibility by surrounding Friedman's essay (along with a featured photograph that portrayed James Roche, chairman of General Motors, standing alone at a podium) with photographs of public servants and activists who had been pressing General Motors' board of directors to take accountability for the company's past and future records of public safety and environmental pollution. In contrast to Roche's closed mouth and seemingly neutral expression, the activists were pictured mid-speech—creating a contrast in which the activists could almost be read as hectoring the comparatively impassive Roche.[12]

The essay laid out what would come to be known as the Friedman Doctrine, also known as shareholder theory: that "the manager is the agent of the individuals who own the corporation . . . and his primary responsibility is to them." The shareholder could use their wealth to advance whatever cause they determined was most deserving. Any other conceptualization of corporate social responsibility, Friedman argued, would be ethically suspect because it would "amount to spending someone else's money for a general social interest." Friedman's argument redefined the pursuit of profit and the accumulation of individual and corporate wealth in civic and moral terms, offering managerial culture a story about the good they were already doing simply by being in business and generating funds that could be used as stockholders saw fit. Consumer activists had lamented excessive corporate profits as exploitation and profiteering, but Friedman framed corporate profits as necessary precursors of social good in a free society. In the process, Friedman's argument redefined the affective textures of managerial life: in place of besiegement, overwhelm, and unpreparedness, shareholder theory invited managerial subjects to translate the affective tensions of the moment into what could feel like principled refusal and moral propriety. Yet, the implications of shareholder doctrine did not leave managers as free to take a hands-off approach as may initially have seemed. Friedman argued that businesses should leave questions of governance to the government, trusting individuals to decide which charities they thought most deserving. But amid increasing demands for corporate social responsibility, business leaders convinced by Friedman's argument would need to change the public opinions that motivated grassroots action and invigorated regulation. To avoid being compelled by law to take actions in the name of social responsibility, corporate managers would have to wage public relations battles.[13]

Other justifications for the social necessity of private enterprise developed outside the realm of the popular press, but with considerable strategic implications for business interests. In summer of 1971, shortly before he was to be nominated to the Supreme Court of the United States, corporate lawyer Lewis F. Powell drafted a memo titled "Attack on American Free Enterprise System," at the request of Eugene B. Sydnor, a retail executive and committee chair for the US Chamber of Commerce. In it, Powell expressed belief that the US economic system ensured every kind of civic and personal freedom, since only capitalist principles could protect liberty. If "respectable elements of society"—including intellectuals, the clergy, the media, and politicians—were engaged in a "broadly based and consistently pursued" effort to destroy capitalism in the United States, Powell argued, then the answer lay in a coordinated defense of capitalism across as many parts of US society as possible—including policy, the courts, the schools, and public discourse. Glickman has argued that contrary to perceptions that the Powell Memo (as it has come to be known) was the opening salvo in a culture war, in fact the memo, which became public knowledge after Powell joined the Supreme Court, was important because it collected and organized twentieth-century notions of free enterprise that had been circulating since the 1930s. The history of sponsored economic education media supports this argument—and viewing the Powell Memo in light of the AAAA/ANA's postwar plans for economic education shows that even Powell's *tactical design* for a broad and coordinated defense of American private enterprise was not entirely novel. Rather, Powell's memo reiterated and reimagined the tactics that the Smock Report had anticipated twenty-four years earlier.[14]

The memo imagined corporate leaders as operations-focused but ultimately appeasement-minded "good citizens" with "little stomach for hard-nose contest with their critics." This portrayal of American business effectively reproduced the arguments Henry Link had made in *Business Screen* twenty-three years earlier, while it ignored business advocates' often-strident attempts to shape public opinion over the course of the twentieth century. Ultimately, Powell portrayed American business management as the caretakers of a system "which provides the goods, services, and jobs on which our country depends," lamenting that, despite their contributions to US abundance, business leaders had been subject to attacks from those who did not approve of or understand the system. Waterhouse observes that the memo was organizationally powerful, helping spur new networks of conservative organizing. It was also rhetorically powerful: Powell's memo told a story that could turn an atmosphere of managerial overwhelm and beleaguerment into what could be imagined as principled resistance and moral concern for the trajectory of the nation.[15]

The notion that business served society simply by pursuing its own commercial imperatives surfaced in a different formulation that same year in Federal Trade Commission (FTC) hearings on the role of advertising in society. As media historian Molly Niesen documents, the advertising reform movement and the reinvigorated FTC of the early 1970s had brought on a full-blown "public relations crisis, unparalleled since the 1930s" for advertisers. In October of 1971 the FTC had called executives from major advertising agencies and trade organizations to testify on topics including advertising to children and advertising's capacity to emotionally manipulate the public. The hearings gave a platform to advertising industry leaders, who described advertising as an unmitigated force for good. Consider, for example, advertising executive Alfred Seaman's defense of his craft as reproduced in a paperback edited summary of the hearings, *The Case for Advertising*, published by the AAAA:

> Advertising is both the sparkplug and the lubricant of the economic machinery which create consumer wealth. Its job is to inform, as all critics and practitioners agree. But its job is not just to inform. Its function is to *sell*. Sell products. Sell ideas. Sell styles of living—which are often better than the ones people create for themselves, as a trip to some backward nation will quickly show. So my philosophy is that selling creates wealth and better social conditions. Selling may not be a noble calling, but it is an honest and constructive and necessary one.

Where Friedman suggested that personal wealth was the predecessor to voluntary civic responsibility and Powell highlighted the role of business in providing social stability by generating jobs, goods, and services, Seaman had suggested that a lifestyle of material comfort was a social good in itself. In doing so, Seaman echoed debates that had been part of US culture since the Sputnik crisis of the late 1950s: was it better for a society to focus on consumer goods, as the United States had done after the Second World War, or to deprioritize consumer goods in favor of developing industry, infrastructure, and social safety nets, as the Soviets had? Advertising industry leaders had grappled with these issues in the aftermath of the Sputnik launches. As historian Robert Zeiger documents, Advertising Council leaders privately worried that the consumption-oriented culture of the postwar US had created a self-indulgent citizenry ill-suited for a protracted struggle of global ideologies, but the council's public messaging around the conflict ultimately avoided casting doubt on the morality of American material plenty.[16]

The Case for Advertising also clarified how advertising leaders, speaking in defense of their own industry's practices, made distinctions between persuasion and deception. For example, the paperback approvingly summarized the testimony of attorney and former FCC commissioner Lee Loevinger, who had argued that advertisements had an obligation to avoid making outright false statements, but *no* obligation to disclose all information that might be relevant to consumers' decision-making. Messages that critics and opponents might describe as misleadingly incomplete were, in this formulation, entirely permissible because they counted as artful persuasion. "Our government can regulate deception and fraud," *The Case for Advertising* declared, but "it must not curtail the freedom to persuade. Persuasion is essential to our political and economic life. Efforts to persuade the voter and the consumer guarantee that they have choices"—a claim that subtly underlined the imagined link between consumer choice and political liberty.[17]

On a similar note, advertising executives such as Tom Dillon, the head of leading advertising agency BBDO, described the industry as being "boldly and openly persuasive to a point of view which is clearly identified with the advertisers—one of the few forms of persuasion in which the interest and the source of persuasion are always clearly labelled." The consumer, Dillon suggested, could use their own reasoning abilities to come to a decision. This formulation placed the responsibility for civic and consumer decision-making squarely in the hands of the individual, but left that individual also with responsibility for finding and understanding relevant information that might have been left out—to say nothing of the power imbalance that resulted when the supporters on one side of a controversy had access to resources that far outpaced their opponents.[18]

In sum, the social context of US business in the late 1960s and early 1970s—including growing economic disruption and consumer activists' demands for corporate social responsibility—contributed to an environment in which popular managerial discourses and affects coalesced around a sense of besiegement and a crisis of public opinion. Key texts such as the Friedman Doctrine and the Powell Memo responded to this perceived crisis, either by redefining the idea of social responsibility to defy the demands of consumer activists (as was the case with Friedman), or by reasserting that capitalism was good for everyone. Leaders from the advertising industry and their allies took a similar tack, describing advertising as intrinsically beneficial and imagining advertising's strategic omissions as patriotic manifestations of free choice. These threads of discourse provided context for how sympathetic executives in the advertising industry and their client corporations could view an Advertising Council campaign about the US economic system as an educational act of unbiased public service, even though its stated purpose was to increase support for US corporations and their practices: they saw public service and persuasion as the same thing.

Constructing Publics and the Public Interest

Examining the development of the campaign shows how the Advertising Council enacted its assumptions about economic knowledge and support for the status quo. The project began with a volley of research that used the methods and scientific jargon of the social sciences, implying a level of objectivity—but the conclusions Advertising Council leaders and their allies drew from this research reflected their assumptions that knowledge of the system would be the same as support for it. These assumptions both helped to justify the developing program, and portrayed critics as lacking the requisite knowledge to make a legitimate critique. In September of 1974, founding Advertising Council member Chester J. LaRoche drafted an internal memo calling for a campaign to promote understanding of the American economic system. LaRoche argued that such a campaign was necessary, given the poor public image of business amid mounting inflation and increased consumer activism. LaRoche observed that it would be crucial to emphasize the benefits the system offered to ordinary people. LaRoche's declarations came at a moment of gathering strength for advocates of private enterprise: as Benjamin Waterhouse shows, a controversial program of price and wage controls implemented from 1971 to 1974 in an attempt to control inflation had galvanized business conservatives, strengthening support for their critiques of government planning.[19]

Just a few weeks after LaRoche's memo, in October of 1974, Commerce Secretary Frederick Baily Dent gave a speech at an Advertising Council board luncheon urging the creation of a campaign to promote economic understanding. Echoing prior sponsored economic education rhetorics, drafts of Dent's comments described the economic liberties of private enterprise as "inseparably linked to political freedoms," warning that "tampering in one area inevitably affects the other." Dent suggested ordinary working people might never take a high school or college course on economics, but could be reached by PSAs—and that these PSAs might influence their votes about economic policy. Indeed, ordinary peoples' opinions about the nation's economic policies were of concern to policymakers. The "inflationary psychology" that had worried lawmakers in the late 1960s was still echoing in the public discourse: Dent had remarked in July of 1973 that "psychological factors" were to blame for inflation, and an August 1974 *New York Times* editorial by Federal Reserve Board chairman Arthur Burns had positioned monetary policy as a way to "discipline" the destructive force of the public's expectations that inflation would continue to worsen. Dent's rhetoric summoned the same notions that had driven the AAAA/ANA's postwar economic education projects: a certainty of the rightness of private enterprise and the tools of commercial persuasion, backed up by the managerial folk knowledge of advertising industry professionals and their allies. Within a month of Dent's speech to the Advertising Council, research was underway at Compton Advertising, the advertising agency that ultimately worked with the Advertising Council to create the campaign.[20]

One of the first steps toward carrying out the "American Economic System" campaign was an open-ended survey of "economic understanding" among US adults, performed under the Advertising Council's instruction. The field research company Coordinated Research Interviewing Service carried out the survey in November and December of 1974. Respondents were asked how they would describe the economic systems of the United States and prompted to explain the roles of business, labor, consumers, investors, and advertising in the economic system. Interviewing was conducted in a variety of locations, with care taken to ensure that the sample was diverse across demographic categories including gender, age, race, community population density, and so on; researchers also considered traits such as an interviewee's income, education, marital status, prior education in economics, union membership, homeownership, and political affiliation.[21]

The survey both constructed the perceived problem and categorized the people the campaign would be designed to reach. The survey followed procedures of social science, with careful attention to sampling and coding. The Advertising Council's public statements on the survey, too, used the language and procedures of social science, asserting the generalizability of the research with claims that "the findings represent the language and logic of the American public." Promotional materials for a published summary of the national survey findings declared that the survey offered detailed information about public attitudes and values based on nearly three thousand open-ended interviews, with almost two thousand participants drawn from a national sample and the balance selected from "special segments of the public," which included people in influential positions in corporations and religious organizations, along with teachers, students, and "community leaders."[22]

Yet, Compton's interpretations of the data yielded from the study seemed to flow from foregone conclusions about the need for economic education and an assumption that support for the American economic system was the same as knowledge about it. In this sense, the economic education proponents of the 1970s were similar to the educational reformers in the 1950s who, when they pressed for better public *understanding* of science, in fact wanted more public *appreciation* for US scientists and the Cold War vision of science as a force for national competitiveness. Compton's summary interpretations of the research suggested that Americans' knowledge of the economic system was spotty—but did not acknowledge the possibility that some respondents' disapproval or criticism of the system may have been caused not by ignorance, but by informed disagreement or firsthand experience with real hardships. Rather, Compton researchers suggested, with an abundance of optimism, that negative assessments of the American economic system came primarily from those who had "not yet realized the benefits of the system"—but, as that "yet" seemed to promise, might enjoy it soon. The report failed to acknowledge that those groups that it identified as being particularly lacking in knowledge were those who were most likely to experience structural inequality—including low-income people, retirees, working-class people, homemakers, and Black people. Critical theories of corporate culture can help make sense of this seeming blind spot. The production and circulation of managerial knowledge, theorist Nigel Thrift argues, is not just practical but affective: it involves "the constant attempt to produce new, more appropriate kinds of *subjects*, what we might call 'souls' that fit contemporary and especially future systems of accumulation. In pursuit of high performance, both workers and managers must be refigured." The Compton Research Department's constructions of economic knowledge produced disparate subjects, configured through their degrees of appreciation for managerial capitalism: on one hand, knowledgeable (and appreciative) workers along with managerial and executive subjects, and on the other, those structurally excluded from and, in many cases dubious of, capitalism's benefits—who were portrayed as subjects without knowledge.[23]

The Advertising Council's external communications about the developing campaign also suggested that knowledge about the system and approval of it were one and the same. Between January and May of 1975, the Advertising Council and the US Department of Commerce negotiated a contract in which Commerce agreed to disburse $150,000 for the initial research study and an additional $89,000 to cover the production and distribution of campaign materials including TV, radio, print, and transit advertisements. The final proposal from the Advertising Council to the Department of Commerce made clear how the council viewed its audiences and the persuasive tasks that lay ahead. It emphasized how the US democratic system imbued ordinary citizens with responsibility for deciding public policy, yet suggested that Americans were poorly equipped for the job, emphasizing "the importance of America adhering to a free-market system when throughout much of the rest of the world the tide is ebbing towards central planning, government ownership and government control." Yet, the proposal presented this *ideological* goal of promoting "a free-market system" as something that could be done in a way that was both unbiased and credible. This was only possible if the principles of a free-market system were understood as self-evident realities and matters of fact—a position that had precedents in prior economic education projects, especially the JCEE's articulations of scientific anticommunism in its 1960s efforts to expand the economics curriculum in schools.[24]

Resistance to the "American Economic System" Campaign

As the "American Economic System" campaign was being set in motion, the Advertising Council was becoming a frequent target for activist critics who saw it as a front for corporate influence laundering. For example, a pair of articles in the December 1974 issue of the New Left magazine *Ramparts* focused attention on the Advertising Council and its activist opponents. The feature on the Advertising Council painted it as a big-business mouthpiece that made a mockery of the very notion of public service. The article included a statement from Congressman Benjamin Rosenthal (D-NY) that encapsulated critics' concerns:

> "The Ad Council," he continued, "is a propagandist for business and government, and with staggering control of the media, it not only makes sure its own side of the story is told, but that the other side isn't. The public has no meaningful access to the media. We're not disputing industry's right to tell its side, but just its monopoly of the time meant for the people."

The article charged that the Advertising Council had an effective monopoly on PSA time because station managers chose Advertising Council PSAs—which were ready to use, made to high production values, and tended to avoid topics that would raise controversy—over PSAs for local organizations, which typically needed to be made in-house using a station's own time, equipment, and production resources. These conditions led critics of the Advertising Council to charge that the council's professionally produced, business-friendly PSAs consumed up to 80 percent of available PSA time and space, and, further, that the Advertising Council's connections to major advertisers and manufacturers resulted in PSAs that held citizens responsible for the nation's problems while obscuring the responsibilities of corporations and the government.[25]

Further, *Ramparts*' coverage of the Advertising Council's critics approvingly tracked the emergence of a "public interest advertising movement" of organizations—including the San Francisco–based Public Media Center; Washington, DC's Media Access Project; and Los Angeles–based media production companies such as Public Communications Inc. and the Public Advertising Council—that produced print and broadcast advertisements for organizations and causes outside of the typical bounds of PSAs, such as environmental conservation, consumer rights, labor rights, and reproductive health. Like the Advertising Council, public interest advertising organizations used the media forms of print, transit, outdoor, and broadcast advertisements; but unlike the Advertising Council, public interest advertising went beyond individual-level calls to action, enfolding critiques of powerful industries and calls for collective grassroots and policy responses.[26]

The FCC's Fairness Doctrine, which the FCC enforced from 1949 until 1987, facilitated the public interest advertising movement's tactics. Aufderheide observes that the Fairness Doctrine rule required broadcasters to present controversy in a balanced manner in all "informational broadcasting including public affairs and news programming, public service announcements (PSAs), program-length commercials, advocacy advertising, appearances by politicians, and political commercials." As the *Ramparts* pieces detailed, public interest advertising activists asked for access to the airwaves of local television stations and, in some cases, filed legal complaints asserting their right to reply to the messages of corporate advertisements and establishment-friendly PSAs. Here, again, Rosenthal—not only a congressman but the chairman of the House Committee on Government Operations' Subcommittee on Commerce, Consumer, and

Monetary Affairs—was mentioned for his support of the Public Media Center's efforts to respond to oil industry public relations advertising. His criticism of the Advertising Council in *Ramparts* foreshadowed a direct confrontation to come.[27]

In mid-July of 1975, just as the Advertising Council was preparing to release the findings of its exploratory research into public understanding of the US economic system, Rosenthal launched an inquiry into the "American Economic System" campaign through the Subcommittee on Commerce, Consumer, and Monetary Affairs. The initial inquiry led to a congressional hearing on July 30, 1975, a day before the Advertising Council's research for the "American Economic System" campaign was set to be released to the public. Rosenthal questioned Commerce's apportionment of funds from the Economic Development Administration and the Office of Minority Business Enterprise, pushing the Department of Commerce's director of policy development Robert Milligan to explain the rationale by which the "American Economic System" campaign fulfilled those offices' missions. Milligan's explanation was simply that better economic "understanding" would both reduce unemployment and encourage more minorities to go into business.[28]

Rosenthal grilled Keim and Milligan on the circumstances of the campaign's provenance, observing that a few years prior in 1973, Howard J. Morgens, the chairman of the board of Proctor and Gamble, had given a speech in praise of the profit motive at an Advertising Council dinner that closed with a call for the Advertising Council to educate the public about "this miraculous business system of ours," cautioning that it could be "gradually crippled by a public and a Congress who do not understand it." Moreover, the advertising agency that volunteered to coordinate the Advertising Council's contribution to the "American Economic System" campaign was Compton Advertising, which also handled Proctor and Gamble's commercial accounts. Members of the House committee raised questions of whether the Advertising Council's decision to create an advertising campaign aimed at raising so-called economic understanding was influenced by the commercial imperatives of the nation's largest advertiser or the opinions of its chairman. Keim, years later, described the hearing as "vicious" and the suggestion of improper influence from Procter and Gamble "a stretch worthy of a Joe McCarthy." In the end, although Rosenthal lambasted the "American Economic System" campaign as a "boondoggle," the General Accounting Office ultimately "termed the contribution both legal and proper."[29]

158   CHAPTER SIX

The day after the congressional hearing, the Advertising Council held its news conference to release the results of its preliminary research study of economic attitudes. Despite suggestions that the campaign and its advocacy for private enterprise would damage the council's reputation, Keim insisted that the Advertising Council's research had uncovered a foundational problem with economic understanding and that the campaign would aim to popularize economics "as science and technology were popularized in the nineteen-sixties," as *New York Times* reporter put it. This comment, perhaps inadvertently, recalled how economic education had become associated with science education and the imagery of the space race during Cold War geopolitical pressures. Similarly, Barton O. Cummings of Compton Advertising remarked that the campaign would "not advocate for or against"—a statement that could only be true if private enterprise were a foregone conclusion and matter of societal consensus. Cummings echoed that same claim months later, attesting at a meeting of the ANA that the PSAs for the campaign would "avoid propagandizing or defensive statements," aiming instead to be "reasonable" and "friendly." From autumn of 1975 onward, preparation was underway for a planned launch on April 22 of 1976.[30]

However, the launch event would create another occasion for resistance to the campaign. Expressions of grassroots criticism became evident in March of 1976 when a patriotic-themed activist group, the Peoples Bicentennial Commission (PBC), launched a critique of the campaign. Historian Simon Hall documents how the Peoples Bicentennial Commission intermixed its "populist radicalism" with the imagery of American patriotism, taking up patriotic symbols to critique corporations' concentrated wealth and power. As Hall notes, the PBC was successful at bringing public attention to critiques of how the bicentennial had seemingly been turned toward partisan and commercialized ends. Jeremy Rifkin, the PBC's founder, declared his intent to launch a public interest advertising countercampaign against what the PBC called the Advertising Council's "massive propaganda campaign to sell the corporate view of the American economic system." The day of the Advertising Council's launch, the PBC hijacked the media narrative by holding a competing press conference immediately after, and across the street from, the Advertising Council's launch event at the Ford Foundation's New York City headquarters. This event reflected the grassroots PBC's activist practices: it had made its name in part by crashing prior patriotic celebration events to protest what it saw as outsized corporate power.[31]

FROM INSTITUTIONS TO MARKETS

The Peoples Bicentennial Commission had become known for pranks designed to emphasize how, in the group's view, ordinary people had become detached from the antiestablishment ideas that had fueled the American Revolution. For example, a *Newsweek* feature in 1975 had reported that PBC members presented Delaware residents with a petition that turned out to be excerpted from the Bill of Rights—which, the activists claimed, the majority failed to recognize and about half refused to sign. The revolutionary theme was reflected, too, in imagery such as the Peoples Bicentennial Commission's use of the coiled snake from the yellow Gadsden ("Don't tread on me") flag as an organizational motif. The *Newsweek* feature remarked that the group drew criticism from business advocates at the US Chamber of Commerce, but also garnered interest from such relatively mainstream groups as the Camp Fire Girls and the National Council of Churches. The Peoples Bicentennial Commission adopted some strategies similar to those of the left-leaning public interest advertising movement: for example, it touted its own countercampaign promoting the organization's paperback book *Common Sense II*, which portrayed US corporations in the villainous role of "the tyrants of our own day."[32]

A coordinated challenge to the "American Economic System" campaign with more powerful backing came from a group calling itself Americans for a Working Economy. Headed up by the Public Media Center, one of the public interest advertising organizations profiled in the 1974 *Ramparts* feature, Americans for a Working Economy was an organizational alliance that listed the National Education Association, the Consumer Federation of America, Friends of the Earth, the national Council of Senior Citizens, and unions affiliated with the AFL-CIO and the United Auto Workers among its sponsor organizations. The Public Media Center's cofounder, Roger Hickey, announced in July 1976 that the group was planning its own countercampaign to address the shortcomings of the "American Economic System" campaign, particularly its lack of attention to the role of the public sector and its inattention to "structural problems that keep the economy from working for all the people." Hickey had stated that the Public Media Center would request stations airing the Advertising Council spot to air their own PSAs as well, and if turned down, the organization would consider a complaint to the FCC under the Fairness Doctrine.[33]

The direct impact of the challenges from Peoples Bicentennial Commission and Public Media Center on networks' approval of the Advertising

Council "American Economic System" spots is not entirely clear, but the networks' reception of the Advertising Council PSAs was unusually lukewarm: while the NBC network and many local affiliates ran the spots starting in August, the other major networks balked, making the "American Economic System" campaign the first Advertising Council campaign to face such rejections. CBS signaled that it would consider airing different commercials that omitted the booklet offer, and ABC simply declined to air the PSAs altogether. When the Peoples Bicentennial Commission requested airtime for their countercampaign, NBC declined, arguing that the PBC's message contained controversial advocacy and that the network believed the PBC's campaign was "not an answer to the Ad Council campaign, which we believe is not controversial." The Public Media Center continued its opposition to the "American Economic System" campaign, not only pressuring networks to air its own PSAs in support of its own booklet, but also calling on the Department of Commerce to provide funding—a request that Milligan rebuffed on the grounds that the booklet was factually correct and unbiased.[34]

Power versus Freedom: Explaining the American Economy

By September of 1976, criticisms of the "American Economic System" campaign—and especially its booklet—were issuing from many sides. Where activists from the left viewed the "American Economic System" campaign as propaganda for business interests, others saw the campaign as disappointingly empty. Economist James Tobin of Yale University warned that "many will be deceived because the smooth Madison Avenue language gives the impression of telling how the economy works without ever doing so." A spokesperson for the conservative American Economic Foundation expressed concerns about the booklet's tolerance for government intervention, calling it "a mishmash of bland platitudes." The Advertising Council's Keim responded, "our goal is to get people to understand more about the system and then they can make up their own minds on whether it is good or bad." To the charges that the booklet was bland and oversimplified, Keim said, "it may be simplistic, but we were trying to draw people in . . . to show that economics isn't that tough." The Advertising Council insisted that the campaign was politically neutral and that "its 'clients are not institutions but the American people.'" While this claim may have seemed far-fetched given the institutional funding and

FROM INSTITUTIONS TO MARKETS

donated corporate resources that launched the campaign, it echoed the logic within the booklet—in which institutions of capitalism and their concentrated power seemed to fade into the background.[35]

A closer examination of the booklet itself clarifies how the booklet could be perceived as by some as propagandizing and by others as saying nothing. The Advertising Council had hoped its booklet would have broad appeal, and vetted it accordingly: leadership on the project noted that its reviewers included "economists, representatives of the Joint Council on Economic Education, [the] Committee for Economic Development, labor and business organizations, government agencies, the members of the Advertising Council's Public Policy committee and its Board of Directors." A later *Fortune* magazine feature on the booklet suggested that writers at the Department of Commerce had been largely responsible for the booklet's text: "the admen wanted it to be upbeat and readable, whereas the bureaucrats insisted on objectivity and lots of information. Commerce won." The feature concluded that "the pamphlet is vague, antiseptically dispassionate, and reads like a textbook." Although the Advertising Council had aimed for an accessible guide to understanding and appreciating the US economic system, *The American Economic System ... and Your Part in It* delivered a limited explanation that, in critics' eyes, left much unsaid.[36]

The booklet's central organizing concept split economic actors in the US into three groups: consumers, "who look for the best value in return for what they spend"; producers, "who seek the best income for what they offer"; and governments, "which seek to promote the safety and welfare of the public, and to provide services in the public interest." This taxonomy elided important inequalities of power and wealth: workers and the labor force were identified as producers, but so were managers, investors, and entrepreneurs. By lumping different class positions and functions together as producers, the booklet tacitly invited readers to imagine that laborers, managers, and the owners of businesses large and small were driven by the same motivations.[37]

This taxonomy obscured (and, to an extent, made unmappable) class-based critiques of capitalism, because under *The American Economic System ... and Your Part in It*'s taxonomy, "consumers" could be individuals, businesses, or governments; and "producers" could be among the ranks of labor or managers. The booklet pointed to the decisions of individual "producers" and "consumers" as having the most influence over the US economic system, and explained supply, demand, and competition as the dynamics by which "producers" and "consumers" interacted. This taxonomy of economic actors blurred the lines between individuals and corporations; as such, it reimagined business advocates' long-standing claims that the civil liberties of citizens and the functional privileges of corporations were intertwined by portraying them as having few meaningful differences. Its definitions of democracy and capitalism played up individual choices as motive forces (claiming, for example, that "democracy is a system based on individual freedoms") while its formulations of socialism and communism identified the government and the political party, respectively, as the crucial actors in such systems.[38]

Moreover, *The American Economic System . . . and Your Part in It*'s performance of objectivity skimmed over existing inequalities. As one *Wall Street Journal* reporter put it,

> On the subject of discrimination, the booklet says: "Differences in incomes associated with race and sex are often the result of discrimination and lack of opportunity." That's all.

Similarly, a writeup in the *Washington Post* noted that critics of the campaign—including former officials who had advised the Kennedy administration, such as Keynesian economist Walter Heller—had raised concerns about the bias of the booklet and charged that "it glosses over such questions as unemployment, minorities, and environmental pollution." The booklet's carefully brief coverage of issues of economic justice lent itself to the appearance of impartiality: it simply stated that inequality existed and mentioned questions to be discussed, avoiding any prescriptive suggestions that might have been interpreted as partisan. However, using omission and superficial mention as tactics for performing nonpartisan objectivity yielded a text that, critics charged, did little to challenge the status quo.[39]

In September of 1976, the Public Media Center released its own PSAs supporting its own booklet, *A Working Economy for Americans*. At its release, it claimed that over eight hundred local television and radio stations had agreed to air the Public Media Center's PSAs. By June of 1977, a Public Media Center spokesperson stated that ten thousand copies of the booklet had been sent out, with an additional twenty-thousand on order. Molly Niesen observes that the two booklets "offered Americans contrasting views of the world": whereas *The American Economic System . . . and Your Part in It* centered "individual freedom, consumerism, and free enterprise," *A Working Economy for Americans* focused instead

FROM INSTITUTIONS TO MARKETS

on "social justice, equal rights, and democracy." Indeed, several differences in tone, complexity, and approach distinguished *A Working Economy for Americans* from *The American Economic System . . . and Your Part in It*. First, *A Working Economy for Americans* approached concepts in greater depth, seemingly assumed a more well-informed reader. Second, the two texts took different approaches to the history of the nation and its implications for the present day. *The American Economic System . . . and Your Part in It* used the occasion of the bicentennial to flit from the practice of bartering in the 1770s to the use of credit cards in the 1970s as an illustration how spending habits had changed. *A Working Economy for Americans* presented more detailed and inclusive historical context, acknowledging both the role of African Americans, unwillingly "brought as slaves from Africa to supply the labor for cotton and tobacco plantations," in the early US' political economy and the dispossession of indigenous peoples, observing that "land seemed to be almost unlimited (after it was taken from the Indians)." Third, *A Working Economy for Americans* challenged prevailing ideas about what it meant for the government to intervene in economic life. Over several pages, it highlighted the involvement of the US government in the rise of corporate power, declaring, "in fact, individuals and free enterprise, often lauded as the prime agents of our phenomenal national growth, could not have accomplished a lot of the things it did without active government support." Fourth and finally, the two booklets differed in how they called readers to action. *A Working Economy for Americans* critiqued the existing system and laid out a detailed set of policy suggestions, including antitrust legislation, tax reform, full employment policies, and cooperative organizational forms such as co-operatives and publicly owned companies. By comparison, the pressures for *The American Economic System . . . and Your Part in It* to maintain the appearance of nonpartisanship seemed to result in a text designed not to call people to action but simply to raise awareness about abstract forces such as supply, demand, and competition, always landing on the observation that the American people would need to make some decisions about these issues—but not saying what those decisions could be. It was this approach that critics, like Ted Howard of the Peoples Bicentennial Commission, called "advocacy by omission," suggesting that such works implicitly endorsed the status quo.[40]

As historian Daniel Rodgers has observed, "the 'market' that came into vogue in the 1970s floated virtually free of corporate or institutional presence," and by the late 1970s would represent a new kind of myth-making about society, defined by its "detachment from history and institutions and from questions of power." Critics charged that power was exactly the thing that was most notably missing from *The American Economic System . . . and Your Part in It*. Indeed, a critique of the "American Economic System" campaign published in the often-radical academic journal *College English* charged that the Advertising Council's very purpose, as crystallized in *The American Economic System . . . and Your Part in It*, was to entrench and conceal existing power relations.[41]

Where *The American Economic System . . . and Your Part in It* made the corporation out to be an economic unit with the same basic economic motivations as an individual, *A Working Economy for Americans* presented multiple critiques of corporate power. For example, *A Working Economy for Americans* declared that "economic power translates into political power. . . . It is this alliance of corporations with elected political leaders from which we have the most to fear, since it endangers democracy itself." Indeed, both booklets ended with a declaration of how the political and the economic intersected. The Advertising Council's booklet stated:

> All of our needs and desires cannot be fully satisfied—nor will they ever be in a world of limited resources. Throughout history, many societies have attempted to solve this problem by dictating what individual needs and wants should be—and by controlling how these needs and wants are met. Yet, economic freedoms and personal freedoms have a way of interlocking.

Perhaps in a riff on that passage, and making clear the differences between the two booklets, *A Working Economy for Americans* declared on its final page that

> the fight for guaranteed jobs and income for all, a clean environment and the economic rights of citizens and consumers requires such cooperation. For the fight is not an easy one; no one said it would be. The struggle is complicated by the fact that economic power and political power are inextricably intertwined. Thus citizens must learn to exert control over their political system in order to effect economic change.[42]

Even though both passages portrayed economy and society as being inseparable, they offered very different visions of the link between those two realms. The Advertising Council centered *freedom*, a state of potential being that could be subject to the cycles of longing and delayed fulfillment

FROM INSTITUTIONS TO MARKETS

that Campbell describes as central to consumer culture, but Americans for a Working Economy centered *power*, a sense of agency and control embedded in a specific time, place, and context.

The American Economic System . . . and Your Part in It suggested that allowing "economic freedoms" would be the best way to preserve a democratic system based on individual freedoms. By making these two moves, the booklet enacted the most distinctive themes Oreskes and Conway identify in their survey of ideological opposition to "big government," both in the sense of imagining commercial imperatives on par with political freedoms and in the sense of imagining "that markets exist outside of politics and culture, so that it can be logical to speak of leaving them 'alone.'" *The American Economic System . . . and Your Part in It*'s exhortations against "societies . . . dictating" and "controlling" consumer decisions implied that market forces had the capacity to democratically distribute power. This formulation invited readers to think of real lived conditions as the natural consequence of market forces, and thus to understand unmet needs not as a failure of the system, but rather as an imbalance that could be properly addressed by the further workings of market forces—thus ensuring the continued protection of personal liberty and, by extension, democracy.[43]

The Complications of Markets and Democracy

The balance of the "American Economic System" campaign proceeded more smoothly, remaining active until 1979 when it was superseded by a new Advertising Council campaign focused on—once again—inflation. Although the public service advertisements associated with *A Working Economy for Americans* were adopted by some broadcasters, they did not see nearly as broad distribution as the Advertising Council PSAs they were designed to respond to. It's not clear what happened to Americans for a Working Economy, the group that had published the booklet: they received no further press coverage after the booklet's publication, suggesting that the coalition was temporary. To be sure, many of its constituent organizations—among them labor unions such as the National Education Association, the United Auto Workers, and AFL-CIO groups representing state employees, machinists, and chemical workers—would have been grappling with the rise of Reagan-style conservatism and its challenges to organized labor by the early 1980s.[44]

166   CHAPTER SIX

Ultimately, the Advertising Council's approach won out, in the sense that additional PSAs related to the campaign were seen as nonpartisan and uncontroversial enough to be broadcasted. The "American Economic System" campaign continued to field critiques along by-then-familiar lines, but nothing on the level of the confrontations with Congress and activist groups that marred the year of the campaign's launch. By January of 1977, meeting minutes of the Advertising Council's Industry Advisory Council projected a mood of calm and careful planning, with the observation that the "American Economic System" campaign had been subject to "practically no organized criticism" for several months. Compton Advertising was developing a new advertising campaign that would focus on "E.Q. (Economic Quotient)," urging each American to improve their knowledge of economics. While the elements that caused the most public controversy were changed, the deeper logic of the campaign was essentially the same. It continued to focus on individual awareness, leaving little room or conceptual framework for discussion of systemic problems of power.[45]

The "E.Q." PSAs were made with two alternate endings: one ending offered the booklet, and the other encouraged viewers to learn more about economics at their local libraries (making it less vulnerable to allegations of bias). Unlike the prior run of PSAs, the new "E.Q."-themed PSAs were approved by all three major networks. As the new PSAs were launched, coverage of the Advertising Council in major US newspapers turned away from the prior year's controversies and toward new figures released from Compton, which showed that almost a third of the 2,016 adults surveyed were familiar with the campaign — a level of public awareness that reflected the size and scope of the campaign's impact. Compton reported gains in both "the public's understanding of our economic system" and "the public's appraisal of the system." The campaign ended, then, as it began: by equating approval of the American economic system with knowledge of it.[46]

The 1970s were a transformative decade for business interests: corporate leaders started the decade describing themselves as besieged by economic and policy changes, but ended it amid the regulatory and cultural changes of an ascendant conservatism. As the late 1960s gave way to the early 1970s, economic and social pressures from inflation to the movement for corporate social responsibility had contributed to a sense of managerial overwhelm and crisis. While organized lobbying pushed for policy changes through direct interaction with lawmakers, public relations efforts sought a more diffuse form of advantage by deliberately cultivating public perceptions of corporate legitimacy. Considering these pressures, managerial discourses insisted that the operations of business were intrinsically socially beneficial, and further, that promoting US corporate leaders' understandings of American private enterprise was, in itself, an act of public service that would ensure ongoing US prosperity. This was the context in which the Advertising Council's "American Economic System" campaign took shape.[47]

The "American Economic System" campaign had aimed to persuade the public to develop an appreciation for, and willingness to defend, private enterprise. The campaign reproduced economic education tropes that conflated civics with promotion: it imagined persuasion to be a form of public service, and it framed appreciation of capitalism as economic knowledge. Yet, the Advertising Council presented its "American Economic System" campaign as apolitical and unbiased; in doing so, it quietly incorporated the anticommunist tenor of prior decades' sponsored economic education efforts. The Advertising Council claimed to be pursuing what it called public understanding of the US economic system, but its attempts to cultivate appreciation and goodwill for managerial capitalism advanced ways of seeing the world that did little to challenge the corporate power.

The public interest advertising movement's opposition to the "American Economic System" campaign foregrounded the issues at stake, calling attention to how economic and political power could go hand in hand. Ultimately, the Advertising Council and its allies won out over their opponents. Yet, the public interest advertising movement's strategic use of countercampaigns both demonstrated the movement's small victories and complicated the long-standing liberal notion that the best remedy for objectionable speech was more speech. Both the Advertising Council and its activist counterparts—at the Peoples Bicentennial Commission and the Public Media Center's Americans for a Working Economy coalition—attempted to introduce counternarratives to the public discourse, but encountered institutional barriers. Nonetheless, the activists mobilized grassroots power, using the stipulations of the Fairness Doctrine to fortify their critique of the Advertising Council and potentially leading some controversy-averse broadcasters to steer clear of the Advertising Council's initial PSAs altogether.

The portrayal of abstract and atomized producers and consumers in the Advertising Council's *The American Economic System ... and Your*

Part in It invited audiences to learn to see in the abstract — to imagine the prerogatives of corporations as inseparable from the rights of the individual, even when lived experience suggested that the two were sometimes at odds — and further to learn to *not* see the imbalances of power, resources, and political influence that co-constructed corporate operational and communicative practices. This way of seeing did more than simply serve companies' economic imperatives; it enabled economic education's allies to imagine themselves as servants of the public interest. In 1976, then president of the Advertising Council Robert Keim declared to a *Wall Street Journal* reporter, "we don't want to change people's views, we just want them to think about economics."[48]

In the end, the "American Economic System" campaign elevated the Advertising Council to a new level of public visibility, but also engendered considerable controversy. Critics had come from many angles. In a 2002 memoir recounting his work with the Advertising Council (titled, grandly, *A Time in Advertising's Camelot: Memoirs of a Do-Gooder*), Keim lamented that "academic economists pooh-poohed us for daring to be simplistic about their holy grail. Our answer was that we were getting people interested in a subject that greatly affected their lives. . . . The beatniks attacked us for 'selling' the capitalist system and some politicians accused us of being the handmaidens of Wall Street and conservative Republicans." Indeed, even some conservative commentators had expressed serious doubts about the campaign in its moment. For example, the influential conservative journalist Irving Kristol dubbed economic education "a threefold confusion of the process of education with the procedures of advertising with the purposes of propaganda," and economist and columnist Paul Samuelson dismissed economic education as a "historically worthless" project "mostly prompted by the vanity of the business leaders." Voices from inside the advertising industry, too, expressed concern: Neal O'Connor, the chairman of the AAAA, had addressed the campaign obliquely in 1976, warning that what passed for economic education could in fact be "economic indoctrination."[49]

Economic literacy is often described in language that seems removed from politics: economic educator Ronald Banaszak, for example, describes it as "knowing and applying fundamental economic ideas" in a "logical, reasoned" way. This was, in effect, the stated promise of the Advertising Council's "American Economic System" campaign, and of many economic education campaigns that had come before it: that it would help the public become more familiar with ideas and ways of thinking related

FROM INSTITUTIONS TO MARKETS

to economics. However, the Advertising Council's "American Economic System" campaign in fact offered a very narrow kind of economic literacy that was focused on "reading" the terrain of everyday life and extracting meanings compatible with market ideologies. This isn't merely to say that the "American Economic System" campaign taught people about market ideologies when it purported to teach people about economics, although that is true. The topics and concepts that were the focus of the Advertising Council's "American Economic System" PSAs and the booklet *The American Economic System ... and Your Part in It* treated some matters as central to economic understanding and other matters as barely important enough to mention. This selective framing rearticulated the affirmative style: it subtly retained the proclivity toward celebratory and confident rhetorics about private enterprise (and lack of attention to ideological alternatives) that had characterized efforts to sell America to Americans from the interwar period forward. Yet, the campaign was a *reimagining* of the affirmative style because the "American Economic System" campaign differed from its predecessors in how it described the economic system and, by extension, how it constructed economic knowledge. In the few years that had passed since 1969, the focus of Advertising Council economic education campaign themes shifted from one that centered what people (and institutions, in the JCEE's contributions) could do to help address society-level problems to one that centered *awareness* of abstract and impersonal economic forces that could, themselves, be imagined to be objective. This view discarded the JCEE's emphasis on institutions but elaborated on the JCEE's framing of economic analysis as objective, transferring the quality of objectivity from economists' analyses of market forces to the market forces themselves.[50]

This shift from individuals and institutions to economic roles and market forces had important consequences. Like many prior economic education campaigns, the 1970s "American Economic System" campaign deployed the promotionally nationalist talking point, publicized by the National Association of Manufacturers in the 1930s, that private enterprise, political liberties, and personal liberties were so intermeshed that a threat to one was a threat to all three. Unlike prior decades' sponsored economic education ideologies, however, the "American Economic System" campaign's portrayal of "producers" and "consumers" placed US corporations and their allies at a distance from inequalities of power. *The American Economic System ... and Your Part in It*'s market fundamentalism imagined that power resided less in individuals or institutions than in economic roles—producer, consumer—and market forces such as supply, demand, and competition. These market forces were presented as self-adjusting mechanisms that seemed to exist apart from politics. Such an approach rendered institutional power effectively invisible because, from a market fundamentalist perspective, individuals and institutions could be understood merely as *the conduits through which the power of apolitical economic forces was made manifest.* The invisibility of power in the *American Economic System* booklet was a target for critics, who charged that the booklet urged readers to see profit-making imperatives as the expression of freedom rather than the exercise of power.

In the process of offering explanations based on a nascent market fundamentalism to its audiences, the campaign constructed virtuous subject positions and affective postures for those who considered themselves to be aligned with business. Communication theorist Zizi Papacharissi observes that affective attunement can be observed in "imbricated layers of storytelling." The "American Economic System" campaign's affective charge emanated not only from the stories *within* the texts of PSAs and booklets, but also from how allies of the campaign circulated stories about why such texts were necessary. The "American Economic System" campaign alluded to the meaning of doing business and the moral legitimacy of being a business leader, both in and beyond the narrative boundaries of booklets and public service advertisements. Campaign supporters' claims about the pressing need for economic education were based on a social and political frame of serious threat. Narrative frames in which business itself was under siege had been part of economic education media discourses for decades. Such discourses had long constructed important but underrepresented constituencies—such as immigrants, working people, retirees, and people of color—as ignorant, misinformed, or downright hostile toward corporations and business leaders. Considering this narrative frame, the proponents of the "American Economic System" campaign could imagine it to be a public service initiative that helped to preserve the standard of living in the United States. Through these layers of narratives about social responsibility and American exceptionalism, the Advertising Council's "American Economic System" campaign generated resources for smoothing the affective textures of managerial identity within a culture that seemed (to many managers, at least) to be running out of patience for corporate power.[51]

The market fundamentalism touted in the "American Economic System" campaign had implications for understandings of democracy: it

FROM INSTITUTIONS TO MARKETS

suggested that market forces could be immediate and accurate manifestations of the popular will. *The American Economic System . . . and Your Part in It* portrayed supply, demand, and competition as organizing principles that helped to coordinate society. From this perspective, government could, itself, be seen as somewhat suspect, to the extent government was imagined to be less constrained by an immediate and automatic discipline imparted by economic market forces. Ironically, the campaign was kick-started with federal funds, but contributed to a growing political discourse that imagined civic institutions were less accountable, and therefore a less vital form of democracy, than the forces of the market. Further, since market ideology suggested that these forces acted automatically to bring about a state of balance, allowing market forces to operate freely could be understood as the best way to prevent injustice or the abuse of power. This reasoning echoed some of the logics in play around 1960s scientific anticommunism, especially the supposition that decentralization was democratic in itself.

The ideas promoted in *The American Economic System . . . and Your Part in It* and the Advertising Council's PSAs came to be increasingly naturalized in the decades to follow. It's too simple to say that the "American Economic System" campaign single-handedly ushered market fundamentalism into the public consciousness, but the campaign did reflect a growing interest in markets and market forces, which corporations could exploit to serve their own ends. The "American Economic System" campaign may be seen as a strategic means of building long-term corporate public legitimacy in the manner business advocates had long envisioned. Yet, the campaign was as least as much a rearticulation of economic education's established tropes, and an updating of those tropes to meet the ideological climate of the moment.

CHAPTER SEVEN

The Triumphs of Economic Education

By the late 1970s, economics had gained ground as a subject of popular imaginings. While the previous chapter examined how multiple constituencies used public service messaging to connect claims about the importance of economic understanding to the ordinary conditions of everyday life in the 1970s, this chapter traces how these ideas found expression in both popular discourse and educational policy. From the late 1970s into the early 1980s, precepts and practices familiar to proponents of sponsored economic education media became increasingly naturalized in popular discourse and institutionally affirmed through state laws. The chapter begins by explaining how, over the course of the 1970s, almost half of the nation's state legislatures put policies into place requiring the teaching of economics or economics-related topics in primary and/or secondary schools. It examines how business interests and educators helped support this policy trend, and how these advocates for economic education won favorable coverage of their projects in the news media. The chapter argues that, taken together, these events pointed to a shift in which economic education, ever perceived by its supporters as an underdog cause, gained new forms of institutional legitimacy even as its precepts proved to be compatible with a growing disdain for institutions themselves. The chapter then considers the simulation-based games that were part of the new curricular offerings to meet these mandates. In particular, it examines how the proponents of simulation games for economic education hoped such games could not only bring economic concepts to life, but could further help young learners develop empathy alongside analytical skills, in contrast to assumptions that economic thinking relied on a detached analytical distance.

State Mandates and the New Conservatism

Over the course of the 1970s, state mandates for economic education had flourished across the nation. Between 1971 and 1982, twenty-four states passed or updated mandates for instruction in economics. Such mandates were compatible with the JCEE's decentralized resource provision model. The JCEE often provided support by training teachers to comport with the new mandates requiring economic education in schools; in Florida, for example, the state legislature not only passed a statute mandating economic education in 1974, but also provided funding for the Florida Council on Economic Education.[1]

Some arguments for the mandates suggested echoes of the affirmative style—that is, the tendency toward rhetorics of celebration, coupled with refusal to engage seriously with ideological opponents. For example, upon the passage of North Carolina's bill in 1975, Democratic state senator and bill sponsor William Kemp Mauney commented to a *New York Times* reporter, "I don't think there's anything wrong with the General Assembly telling school teachers [sic] what to teach.... It's not that important that school children be taught Marxism. It's already being taught just like free enterprise ... in some schools." Mauney's comment showed how advocates managed the contradictions of economic education by the mid-1970s: if education was required to promote private enterprise, one way to reconcile the seeming bias of this approach was by using a rhetorical move that framed the promotion of conservative ideas as a needed counterbalance against Marxism in schools. Lewis Powell's infamous memo, for example, had framed its strategic recommendations for the promotion of private enterprise in universities as a counterforce to an existing "attack on the free enterprise system," in his phrasing.[2]

A comprehensive study of 1970s economic education mandates carried out a few years later by educators Dennis C. Brennan and Ronald A Banaszak through the Center for the Development of Economic Education at the University of the Pacific in Stockton, California (itself financially supported by the Foundation for Teaching Economics) examined the laws and educational standards set by the states. It found that in practice, these mandates could serve a range of instructional goals, including promoting "the benefits of the free enterprise system"; teaching students about the US economy and how to behave within it; and fostering "consumer survival skills." Further, the study noted factors that were associated with the mandate trend: popular interest in economics was up, as was business leaders' interest in "lobbying for mandates in economics education." The figure of twenty-four states mandating economic education only partly reflected the degree to which economics was being embraced in the nation's schools: even in many states without formalized mandates, the report noted interest in teaching economics.[3]

The report's mention of business support for mandates warrants closer examination. For example, the details around the passage of Oklahoma's economic education statute in 1974 shows how local business advocates and their allies—including the Oklahoma City Chamber of Commerce, local businesses, and the JCEE-affiliated local Council on Economic Education (CEE) promoted economic education at the state level. An April 1973 *Chicago Tribune* article reported on economic education efforts in the state, including a new economic education curriculum guide for primary and secondary schools, distributed by the state department of education and prepared with input from the Oklahoma CEE. It further described a contest that offered a $1,000 prize for the best use of the guide in the classroom, sponsored by the Liberty National Bank and Trust of Oklahoma City—noting that the bank's executive ranks included the president of the Oklahoma CEE. Oklahoma passed its statewide Economic Education Act of 1974 with lobbying support from the Oklahoma City Chamber of Commerce and sponsorship by Democratic state congressmen. Supporters of the mandate in the years to come would emphasize the value of economics as a discipline and way of thinking. For example, in 1976, Oklahoma City's *Daily Oklahoman* newspaper included a feature on economist and educator Lorraine Scheer, who noted that Oklahoma's mandated economics curriculum had "considerably" helped economic educators, even though, as she pointed out, the legislature had passed the law without providing funding to implement it. The Oklahoma mandate illustrated how state mandates brought together different constituencies: supportive institutions and individuals worked to pass and implement economic education requirements that they saw as affirming private enterprise, and educators such as Scheer focused on how instruction in economics could not only build students' understanding of economic systems in the US and elsewhere, but could also help students, as individuals and as citizens, "to better make decisions that would enhance their well-being," as she put it.[4]

The seeming accord between business advocates and educators illustrated how popular discourses about economics had changed from the early

THE TRIUMPHS OF ECONOMIC EDUCATION   175

1960s to the mid-1970s. Conservative critics of the JCEE and the National Task Force on Economic Education's joint efforts to build students' knowledge of comparative economic systems in the 1960s had received these organizations' projects with skepticism, suggesting that they didn't do enough to foster support for and appreciation of American capitalism and its freedoms. By the mid-1970s, however, such conflicts seemed less evident.

Further, news discourses identified economic education as a growing trend. A 1975 commentary by columnist, economist, and *Ethics and Profits* coauthor Leonard Silk framed the spate of rising interest in teaching economics as the culmination of a twenty-year trend, brought to fruition by a "time of crisis in both economics and education"; the piece featured George Leland Bach, who had chaired the National Task Force on Economic Education, approvingly mentioning Bach's efforts to find more engaging and personalized ways of learning. Follow-up reporting from Silk the following year commented on the JCEE's forthcoming *Master Curriculum Guide in Economics for the Nation's Schools*, emphasizing how it laid bare the vexing complexity of economic problems, especially when it came to matters such as "equity and social justice." Reflecting on how questions about economics were interwoven with "conflicts in philosophies and values," Silk suggested that the task force offered little guidance. Here, Silk's comments were similar to the critiques leveled by the left-leaning Americans for a Working Economy and other critics—that the institutional voice of economic education failed to help learners develop insights into what to do about structural conflicts within US society. Just a few years later, a 1978 news feature reported on a rightward shift in "economic thinking," accompanied by an uptick in corporate support for "economic education aimed at defending the free market system."[5]

Another indication of a shift in attitudes toward economic education could be seen in the nonfiction programming being prepared for the nation's television screens by the late 1970s: while corporations and their charitable foundations were eager to fund libertarian economist and public intellectual Milton Friedman's PBS miniseries *Free to Choose*, John Coleman—the once-celebrated "National Teacher" of the JCEE's 1962 *The American Economy* telecourse—failed to raise sufficient funds to underwrite the broadcast of a new educational television program about economics. Coleman suggested at the time that his fundraising difficulties may have been caused by major corporations' shifting expectations for sponsored programs: perhaps they assumed, Coleman remarked, that he would be "too liberal or too objective," possibilities Coleman described as "frightening to companies." In the sixteen years since the production of *The American Economy*, sponsors' expectations of sponsored economic education seemed to have shifted away from Coleman: the scientific anti-communism of a program like *The American Economy*, it seemed, would no longer be enough for corporate sponsors invigorated by the popular discourses around business, economics, and public opinion that aligned with a growing market fundamentalism.[6]

Computers, Simulation, and Economic Education

The formalization of state mandates and the shift in news coverage pointed to a growing popular fascination with economics over the course of the 1970s and beyond; this fascination was also made manifest in the use of computerized simulation games as tools for teaching children about economics and business operations. Simulation games were championed by the JCEE in the late 1960s, and later included in a semester curriculum program developed by the business education organization Junior Achievement. Tracing these developments suggests that simulation's value for teaching economics in the 1970s and early 1980s United States among disparate constituencies within the broader economic education movement lay not entirely in its power to teach economic principles, but in its power to capture attention and teach a suite of affective tendencies—including empathy for managerial decision-makers—through role play. I argue here that economic educators' fascination with games and simulations for teaching can be understood as connecting to traditions of twentieth-century thinking around economic education media, especially the assumption that media could help stir an affective attachment to private enterprise (as was expressed in earlier sponsored economic education media projects), and also the hope that teaching students economic principles would lead them to become better citizens.

By the late 1960s, educators at the JCEE had documented a growing interest in simulation games for teaching economic concepts in primary and secondary classrooms. *Games and Simulations for Teaching Economics*, a booklet authored by JCEE economists Darrell R. Lewis and Donald Wentworth and first published in 1968, gives insight into how economists and educators conceived of simulation games and their value in the late 1960s and early 1970s. In the early 1970s, these games and simulations were largely analog, tabletop games; though some mainframe digital economic simulations existed in the 1970s, they were far out of the average schoolteacher's reach. The discursive themes established during this time, however, carried over into subsequent discussions of digital simulation and games for what would become a growing personal computer market.[7]

Games and Simulations for Teaching Economics indicated that economics teachers were integrating ideas from other realms of social science into their understandings of the learning possibilities of simulation. Lewis and Wentworth's tentative explanation of what simulations could make possible had drawn on writings from educational psychologist Paul A. Twelker, who had expressed hope that simulation could help students learn by experience, and sociologist Hall T. Sprague, who suggested that simulation might help students build students' motivation, make their thinking more nuanced, and build their interpersonal competencies. Lewis and Wentworth had followed these optimistic views of simulation's potential with a set of limited empirical findings about the efficacy of games for teaching economics. These findings had in some ways verified Twelker and Sprague's speculations: for example, the researchers had found that the "amount of cognitive learning" gained from simulation wasn't significantly higher than what could be attained through "conventional" classroom instruction, but did find that such exercises increased students' interest in the lessons. Further, Lewis and Wentworth had reported that simulation exercises may have helped students develop "more empathy for the roles they are assuming and the complexities of the environments they are dealing with," better "decision-making strategies," and better understandings of the complexity of social systems. Taken as a whole, then, the booklet emphasized how simulation games for economic education could cultivate student involvement, social skills, and systems-level thinking *in the process of teaching* economic concepts.[8]

This attention to interpersonal processes and empathy for decision-makers was evident not only in JCEE materials, but also in projects from other economic education-adjacent organizations that experimented with simulation games. The business advocacy nonprofit Junior Achievement (JA), for example, had long maintained a tradition of experiential offerings that it positioned as educational: for much of the twentieth century, Junior Achievement had organized after-school programs in which secondary school students created and managed their own small "companies." By the late 1970s, though, Junior Achievement developed a new approach to its educational activities, offering an example of how legacy ideas from economic education carried forward into the 1980s.[9]

In March of 1980, the National Board of Directors of Junior Achievement distributed the results of a seven-month study of "the teen environment" to its sponsors, affiliated youth organizations, and the media. The report, funded by aluminum manufacturer ALCOA and prepared by management consultancy the Robert Johnston Company, suggested that youth in the US had become unmoored from the hopes and values that had inspired prior generations. "The world of business," the report declared, "should seek to fill this void." Doing so, the *Teen Environment Report* suggested, could improve youth attitudes toward business.[10]

Junior Achievement developed a program in the early 1980s that seemed oriented toward these hopes to engage a new generation: Applied Economics, a classroom curriculum that combined JA's traditions of experiential learning with simplified lectures on economic concepts and computerized business simulation games. In 1984, an evaluation of Applied Economics for Junior Achievement polled teachers of Applied Economics and standard economics teaching approaches, finding that both approaches contributed to student improvement not only in students' knowledge of business and economics, but also in their understandings of themselves and others. Junior Achievement differed from the JCEE to the extent that many of its efforts under the name of economic education emphasized business operations rather than economic reasoning. Yet, both organizations seemed to embrace the idea that learning economics could help students develop both intellectually and socially.[11]

Lewis and Wentworth's observations, examined alongside JA's approach to assessing student learning, offer perspectives on how different traditions within economic education conceptualized economic thinking and its relation to feelings and personal values in the early 1980s. They suggest that economic educators of the 1970s and 1980s saw themselves as cultivating economically knowledgeable citizens who were capable of empathy and human connection. This empathetic economic subject showed up in teaching materials on the cusp of an era of increasing liberalization and privatization. The vision of an economically *and* emotionally literate capitalist subject was relevant not only for what it said to students about how to be a businessperson, but also for how it permitted businesspeople and economic educators in the US to understand their *own* place in the social imaginary and the moral order.

The enactment of state mandates, along with approving news coverage of economic education, reflected how economics was coming to be understood by many policymakers and members of the public as a self-evidently necessary body of knowledge for youth in the United States. Organizations like Junior Achievement took advantage of the new state mandates and the mood of popular receptivity to economic education to launch programs that rearticulated prior linkages between economic education, affect, and notions of civic preparedness.

To be sure, these developments did not go uncontested—but critics faced an increasingly uphill battle, as companies invested more money in educational materials and the precepts of sponsored economic education gained further ground. Corporation funding for education had almost doubled over just a few years, rising to a reported $870 million by 1979. That same year, the Ralph Nader–affiliated Center for the Study of Responsive Law published *Hucksters in the Classroom*, an exposé and critique of corporate-funded educational materials written by researcher Sheila Harty. Such sponsored materials, of course, were nothing new: as Inger Stole documents, corporations' attempts to access the classroom through sponsored and branded teaching materials had been the object of consumer activism since the 1930s. *Hucksters*'s chapter on sponsored economic education materials called attention to state mandates, observing (for example) how Texas had passed a mandate for free enterprise education, but "appropriated no state funds to finance it," echoing educator Lorraine Scheer's observations about her own state's mandate. Texas's failure to apportion funding, Harty argued, enabled the approval of privately financed teaching materials from local utility companies and antilabor organizations. The chapter offered a view, too, onto the roles the JCEE and local CEEs played in supporting such materials. Harty acknowledged that JCEE president M. L. Frankel had advocated for impartial approaches to teaching economics, but the chapter leveled critiques at privately funded economic education materials that had been developed by utilities and oil companies in partnership with state Councils on Economic Education. Ultimately, *Hucksters* charged, such corporate-sponsored economic education materials could be misleading in their "focus on government policies which are favorable to business" and their tendency to skirt discussion of policies meant to reign in such problems as monopoly and pollution.[12]

When confronted with such critiques, some corporate sponsors retorted that their materials represented particular industries' or companies' points of view, and that people with other points of view were free to fund their own materials. However, few nonprofit organizations critical of corporate power had as much money to spend on publicity as corporations did.

Further, the FCC stopped enforcing the Fairness Doctrine in 1987, meaning that activists could no longer demand airtime for opposing viewpoints.[13]

In addition, the grounds of both public rhetoric and public outreach seemed to shift in the 1990s, with "financial literacy" gaining ground. Scholars have critiqued financial literacy programs for eliding questions of power and politics while claiming to be neutral and empowering—dynamics that are familiar from this history of sponsored economic education media. A few factors seem salient to this seeming enthusiasm for financial literacy, including institutional interest and larger ideological shifts. Journalist Helaine Olen links financial institutions' involvement in public-facing financial literacy programs to incentives set in place by the Community Reinvestment Act of 1977. Demand for financial literacy in the schools has grown as well; the former JCEE, known today as the Council for Economic Education, offers financial education alongside economic education in its suite of offerings. Further, historian Gary Gerstle points out that the dissolution of the Soviet Union in 1989 and 1990 drastically changed the terms of ideological conflict in the early 1990s. Without the looming threat of communism, selling the public on the virtues of capitalism seemingly became a less pressing priority for corporations and other business-friendly organizations. Financial literacy programs emphasized consumers' responsibility for their own participation in an increasingly risk-laden and deregulated financial system.[14]

In schools, too, sponsored educational materials continued to gain a foothold in the 1990s—despite the objections of advocates for commercial-free education. In 1997, a *New York Times* feature on the commercialization of education in the US reported that corporations had "dramatically increased their involvement in education"; the feature highlighted how public schools facing "dwindling" funding grappled with whether—and how—to use such materials. The growing production of sponsored classroom materials in the early 1980s and beyond signaled that for-profit corporations still saw education as a venue for cultivating goodwill.[15]

Conclusion

Despite being made for a particular moment, ephemeral media don't necessarily disappear once their moment has passed. They can recirculate in surprising ways. This was the case when a spate of social media posts in the late 2000s and early 2010s drew attention to Harding College's short cartoon film *Make Mine Freedom*, which had been largely forgotten since its circulation heyday in the late 1940s. Social media users circulated an uploaded digital version of the cartoon film on social media platforms and discussion boards, in some cases echoing conservative memes that linked the candidacy, and then the presidency, of Barack Obama to socialism. These commenters were unlikely to have known that the cartoon had incorporated themes from the Smock Report, a blueprint for postwar sponsored economic education media that was designed to defend the interests of the US advertising industry and its allies in manufacturing and publishing. A combination of ephemerality, digital availability, and political rhetoric had led to this postwar artifact of sponsored economic education media being circulated on social media networks in the 2000s, far from its original context.

Bloggers' and social media users' circulation of an ephemeral cartoon film as an artifact, and some social media users' comments alluding to the sensibilities of the past, seemed to show that the politics of opposition to the mid-twentieth-century New Deal political order lived on in twenty-first century political culture. Some of those who posted the video may have done so because they found something in the film that resonated with their own political positions, while others may have circulated the film more strategically, turning online debate toward the trope of socialist threat and away from the reckonings on race and inequality that Obama's candidacy and subsequent presidency seemed to invite. Either motivation would have been in line with the prior century's traditions in economic education discourses. Social media users' embrace of the film suggested that the Smock Report's postwar strategic communications plan for the promotional industries had met its designers' aspirations sixty years after the fact: for many of these commentators, private enterprise seemed intrinsically American.[1]

The world has to be made to mean, as Stuart Hall observed. This book has examined the meanings of sponsored economic education media and how these media, and their proponents, attempted to make worlds have meaning. Sponsored economic education media helped their supporters to imagine themselves as particular kinds of people—knowledgeable, public service–minded experts—in a world where the celebration of capitalism, and optimism about a capitalist future, were neutral and objective matters of fact. And, as shown by social media users' repurposing of sponsored film a good sixty years after the fact, sponsored economic education media allow today's advocates for private enterprise to represent the past in ways that further naturalize their own imaginings of the past, present, and future.

Yet, contrary to some assumptions about ephemeral films from the age of the "great free enterprise campaign," sponsored economic education media are not evidence of a bygone time of commonsense consensus. The production of these materials was controversial. It was almost always accompanied by critiques of their aims and methods from labor organizers, educators, activists, policymakers from across the political spectrum, and even some business leaders. The arc of sponsored economic education in the twentieth century raises a question: if economic education was seen by so many as a waste of time and money, why did it flourish and endure? One explanation is that economic education media were intended to be meaningful to the general publics they were putatively meant to reach, but they were in fact also meaningful to a *managerial* audience. More specifically, the history of economic education in the twentieth-century US suggests that for some business executives and their allies, sponsored economic education media offered valuable stories that helped managerial subjects to make sense of their role in society. In contrast to popular and consumer activist discourses that regarded advertisers and manufacturers as untrustworthy takers of profit and manipulators of public attitudes, sponsored economic education media and the discourses around

CONCLUSION   183

them portrayed businesses as civic-minded and useful institutions whose leaders could serve the public while pursuing profits. This strategy had obvious public relations value, but also provided rationales for continuing with business as usual by addressing managers' possible moral, political, or ethical qualms.

Sponsored economic education media also reinforced managerial constructions of the promotional industries, reifying folk beliefs about the expertise of promotional specialists. It validated advertising industry leaders' economic doxa, reinforcing folk beliefs that advertising was the keystone of a free press and, by extension, a necessary part of a free society—a rationalization that built on existing traditions of promotional nationalism. The affirmative style of sponsored economic education media further entrenched this promotional nationalism, expressing optimism about the future while excluding competing ideologies from the discourse.

Moreover, the story of sponsored economic education media suggests an insight as regards the political and ideological uses of pleasurable imagining. For the creators and allies of economic education media, the pleasure of imagining a unified US society with private enterprise as its virtuous core seemed to require the urgency of an immediate crisis: if not the international crises of war and geopolitical ideological competition, then the perceived domestic crises (or, events that were defined as crises by some constituencies, at least) of national identity, immigration, labor unrest, consumer rebellion, and economic malaise. The crises changed between the 1930s and the 1970s, but the sense of crisis endured in a permanent now of ideological urgency. Many proponents of sponsored economic education media used the affirmative style as they intervened in these points of perceived crisis, promising that private enterprise would deliver the most benefits to all parts of US society while lifting morale and preserving democracy and personal liberty. This finding highlights how political rhetoric that promises a bright future facilitates imaginative pleasure in its framings of virtue and crisis—whether or not those framings stand up to scrutiny.

Despite the inherent contradictions of sponsored economic education media, its proponents characterized these media as both persuasive and educational. In light of Raymond Williams's suggestion that scholars of media should study the contradictions of media in social context, the history of sponsored economic education media suggests that scientization was a crucial element of the social order that made it possible for sponsored economic education media to seem to be both promotional and educational within the New Deal political order. More specifically, the NAM, AAAA/ANA, and other business advocacy organizations peppered their persuasive campaigns about the US economic system with appeals to efficiency and expertise, followed by the JCEE's characterization of economics itself as a universal technique for intellectual analysis and civic participation. These forms of scientization allowed for claims about *educational* goals of shoring up everyday peoples' knowledge of the economic system to shore up the *ideological* goals of securing public assent for the corporations' power in the US.

Underneath these claims about education laid an assumption that physicist Simon Brown has called the *deficit model*: an erroneous but pervasive assumption, common among science practitioners, that "there is a knowledge 'deficit' that can be 'fixed' by giving the public more information." Something similar to the deficit model seemed to be in play for the creators and supporters of sponsored economic education media, who imagined anything other than full-throated support for private enterprise to be the product of ignorance and misinformation. Seen in this light, the tensions between education and selling could begin to resolve into an internally harmonious regime of knowledge claims and trajectories to a better tomorrow. This rationale enfolded three distinctive dimensions that, combined, gave sponsored economic education its texture: a promotional nationalism whose ideological assumptions constructed private enterprise as an integral part of American freedom; scientization, as expressed through claims about expertise, knowledge, and systematic methods; and affect, as expressed in the articulation of an affirmative style that centered self-assurance and optimism.[2]

Promotional Nationalism and the Construction of Private Enterprise as Free

The notion that the economic privileges of corporations were analogous to, and intertwined with, the political and personal liberties of individuals — that democracy and capitalism were the political and economic expressions of a singular virtue of liberty — was a well-worn trope in economic education. Sponsored economic education media mobilized patriotic sentiments and ideas of national identity to advance the interests of private companies, a rhetorical strategy I refer to as promotional nationalism. The use of national imagery and sentiments for self-interested ends was nothing new in the twentieth century, but it played a particular role in that era through sponsored economic education media that purported to primarily serve the public benefit. There's no way to know how much of the promotional nationalism evident in sponsored economic education media was the sincere expression of true believers versus how much was cynically deployed for purposes of profit, but in terms of the material outcomes of economic education, the sincerity or cynicism of its supporters didn't much matter. The mobilization of promotional nationalism created, maintained, and reconfigured articulations of cultural meaning that could have far-reaching results including project funding, interorganizational alliances, and policy outcomes. Even if the claim seemed far-fetched to some observers, claiming to act in service of the nation was a strategy for countering impressions of unseemly self-interest. This constellation of ideas, linking national identity to private enterprise and public service, found expression again and again in twentieth-century sponsored economic education efforts.

Starting in the 1910s, the Americanization movement attempted to invoke notions of the national interest to acculturate immigrant workers to an industrialized social order, mixing notions of proper language, manners, and lifestyle in with assent to managerial imperatives. Such projects fed into the Americanism drive of the first Red Scare following World War I—for example, cabinet-level government officials collaborated with the motion picture industry on projects that, they hoped, could deflect radical critique and conflict by stirring patriotic sentiment among the swelling working-class populations of the nation's industrial cities. Promotional nationalism did important cultural work, too, in the developing regions of the American West, where ideas of national connectedness and distinctiveness offered promoters a useful tool for playing up the possibilities of domestic tourism and business development. In these ways, by the early 1920s ideas of patriotic national identity and separateness from Europe had become intertwined with notions of business growth and private enterprise. These associations were articulated more aggressively in the late 1920s by groups like the American Hour Broadcasting Committee, whose antiradical and xenophobic positions informed an aggressive patriotism typified by loyalty oaths and unabashed militarism.

The Great Depression and the policy responses of the New Deal brought forth new expressions of promotional nationalism. In the context of the New Deal, antiradicalism could express opposition not only to imagined foreign threats but also to the New Deal's coordinated domestic programs in the wake of an economic collapse. While political groups like the California Crusaders presented their opposition to the New Deal as a natural step for those who thought themselves to be defenders of Americanism, industrial advocacy groups like the NAM were publicizing a claim that would come to be an influential and enduring formulation of promotional nationalism: the assertion that private enterprise, political freedom, and personal liberties were so deeply interdependent that a threat to one was a threat to all.

Advertising industry leaders in the Association of National Advertisers and the American Association of Advertising Agencies—faced with public suspicions that advertising misled the public and harmed consumers—adopted a similar formulation of intertwined liberties in 1941. This allowed leaders in the AAAA and ANA to shift the framing of their public communications strategies from defense of the advertising industry to defense of the free press and the US economic system, justifying and facilitating the formation of the Advertising Council to assist in war efforts. During the war, the Advertising Council prepared prefabricated public service advertising that made promotional nationalism available to sponsoring companies at a range of degrees of intensity, normalizing advertising practices that promoted brands alongside domestic war efforts. When the war ended, the Advertising Council continued its schedule of public service advertising on radio, crystallizing a new expression of peacetime promotional nationalism that linked the media form of advertisement itself to the notion of the national interest.

Expressions of promotional nationalism gained steam in the period after the war, facilitated in many cases by the AAAA and ANA's shared plans to promote US corporate practices as a stable, natural, and self-governing economic *system*, which they called the American economic system. Nationwide publicity gambits such as the Freedom Train narrated the nation's past and present with an emphasis on unity and a subcurrent of support for private enterprise; business advocates praised the Freedom Train's capacity to portray private enterprise as the source of the nation's success. The Advertising Council's postwar "American Economic System" campaign and *Miracle of America* booklet advocated for higher productivity as the key to continued prosperity, drawing on a simplified retelling of the nation's past that centered private enterprise. Yet, the advertising industry's attempts to shape public opinion came up against perceptions of bias that limited their ambitions to exert influence in the nation's schools. In the 1950s and 1960s, the JCEE's scientific anticommunism, supported by the donations of corporations and corporation-affiliated charitable

CONCLUSION

foundations, represented a shifted version of economic education in which promotional nationalism played a subtler background role. Still, the JCEE's projects ultimately aimed toward the same end: public assent for private enterprise (recall, for example, how late 1950s discourses framed economic growth as an ideological weapon in the Cold War).

Advertising Council campaigns in the late 1960s and beyond reflected a rearticulation of promotional nationalism in which PSAs urged everyday people to take steps to understand and support the US economy, as a means of managing Americans' individual and collective wealth. The notion of anticommunism did not completely fade away but seemed to recede to the subtext. The Advertising Council's 1970s "American Economic System" campaign and its booklet, *The American Economic System . . . and Your Part in It*, rearticulated the rhetoric of inseparable freedoms for new generations, emphasizing citizens' role in defending what it called economic freedoms. These campaigns, too, expressed promotional nationalism in a more subtle fashion—but the campaigns nonetheless used corporate funding to advance ideological positions and framings of the US economy that were favorable to the interests of businesses.

The use of promotional nationalism in sponsored economic education media was an indication of how, during the twentieth century, businesses and industries were sensitive to public perceptions of corporate malfeasance but reluctant to cede power. Instead, sponsored economic education media offered powerful illustrations of how companies, industries, and sympathetic public officials used promotions and publicity to smooth and cushion critical public sentiments about the impacts managerial capitalism had on society. At its heart, claims that liberty and capitalism were simply two manifestations of the core principle of freedom expressed promotional nationalism in a way that conflated the civil liberties and political rights of people with the profit-making imperatives of corporations, a tendency that would find broader expression in the turn toward neoliberalism in the latter decades of the twentieth century. As a rhetorical strategy, then, promotional nationalism ended up affirming the politics of corporate power while delegitimizing its ideological opponents. Promotional nationalism not only insisted that private enterprise was intrinsically American, it implied that anything other than private enterprise must be alien and threatening to the social order. Promotional nationalism left an enduring residue on US culture that helped to clear a path for privatization and market fundamentalism at the end of the twentieth century and beyond.

Scientization, Media, and Expertise

The scientization of economic education developed from the 1910s through the end of the 1970s—first in the ways projects to promote private enterprise lauded the persuasive expertise of media production professionals, then in the ways corporate-funded economic education programs (like those organized by the JCEE) positioned economics as a universal technique for both intellectual and civic reasoning under conditions of private enterprise. Supporters of economic education, in other words, overlaid their work with a legitimizing veil of scientific rigor. Remarkably, this allowed them to adopt many of the dynamics of interactions between experts and the public that were distinctive to the public communication of science. This historical arc began with the emphasis on efficiency, scalability, and systematization that developed in tandem with US industrial culture during the late nineteenth and early twentieth centuries. Logics of scientization could be seen not only in the physical optimizations of factory work that were the hallmark of industrial scientific management, but in sales and marketing as well. Proponents of scientific advertising deployed principles from the nascent social science of psychology to argue that the most efficient advertisements would combine persuasive appeals to the intellect, the emotions, *and* the senses.

Embedded in the aspirations of scientific advertising was a faith in the scalability of mass media—including radio, print media, and film. Such mass media forms, proponents imagined, could reliably deliver sophisticated, efficient persuasive appeals to the hearts and minds of mass audiences. The Committee on Public Information's propaganda successes in the First World War seemed to bear out these ideas, bringing even more of an aura of power to mass media. In this light, the slogan of selling America to Americans enfolded hopes that advertising techniques, applied to mass media, could triumph in peacetime by systematically and efficiently instilling not only sentiments of patriotism, but also assent to managerial imperatives.

In the time between the 1929 market crash and the Second World War, the NAM and, in its wake, the AAAA/ANA and the Advertising Council made legitimacy claims premised on professionalism and expertise. These claims to expertise were propped up by managerial folk knowledge, both about media production and about ways of doing business in the United States. The NAM's internal sense-making about their public relations

CONCLUSION   189

practices found expression in booklets like *Experts All*, which emphasized how seasoned media professionals could carry out effective mass media public information campaigns that blended factoids, emotive appeals, and entertainment value. Leading up to World War II, members of the AAAA and ANA had adapted and elaborated such ideas to arrive at a sense of advertising as a systematized and specialized field of practice. The techniques of advertising, they argued, could be used to promote public service projects—with desirable public relations benefits for the advertising industry itself. By 1942, with the war fully underway, Advertising Council organizers' sense of advertising as a persuasive *method* was so well entrenched that they could imagine themselves as experts not only in crafting persuasive messages but also in delivering them to precisely defined audiences using the infrastructures of privately owned, advertising-funded mass media. This sense of advertising's precision and efficiency found expression after the war, too: we can see it in the Smock Report's reliance on market researchers to set the terms of its projects; in the claim that US companies' ways of doing business were best described as a *system* with its own internal logics, seemingly timeless and natural; and in advertisers' confidence that they could create messages that would be repeated until they became virtually indelible.

In contrast to the themes of media expertise and efficient persuasion that characterized the scientization of economic education in the first half of the twentieth century, in the 1950s and beyond the JCEE developed a different approach: they would scientize ideology itself through the methods of economic analysis. The leaders and affiliates of the JCEE imagined economics to be a systematic and objective style of reasoning that could be applied to any problem—and one that would objectively demonstrate that capitalism was better than other economic approaches. Economic thinking, they argued, would be uniquely well suited to prepare American youth for the responsibilities of adulthood in a democratic, capitalist society. Like the Advertising Council, the JCEE counted business executives and nonprofit coordinators among their supporters. However, the JCEE distinguished itself from other corporate-funded efforts that adopted the title of economic education by centering the expertise of economics professors and K–12 educators rather than advertising and promotional specialists. Accordingly, the JCEE's version of economic education offered a softer promotional nationalism, deploying scientific anticommunism to suggest that properly trained students would use careful and rigorous analysis to discover that private enterprise was the most desirable organizing principle for society. In playing up a conceptualization of economic education as objective and scientific, but still ultimately appreciative of capitalism, the JCEE and its supporters leveraged national anxieties that the United States was falling behind the Soviet Union's scientific and intellectual achievements in the late 1950s. Under these circumstances, the JCEE's style of teaching economics in schools opened up an ideologically resonant path forward, and it used mass media to train schoolteachers at scale while preserving the complexity of the lessons set forth by an economist acting as "National Teacher." Yet, the JCEE's struggles to reconcile its own philosophical commitments with the Advertising Council's affirmative style of promotional nationalism in the late 1960s prefigured coming shifts in popular understandings of economics.

Amid the social disruptions of the late 1960s and early 1970s, many of the themes of efficiency and rigor that had characterized economic education from the 1920s through the 1960s were rearticulated by a different group of political and cultural actors such as Lewis Powell and Milton Friedman, whose support for private enterprise was paired with a suspicion that many institutions were impediments to it. Where the JCEE's scientific anticommunism had suggested that an economic mode of *analysis* would guarantee objective decision-making among the leaders of institutions and ordinary people alike, the emergent neoliberalism of the 1970s instead suggested that market forces *themselves* were efficient and disinterested powers whose workings could be understood, predicted, and harnessed—and therefore, that the most neutral social principle would be to facilitate the functioning of those market forces.

Echoes of prior articulations of scientization to economic education could be seen, too, in the framing of the Advertising Council's mid-1970s "American Economic System" campaign. The Advertising Council not only used social scientific research methods to construct agreement with the status quo as a sign of economic knowledge (as its precursors, indeed, had done); its leadership rebuffed accusations of bias by comparing the social and political significance of economics in the 1970s to that of science and technology in the late 1950s. In so doing, they made an implicit claim that economics, like science, was an unbiased way of knowing whose putatively impeccable objectivity could be harnessed to enhance the global standing of the United States. Such assumptions—about the rigor of economics as a scientific way of thinking and knowing, and about the importance of economics for a nation enmeshed for decades in a geopolitical and ideological Cold War—informed the flourishing of mandates

CONCLUSION   191

for economic education that, by the early 1980s, were in place in almost half of the US states.

Yet, the story of sponsored economic education media shows how it wasn't *merely* steady repetition that led to the uptake of economic education ideas in the popular imagination. The infrastructures of media distribution, the media form of the PSA, the political economy of advertising-funded media, and the prevalence of the affirmative style all contributed to how opposing perspectives, which could distract from or challenge the constant drip of affirmation of private enterprise, had little presence in the public conversation. Supporters' insistence that sponsored economic education media was unbiased both enabled and obscured this unequal representation that, in time, came to be nearly univocal.

The scientization of economic education dressed an essentially ideological project in borrowed garments of efficiency, systematization, rigor, and objectivity. Together, these attributes pointed to a scientization of the promotion of private enterprise in US culture during the twentieth century, inflected by the currents of media technological development and geopolitical tensions. Portraying ideological projects as essentially scientific in nature had the obvious benefits of furnishing sponsored economic education media projects with a counterpoint to accusations of bias and propaganda. The seeming naturalization of market forces, and their portrayal as something akin to forces of nature by the 1970s and 1980s — as opposed to an understanding of economics as inherently institutional, social, and political—came in the wake of six decades of corporate leaders, managers, promotional specialists, and their allies mobilizing the legitimacy of science to accomplish ideological and commercial goals.

Affect and the Affirmative Style

One of the ways sponsored economic education media expressed promotional nationalism was by using patriotic emotional and moral appeals. Sponsored economic education media included affective and moral elements that attempted to draw out the audience's sentiments of optimistic patriotism and faith in private enterprise, especially as expressed in hope for a better future. These appeals helped to ease the reconciliation of education and persuasion in sponsored economic education media. The emotional appeals and moral sense-making that threaded through sponsored economic education media fitted with early twentieth-century assumptions about optimally efficient advertising methods. Further, they compensated for the perceived dryness of economic concepts, which economic education advocates feared would limit audiences' attention, and they offered the building blocks for narratives and subject positions that could counter anticorporate public sentiment.

A prehistory of the use of feelings appeals in sponsored economic education can be found in the scientific advertising and Americanization movements of the early twentieth century. Psychologist Walter Dill Scott's scientific advertising reconfigured late nineteenth-century sales techniques for use in mass media persuasion, placing sensory and emotional appeals alongside product information. The Committee on Public Information's successful propaganda efforts during World War I seemed to bear out Scott's theories, leading to wider use of feelings-oriented persuasive appeals. The combination of such feelings-based persuasive appeals with the politics of private enterprise could be seen after the First World War in Franklin Lane and the motion picture industry's joint efforts to inspire patriotic zeal and fervor that, they hoped, would eclipse the stirrings of political radicalism. Lane and other creators of Americanism media in the 1920s imagined that such media would ignite in immigrants an inner spark of patriotism, kindness, and loyalty to ideals of private enterprise. When promoters described such materials as "selling America to Americans," they made an implicit suggestion that American identity in a time of mass immigration was not simply a matter of having proper paperwork or residing in the country; it was something ineffable that had to be *felt*. Moreover, these media productions associated a particularly optimistic affective valence with their celebrations of patriotism and private enterprise. I argue that they express what would come to be recognizable as an affirmative style in economic education media: a tendency toward rhetorics of celebration and certainty, paired with an unwillingness to discuss ideological counterpoints at anything deeper than a superficial level.

This affirmative style was expressed in the 1930s through emphases on raising morale and providing entertainment value, in which those who would "sell" American private enterprise imagined mass media to be the antidote to the perceived dryness of economic ideas and topics. George Creel's ambitions to represent the nation at the 1939 International Exposition through showmanship rather than statistical detail offered an example of the impulse to instill patriotism through spectacle that would find later expression in sponsored economic education media. Both institutional advertising and news commentary touted affirmative visions

CONCLUSION

of how better public morale might elevate the nation's economic and financial outlook, as with Anheuser-Busch's attempts to assure the public of America's bright future, or the celebratory and affective rhetorics of columnists like Boake Carter and Benjamin De Casseres.

These threads of meaning, all articulated to the notion of "selling America to Americans," set precedents for how private enterprise and national identity would be promoted together during and after the Second World War. During the war, the Advertising Council's public communications campaigns played to the advertising industry's strengths in delivering upbeat expressions of patriotic resolve. In the aftermath of the war, Advertising Council campaigns such as the Rededication Week activities and the first "American Economic System" campaign aimed to inspire confident unity in publics riven by social conflicts and the trauma of war, drawing on mythological figures like Uncle Sam to convey authority and construct a veneer of historical continuity. In a similar vein, cartoon films presented by George Benson's Harding College interpreted the dictates of the Smock Report through a lens of humor and high-budget entertainment value.

Even the turn toward scientific anticommunism in the 1950s and 1960s telegraphed a set of affective appeals. In place of the upbeat patriotism that had characterized the Smock Report era, however, the JCEE's scientific anticommunism struck an affective posture of unruffled mastery. The JCEE responded to panic and embarrassment over the technological and educational successes of the Soviet Union, touting the power of American economic reasoning to produce good decisions and telegraphing a sense of self-assured confidence. Even as this approach strained some business conservatives' expectations of affirmation in sponsored economic education media—as with the *Wall Street Journal* commentary that dismissed the National Task Force's approach as inadequately celebratory and even apologetic—it had the advantage of aligning with the seeming indisputability of science. This affective posture of self-assured confidence was present, too, in the Advertising Council's 1970s "American Economic System" campaign, in which economic forces were themselves portrayed as objective and predictable.

Despite sponsored economic education media proponents' consistent worries that economic concepts would be seen as a collection of dry facts in which ordinary people would have little interest, discourses *about* popular economic knowledge were inflected with, and situated within, turbulent currents of managerial affect. These currents of affect included the anxieties and grievances of corporate leaders, the fears of managers and lawmakers alike that ideological conflict and rebellion could fundamentally reshape their industries and fortunes, and the optimistic, future-facing affirmative rhetorics that attempted to address and resolve these uncomfortable tensions. Taken together, these findings cannot fully reconstruct what Raymond Williams termed structures of feeling—the historically specific and evanescent textures of experience that ineffably inform sense-making—but they can indicate some of the pressures that corporate managers and executives imagined themselves to be responding to at the time. The everyday experiences of managerial capitalism in the twentieth century invoked peculiar affective pressures for those in the managerial ranks; sponsored economic education media offered resources for making sense of these affective pressures by offering interpretations of the self and society that incorporated imaginative pleasures of self-construction along with ideologies of private enterprise and national identity. In this context, the affirmative style in sponsored economic education media can be seen as an instrument of ideological and affective *soothing*, one that transmuted feelings of fear and besiegement into self-assured certainty while asserting that the fundamental rightness of private enterprise was beyond debate.

Three dynamics, working together—the scientization of sponsored economic education media, its articulations of private enterprise ideology to national identity, and its capacity to channel the anxious and aggrieved affect of managerial capitalism into optimistic sense-making—helped to reconcile the contradictions of economic education. They made it possible for the proponents of sponsored economic education media to understand these media productions as services to the nation, both in their capacity to persuade and their capacity to inform. Indeed, given the assumption that public understanding of economics was equivalent to public support for managerial capitalism, education and persuasion could be seen as one and the same.

Beyond the Rise and Fall of Neoliberalism

One of the reasons why the history of sponsored economic education media matters is because sponsored economic education media projects anticipated rationales and strategies associated with the ascent of neoliberalism in the late twentieth century, especially around the idea of

CONCLUSION   195

freedom—and at least some of those ideas have endured, outliving the neoliberal era itself. Historian Gary Gerstle argues that the last hundred years witnessed the rise and fall of two political orders: the "New Deal order," in place from the 1930s through the 1970s, and the "neoliberal order," which reigned over the end of the twentieth century and the beginning of the twenty-first before appearing to disintegrate in the 2010s. The neoliberalism that would come into focus in the 1980s and 1990s reiterated ideas that capitalism and freedom were the same thing (or at least very similar things), and that supposedly ignorant publics had to be convinced to adopt this belief lest they support and vote for economic policies that curtailed freedom. These were ideas that business interests had been circulating under the banner of educating the public for much of the twentieth century. Crucially, though, neoliberal ideologies reworked New Deal–era economic education discourses' fascination with the appearance of objectivity by according agency to market forces—forces that, in the neoliberal era, were often imagined to be impersonal and apolitical.[3]

Sponsored economic education media, and their expression of promotional nationalist ideas in an affirmative style, contained ideas that informed the neoliberal political order. This finding fits with historians' examinations of neoliberalism as a term of analysis. Historians such as Angus Burgin argue that the positions that are now identified as neoliberal originated in the mid-twentieth century with thinkers who often held a more ambivalent orientation toward government intervention in markets, before being reimagined for the Cold War era by such popular intellectual figures as Milton Friedman. But while the term was used in earlier times to refer to particular strains of economic or political thought, the *idea* of neoliberalism as it is used today refers to something that, as Kim Phillips-Fein observes, points to "the broadest dynamic of contemporary politics, and the emergence of a political sensibility that spans both political parties."[4]

Indeed, it is notoriously difficult to define neoliberalism, or to find agreement on what political positions are most central to it. Gerstle argues that "laissez-faire capitalism," with its admiration for "dynamism, creative destruction, irreverence toward institutions and to the complex web of relations that imbed individuals in those institutions," forms the destabilizing core of this political order; he points out that retaining the term *neoliberalism* as opposed to *laissez-faire* or *conservatism* reminds us how neoliberalism attempted to echo "the principles of classical liberalism." Historian Daniel Rodgers argues that neoliberalism is a cluster of four distinct elements: finance capitalism, market fundamentalism, disaster capitalism, and a totalizing cultural logic of commodification by which every element of human life is understood in market terms. Indisputably, market forces were central to neoliberalism.[5]

As the 1960s gave way to the 1970s, economic education media demonstrated a thematic shift toward centering market forces. Rodgers describes market fundamentalism as "an intellectual project: the restructuring of late-twentieth-century economic thought around the paradigm of the efficient market." Economic education often promoted simplified ideas about economics that met with scorn or dismissal from those in the profession of economics. The supporters of economic education promoted these simplified notions of market forces as clear and reliable principles that explained the economy's workings and justified managers' claims to jurisdiction over it. However, for at least some of sponsored economic education's supporters, market fundamentalism was less an end in itself than a practical means of creating a favorable cultural and policy environment for the pursuit of profits, and a cultural means of framing that pursuit as morally and civically beneficial.[6]

I contend that the enduring cultural residues of sponsored economic education media go beyond their influence on ideas about markets. As Gerstle declares, "the threat of communism . . . inclined capitalist elites to compromise so as to avert the worst"—and "communism's collapse" made room for the ultimate triumph of a neoliberal political order over the New Deal order that preceded it. The story told in this book recounts how the proponents of sponsored economic education media, influenced (as they often were) by antiradical or anticommunist sentiments, aspired to spread ideas that became accepted as common sense: so naturalized as to seem beyond question. Thus, it seems that ideas, logics, and styles informed by anticommunism became part of the easily overlooked ideological infrastructure of American culture, even after the perceived threat of global communism dissipated, and in forms that have outlived the neoliberal political order itself.[7]

This ideological hangover, so to speak, could be seen in the triumph during the neoliberal era of what historians of science Naomi Oreskes and Erik Conway call the indivisibility thesis: an idea, so endemic to sponsored economic education and its forebears and so useful to those wielding promotional nationalism, that capitalism and freedom are tightly linked (if not one and the same). And that hangover can be seen today, I contend, in the rearticulation of the affirmative style. Popular social media culture is suffused with promotion and content marketing in ways of which the advertising industry leaders of the midcentury period could only have dreamed. The overlapping commercial realms of sponsored social media content, influencer marketing, direct and network marketing, the self-help and personal coaching industries, and the entrepreneurial culture often associated with the tech industry all show some tolerance of a style of sense-making that favors positivity and celebration, paired with reluctance or outright refusal to seriously address critics' concerns. The New Deal political order and the neoliberal order that replaced it may both be dead, but the affirmative style lives.

The case of sponsored economic education media shows how individual media texts contributed to a continuous flow of culture from which people could derive meaning. The archival organizational and governmental records, ephemeral media texts, and press accounts related to economic education show how, for the sponsors of economic education media, shaping public opinion was a matter of perpetual urgency, driven by wariness about the implications of democratic governance amid inequalities of wealth and power. The remarkable amounts of money, time, effort, and coordination that went into the creation and circulation of sponsored economic education media demonstrate how urgently business leaders and their allies sought to align private enterprise with national identity and political liberty in the popular imagination. Proponents of economic education assumed that capitalism is freedom, and worked with incredible ardor to make corporate power, styled as free enterprise, appear to be something natural and inevitable. Critically examining the efforts of the Advertising Council, in particular, highlights the complexity of even sincere efforts to serve the public under the conditions of capitalism, and emphasizes the insufficiency of awareness-raising campaigns in accomplishing social change. Campaigns aimed at fostering public understanding can imply that raising awareness counts as *doing something* about a problem, yet awareness often seems to fall short of creating social change. To accept such a model of public service is to fall prey to what pioneering media theorists Paul Lazarsfeld and Robert Merton called "narcotizing dysfunction," in which awareness takes the place of meaningful social action, leading to a passive citizenry.[8]

The romance of business is far from perishing in debris. Indeed, one of the lasting consequences of the twentieth-century campaigns for private enterprise was how corporations, trade groups, their leaders, and their allies left behind narratives and media texts that could be taken up later to tell stories about the past. This book has aimed to tell a story, through a critical lens, about how sponsored economic education media came to be a distinctive media genre, what their supporters imagined these media could accomplish, and how the ideas they contained came to be framed as natural, inevitable, and common sense. It is a story about how these people, and their projects, narrowed the range of popular understandings of what it could mean to be American, in alignment with their own priorities and interests. The historical arcs of sponsored economic education media illustrate how processes of imagining, and the reconciliations of contradiction through the mechanisms of imaginative pleasure, have contributed to the construction of meaning. Managerial subjects could imagine themselves to be unambiguously good: servants of the public interest, stewards of knowledge, protectors of liberty.

Acknowledgments

I am very fortunate to have so many people to thank for their support of this book.

I want to thank to the archivists who helped me navigate archival collections of records, including Lucas Clawson and the staff at the Hagley Museum and Archive; Carol Leadenham and the Hoover Institution Library and Archives staff at Stanford University; Rory Grennan and the University Library staff at the University of Illinois Urbana-Champaign; Lee Grady and the Archives and Special Collections staff at the Wisconsin Historical Society; Hannah Wood and the staff at the Ann Cowan Archives and Special Collections at Harding University; Rick Prelinger and the staff of the Prelinger Archives; and the staff of the Internet Archive (archive.org). I especially want to thank Hannah D. Cox and the staff at the University Library of Indiana University–Purdue University Indianapolis, who not only welcomed me to their library but supported my research on sponsored economic education media with a Ruth Lilly Philanthropic Library Research Award.

At the University of Chicago Press, my editor Timothy Mennel unwaveringly championed this project from our first meeting and patiently answered my many, many questions throughout the publishing process. I'm grateful to him, and to Susannah Engstrom, Andrea Blatz, Anne Strother, and Mark Reschke for their support and guidance—and I'm grateful to the Board of University Publications for their enthusiastic support of the project. My sincere thanks to James Toftness for images and permissions research. I also want to thank the reviewers of the manuscript for their detailed and thoughtful feedback, which improved this work tremendously.

This project developed during my doctoral training at Cornell University. It benefited beyond measure from the mentorship of Lee Humphreys, Bruce V. Lewenstein, Jonathan Sterne—and, especially, Tarleton

200   ACKNOWLEDGMENTS

Gillespie. Tarleton approached this project with his characteristic intellectual curiosity, kindness, and careful attention to the crafts of research, argumentation, and writing. I thank him for his tremendous generosity of time, resources, and care. I am grateful, too, to those at Cornell University who offered intellectual community, fellowship, mentorship, and feedback on this project's early iterations, including (but not limited to) Jenni Lieberman, Steph Jordan, S. E. Eisterer, Sara B. Pritchard, Ron Kline, Steve Jackson, Phoebe Sengers, Paula Jarzabkowski, Sandy Payette, Megan Halpern, and Justine Lindemann.

This project's interdisciplinary flavor owes much to the intellectual home communities that have welcomed me and this project over the past several years. I owe tremendous thanks to danah boyd for nurturing the kernel of misinformation and disinformation studies in my work by bringing me into the Data and Society Research Institute as a postdoctoral scholar in 2016, where I was able to continue developing this project. At Data and Society, an incredible range of scholars, artists, and practitioners helped me find new ways of seeing. Deep thanks to my colleagues there for intellectual sustenance and community, and in particular to folks who offered feedback on this project, including danah, and also Alice Marwick, Becca Lewis, Joan Donovan, Robyn Caplan, and Alex Rosenblat.

I am deeply grateful as well to the Social Media Collective at Microsoft Research (MSR), which generously hosted me first as a visiting graduate student and then as a PhD intern—with special thanks to Mary Gray, Nancy Baym, Kate Miltner, Lana Swartz, Kevin Driscoll, Dan Greene, Dylan Mulvin, Stefanie DuGuay, and Shannon McGregor. Deep thanks, as well, to Vicki Nash and the Oxford Internet Institute's Summer Doctoral Programme, and to the Comparative Media Studies/Writing Program at the Massachusetts Institute of Technology, where T. L. Taylor and the Comparative Media Studies program welcomed me as a visiting graduate student—with special thanks to Heather Hendershot, who has been an extraordinarily kind mentor and friend.

I want to express my thanks to the many organizations who have given me opportunities to present work in progress related to this project. Thank you to the International Communication Association, the Business History Conference, the Society for the History of Technology, the Society for Social Studies of Science, and the Association of Internet Research, and to the scholars across conferences, departments, and institutions who generously offered their insights about this work in progress—including Lawrence Glickman, Fred Turner, Siva Vaidhyanathan, Josh Lauer, Tom

Streeter, Mike Ananny, Paul Dourish, André Brock, Jeff Pooley, Dave Park, Victor Pickard, Zizi Papacharissi, Melissa Aronczyk, Meryl Alper, Nathan Ensmenger, Pamela Laird, Richard R. John, Kira Lussier, Aaron Trammell, Aaron Mendon-Plasek, Andrea Dixon, Benjamin Waterhouse, C. W. Anderson, A. J. Bauer, and the many anonymous reviewers who have given feedback to my submissions to conferences and workshops. Thank you, as well, to the faculty, staff, and graduate students who invited me to present work in progress, including the Science Studies Program at the University of California, San Diego; the University of Massachusetts Amherst; Miami University; the Massachusetts Historical Society; and the Massachusetts Institute of Technology.

The University of California, San Diego created a truly affirming environment for this project to grow. Even in the most isolating days of the COVID-19 lockdown and its long aftermath, my UCSD colleagues sustained me with loaves of freshly baked bread, camaraderie, and nourishing discussions—first on Zoom or telephone, and then, joyfully, in person. Thank you to Matilde Córdoba Azcárate, Andrew DeWaard, Alex Fattal, Kelly Gates, Erin Hill, Shawna Kidman, and Stefan Tanaka for nuanced feedback on drafts of this work; and to Boatema Boateng, Lilly Irani, Kelly Gates, Patrick Anderson, and Martha Lampland for insightful advice, encouragement, and mentorship.

Thank you to the Hellman Society of Fellows at UCSD for supporting this work with a fellowship in the 2021–22 academic year, and to UCSD and the School of Social Sciences for their ongoing support of this research. Thank you to Marwa Abdalla, who provided stellar graduate research assistance for this project. Special thanks to UCSD's Center for Faculty Diversity and Inclusion for supporting my participation in the National Center for Faculty Development and Diversity (NCFDD)'s Faculty Success Program, and personal thanks to my peer group members Karen and Portia, for their insight and friendship.

Many of the people I have mentioned are not only valued colleagues but, indeed, deep soul friends. I am so grateful to them, and to all those people whose love and care has sustained me throughout this work (many of whom I have not had chance to mention). If you, dear reader, think you might be in this category, I hope you will allow me to affirm that you are. Deep personal thanks to Kate, Chris, Bonnie, Brian, Lily, Chris, and Teddy; and to Robin, Susan, and Jen. Finally, I want to express love and gratitude beyond measure to my mum, Helen, and my sister, Suzie: you have been with me from the beginning, and you have helped me every step of the way.

Notes

Introduction

1. This book is deeply indebted to those historians and their works. See, in particular, Elizabeth A. Fones-Wolf, *Selling Free Enterprise: The Business Assault on Labor and Liberalism, 1945–60* (Urbana: University of Illinois Press, 1994); Alex Carey, *Taking the Risk Out of Democracy: Corporate Propaganda versus Freedom and Liberty* (Urbana: University of Illinois Press, 1995); William L. Bird Jr., *"Better Living": Advertising, Media, and the New Vocabulary of Business Leadership, 1935–1955* (Evanston, IL: Northwestern University Press, 1999); Robert Jackall and Janice M. Hirota, *Image Makers: Advertising, Public Relations, and the Ethos of Advocacy* (Chicago: University of Chicago Press, 2000); Roland Marchand, *Creating the Corporate Soul: The Rise of Public Relations and Corporate Imagery in American Big Business* (Berkeley: University of California Press, 1998); Inger L. Stole, *Advertising on Trial: Consumer Activism and Corporate Public Relations in the 1930s* (Urbana: University of Illinois Press, 2006); Sharon Beder, *Free Market Missionaries: The Corporate Manipulation of Community Values* (Sterling, VA: Earthscan, 2006); Wendy L. Wall, *Inventing the "American Way": The Politics of Consensus from the New Deal to the Civil Rights Movement* (New York: Oxford University Press, 2008); Kim Phillips-Fein, *Invisible Hands: The Businessmen's Crusade against the New Deal* (New York: W. W. Norton, 2009); Bethany Moreton, *To Serve God and Wal-Mart: The Making of Christian Free Enterprise* (Cambridge, MA: Harvard University Press, 2009); Inger L. Stole, *Advertising at War: Business, Consumers, and Government in the 1940s* (Urbana: University of Illinois Press, 2012); Benjamin C. Waterhouse, *Lobbying America: The Politics of Business from Nixon to NAFTA* (Princeton, NJ: Princeton University Press, 2014); Kevin Kruse, *One Nation under God: How Corporate America Invested Christian America* (New York: Basic Books, 2015); and Lawrence B. Glickman, *Free Enterprise: An American History* (New Haven, CT: Yale University Press, 2019).

2. Rick Prelinger, *The Field Guide to Sponsored Films* (San Francisco: National Film Preservation Foundation, 2006). Quoted text appears on vi.

3. On content marketing, see William M. O'Barr, "What Is Advertising?," *Advertising and Society Review* 16, no. 3 (2015), https://muse.jhu.edu/article/594485, and Jonathan Hardy, *Branded Content: The Fateful Merging of Media and Marketing* (London: Routledge, 2022). On ideology and the making of meaning, see Stuart Hall, "The Rediscovery of Ideology," in *Culture, Society, and the Media*, ed. Michael Gurevich, Tony Bennett, James Curran, and Janet Woollacott, 52–86 (London: Routledge, 1982/2005). Quoted passages appear on 63 and 83.

4. On advertising's influence over the content of news and entertainment media, see Edward S. Herman and Noam Chomsky, *Manufacturing Consent: The Political Economy of the Mass Media* (New York: Pantheon Books, 1988/2002); Inger L. Stole, *Advertising on Trial*; and Robert McChesney, *The Political Economy of Media: Enduring Issues, Emerging Dilemmas* (New York: Monthly Review Press, 2008). On the rhetorical construction of "enterprise" as "free" or "private" in ways that obscures governmental infrastructures, see Lawrence B. Glickman, *Free Enterprise*, and also Naomi Oreskes and Erik M. Conway, *The Big Myth: How American Business Taught Us to Loathe Government and Love the Market* (New York: Bloomsbury, 2023).

5. On impermanence as a defining trait of sponsored media, see Jim Burant, "Ephemera, Archives, and Another View of History," *Archivalia: The Journal of the Association of Canadian Archivists* 40 (Fall 1995): 189–98, quotation on 190. Haidee Wasson and Charles R. Acland, "Introduction: Utility and Cinema," in *Useful Cinema*, ed. Charles R. Acland and Haidee Wasson (Durham, NC: Duke University Press, 2011), quotation on 3.

6. Some works do examine corporate-sponsored media, but without making economic education as a media genre the central object of analysis. See, for example, William L. Bird Jr.'s *"Better Living,"* which examines economic education media within broader trends of sponsored media in public relations, and Lawrence Glickman's *Free Enterprise*, which analyzes Leonard Read's pamphlet *I, Pencil*; other scholars, such as Kim Phillips-Fein in *Invisible Hands*, and Naomi Oreskes and Erik Conway in *The Big Myth*, have surveyed the broader aims and purposes of US corporate public relations at various points of the twentieth century.

7. Scholars of media and communication have long grappled with how to accurately conceptualize and measure the ideological influence of media: in the field of communication studies, we talk about this in terms of "media effects," whether direct or indirect. I am influenced by the many scholars of media who argue that the effect of media on ideology can be best understood by approaching it holistically. In this vein, critical scholars have long argued for understanding mass media collectively as a set of practices and artifacts that can attune people to the hegemonic expectations of the society in which they live; from this perspective, access to media infrastructures and the resources to create and distribute media broadly allow some perspectives to become crucial influences on the cultural norms and ideas perceived as dominant in a society. For approaches to media and its influence

NOTES TO PAGES 6–8

that examine media on a broad scale, a few notable examples include Max Horkheimer and Theodor W. Adorno, "The Culture Industry: Enlightenment as Mass Deception," in *Dialectic of Enlightenment: Philosophical Fragments*, ed. Gunzelin Schmid Noerr and trans. Edmund Jephcott (Stanford, CA: Stanford University Press, 2002), 94–136; Jacques Ellul, *Propaganda: The Formation of Men's Attitudes*, trans. Konrad Kellen and Jean Lerner (New York: Vintage Books, 1965/1973); George Gerbner, "Toward 'Cultural Indicators': The Analysis of Mass Mediated Public Message Systems," *AV Communication Review* 17, no. 2 (Summer 1969): 138; and/or Herman and Chomsky, *Manufacturing Consent*.

8. Quotation from Warshaw is sourced from Joseph Kahn, "Trademark Detective: The Colorful Past of American Business Is the 'Beat' of a Sleuth Who Has Pioneered a New Kind of History," *Rotarian* 91, no. 6 (December 1957): 28–31 and 55–57, quotation on 57.

9. Geographer Nigel Thrift's fascination with "the romantic notion of a kind of passion for business" is another point of inspiration; see Nigel Thrift, "'It's the Romance, Not the Finance, That Makes Business Worth Pursuing': Disclosing a New Market Culture," *Economy and Society* 30, no. 4 (November 2001): 412–32, quotation on 414. On managerial responses to Warshaw and his collections, see "Cashing in on Old Office Records," *Business Week*, December 6, 1958, 125–30, quotations on 130.

10. On the economy as epistemological object, see Timothy Mitchell, "Economists and the Economy in the 20th Century," in *The Politics of Method in the Human Sciences*, ed. George Steinmetz (Durham, NC: Duke University Press, 2005): 125–41, especially 126–30. On the different senses in which the term "economic" was applied, Inger Stole's *Advertising at War* discusses how advertisers came under fire for using their craft in ways that, regulators charged, could limit competition in the market, citing an article in the advertising trade paper *Printers' Ink* that described certain behaviors as "uneconomic"; see Stole, *Advertising at War*, 26–27, quotation on 27, and also the cited article, "War on Advertising as Monopoly Breeder Is More than Talk," *Printers' Ink*, August 30, 1940, 9–10.

11. Melissa Aronczyk, "Raw Materials: Natural Resources, Technological Discourse, and the Making of Canadian Nationalism," in *National Matters: Materiality, Culture, and Nationalism*, ed. Geneviève Zubrzycki (Stanford, CA: Stanford University Press, 2017), 58–82, quotations on 60 and 61.

12. On style as a way of belief, see Richard Hofstadter, "The Paranoid Style in American Politics," *Harper's Magazine*, November 1964, 77–86, quotation on 77. According to Hofstadter, the paranoid style was not just about viewpoints themselves, but the urgency and absolutism with which they were expressed. He suggests that style opens the imagination of its adherent to "new points of fascinating interpretation" (81) and creates feedback loops that strengthen its holders' existing beliefs. On the economic style of reasoning, see Elizabeth Popp Berman, *Thinking Like an Economist: How Efficiency Replaced Equality in U.S. Public*

206   NOTES TO PAGES 9–18

Policy (Princeton, NJ: Princeton University Press, 2022), quotation on 5. On styles of scientific reasoning, see Ian Hacking, "'Style' for Historians and Philosophers," *Studies in the History and Philosophy of Science* 23, no. 1 (1992): 1–20, quotations on 10 (on "reasoning rightly"), 3 (on the public qualities of style), and 13 (on self-authentication).

13. M. Brook Taylor, *Promoters, Patriots, and Partisans: Historiography in Nineteenth-Century English Canada* (Toronto: University of Toronto Press, 1989): quotation on 11. On celebratory rhetorics, see Glickman, *Free Enterprise*, especially 66–68.

14. On the strengthened political and economic position of the advertising industry after the Second World War, see Inger L. Stole, "The Fight against Critics and the Discovery of 'Spin,'" in *The Routledge Companion to Advertising and Promotional Culture*, ed. Matthew P. McAllister and Emily West (New York: Routledge, 2013/2015), 39–52, see 48–49.

15. On the promotion of an "American Way of Life," see Wall, *Inventing the American Way*. See also Dawn Spring, *Advertising in the Age of Persuasion: Building Brand America, 1941–1961* (New York: Palgrave MacMillan, 2011). I refer to the American Association of Advertising Agencies here as the AAAA, reflecting how it is represented in historical documents, but it has been and continues to be colloquially known as "the 4A's."

Chapter One

1. On the distribution of *It's Everybody's Business*, see Chamber of Commerce of the United States (1955), "Press Release for Afternoon Newspapers, Tuesday, February 22, 1955," Hagley Library Manuscripts and Archives Collection, DuPont Public Affairs History Files, Accession #1410: box 37, Du Pont films folder. For promotional materials containing rhetoric on inseparability, see Chamber of Commerce of the United States (1954), *Explaining Business in Your Community* (pamphlet), quotation on 16. On NAM rhetoric around the inseparability of enterprise and freedoms—which the authors call the "indivisibility thesis"—see Naomi Oreskes, Erik M. Conway, and Charlie Tyson. "How American Businessmen Made Us Believe That Free Enterprise Was Indivisible from American Democracy: The National Association of Manufacturers' Propaganda Campaign, 1935–1940," in *The Disinformation Age: Politics, Technology, and Disruptive Communication in the United States*, ed. W. Lance Bennett and Steven Livingston (New York: Cambridge University Press, 2021), 95–119, quotation on 101, and further Oreskes and Conway, *The Big Myth* (which discusses *It's Everybody's Business* as an example of the indivisibility thesis on 231).

2. Quotation on "interlocking" freedoms sourced from Advertising Council, *The American Economic System . . . and Your Part in It* (New York: Advertising Council, 1976), 18.

NOTES TO PAGES 18–24

3. For claims about the broadcast opportunities for *It's Everybody's Business*, see Chamber of Commerce of the United States, Education Department (1955), *A Workbook to Help You Use the Film* It's Everybody's Business *Effectively in Your Community* (Washington, DC: Chamber of Commerce of the United States, 1995), Hagley Library Manuscripts and Archives Collection, US Chamber of Commerce Records, series 2 publications, box 21 (quotation on 10). For circulation estimates, see Chamber of Commerce of the United States, "Press Release for Afternoon Newspapers." For audience size estimates, see Chamber of Commerce of the United States (n.d.), "Introduction for *The Story of Creative Capital*," Hagley Library Manuscripts and Archives Collection, Chamber of Commerce of the United States Administrative Files, Accession #1960: series 3, box 2, Administrative Correspondence 1947–64 folder. The figure of ten million pamphlets may be found in Seth N. Fried (April 6, 1978), *Correspondence to George N. Hayden*, Records Group 13/2/219, Box 14, Advertising Council Papers, University Archives, University of Illinois, Urbana-Champaign.

4. On the history of the ideological campaign to define the US through "free enterprise," and the siege mentality of the managerial class in the midcentury period, see Phillips-Fein, *Invisible Hands*, and Fones-Wolf, *Selling Free Enterprise*. A notable voice of opposition in the midcentury period was journalist and writer William Whyte and his book *Is Anybody Listening? How and Why U.S. Business Stumbles When It Talks to People*—which is discussed at the opening of this book's chapter 4.

5. On contradictions in the social system, see Raymond Williams, *Television: Technology and Cultural Form* (New York: Routledge Classics, 1974/2003), quotations on 126.

6. On "common sense," see Sophia Rosenfeld, *Common Sense: A Political History* (Cambridge, MA: Harvard University Press: 2011), quotations on 227 and 228.

7. On framing advocacy for private enterprise as "common sense," see, Glickman, *Free Enterprise*, 170–71.

8. On the third-person effect in communication theory, see W. Phillips Davison, "The Third-Person Effect in Communication," *Public Opinion Quarterly* 47 (1983), quotation on 3. On advertising professionals' assumptions about their audiences, see Inger L. Stole, *Advertising on Trial: Consumer Activism and Corporate Public Relations in the 1930s* (Urbana: University of Illinois Press, 2006), quotation on 18. Stole notes how advertising professionals in the 1920s and 1930s drew gendered and classed contrasts between themselves and their imagined audiences, imagining themselves as men whose powers of discernment far exceeded that of the mass audiences they targeted.

9. On the organizational networks fostered by economic education projects, see Benjamin C. Waterhouse, *Lobbying America*, quotations on 73 and 74 and "Mobilizing for the Market: Organized Business, Wage-Price Controls, and the Politics of Inflation, 1971–1974," *Journal of American History* 100, no. 2 (September 2013): 454–78.

10. On consumer culture and the pleasure of unfulfilled consumer desire, see Judith Williamson, *Decoding Advertisements: Ideology and Meaning in Advertising*

(London: Marion Boyars, 1978/2002), and Colin Campbell, *The Romantic Ethic and the Spirit of Modern Consumerism* (London: Blackwell Publishers, 1987). On rounds of pleasurable imagining, see Campbell, quotation on 88. Still, while these dynamics seem applicable to consumer logics of the twentieth century and beyond in the currents of deregulating, globalizing capitalism, critics have long conceptualized not just neoliberal capitalism but capitalism itself as involving destabilization and precarity. See Karl Polanyi, *The Great Transformation* (Boston: Beacon Press, 1944/2001).

11. On structure of feeling, see Raymond Williams, *The Long Revolution* (New York: Columbia University Press, 1961), quotation on 48. On the nature of postwar consumer culture, see Lizabeth Cohen, *A Consumer's Republic: The Politics of Mass Consumption in Postwar America* (New York: Vintage Books, 2003).

12. On narratives in advertising that offer materials for constructing future visions of self, see Williamson, *Decoding Advertisements*, and Michael Schudson, *Advertising: The Uneasy Persuasion* (New York: Basic Books, 1984), 221. On audience interpretations of media depictions, see Stuart Hall, "Encoding/Decoding," in *Media and Cultural Studies Keyworks*, ed. M. G. Durham and D. M. Kellner (Malden, MA: Blackwell. 2006), 163–73, see 169–72.

13. Zizi Papacharissi, *Affective Publics: Sentiment, Technology, and Politics* (New York: Oxford University Press, 2015), quotations on 118.

14. On how media allows audiences to construct imagined communities, see Benedict Anderson, *Imagined Communities* (New York: Verso, 1983/2006), quotations on 6, and Walter Lippmann, *Public Opinion* (New York: Free Press, 1922/1997).

15. David E. Nye, "Technology, Nature, and American Origin Stories," *Environmental History* 8, no. 1 (2003): 8–24, quotation on 19. On imaginaries, temporality, and technology, see Sheila Jasanoff, "Future Imperfect: Science, Technology, and the Imaginations of Modernity," in *Dreamscapes of Modernity: Sociotechnical Imaginaries and the Fabrication of Power*, ed. S. Jasanoff and S. Kim (Chicago: University of Chicago Press, 2015), 1–33, quotation on 4.

16. I have written in a similar vein about economic imaginaries and their connections to perceived legitimacy in a prior publication: Caroline Jack, "Producing Milton Friedman's *Free to Choose*: How Libertarian Ideology Became Broadcasting Balance," *Journal of Broadcasting & Electronic Media* 62, no. 3 (2018): 514–30, see 518. On imagined communities, see Anderson, *Imagined Communities*, 5–6.

Chapter Two

1. Henry C. Link, "How to Sell America to the Americans," *Business Screen* 9, no. 1 (1948), 20–21, quotations on 21. Historian Kevin Kruse has extensively documented how proponents of private enterprise in the US used spiritual, and specifically Christian, themes to bestow a gloss of moral upstandingness on private enterprise—see Kruse's *One Nation under God*.

NOTES TO PAGES 29–34

2. Quotations on rhetorics of selling in the first sentence of this paragraph are sourced from Frank Fox, *Madison Avenue Goes to War: The Strange Military Career of American Advertising, 1941–45*. (Provo, UT: Brigham Young University Press, 1975), quotation on 56; Wall, *Inventing the American Way*, quotation on 105; Fones-Wolf, *Selling Free Enterprise*, quotation on 38; Robert Griffith, "The Selling of America: The Ad Council and American Politics, 1942–1960," *Business History Review* 57, no. 3 (Autumn 1983): 388–412, quotation on 389; and Stole, *Advertising at War*, quotation on 37. On the "purchaser consumer," see Cohen, *A Consumer's Republic*, 54.

3. On the mobilization of "free enterprise" as a keyword and a central motif of business conservatism in the twentieth century, see Glickman, *Free Enterprise*. On "popular economic proselytizing," see Carey, *Taking the Risk Out of Democracy*, quotation on 37. On the ideological development of "free enterprise" as a keyword in the 1920s and 1930s, see Glickman, *Free Enterprise* (especially chapter 2).

4. On editorial commentary advocating for literacy to increase the audience for advertising, see William C. D'Arcy, "President D'Arcy Rallies A. A. C. of W. to Support Americanization Bill," *Associated Advertising* 10, no. 3 (March 1919): 10, https://babel.hathitrust.org/cgi/pt?id=iau.31858034256317. On the "Americanization" movement of the 1910s, see Carey, *Taking the Risk Out of Democracy*, 37–46, quotation on 39. On the role of film in this movement, see Cristina Stanciu, "Making Americans: Spectacular Nationalism, Americanization, and Silent Film," *Journal of American Studies* 56 (2022): 1–37, quotation on 20, see 23 on NAM distribution.

5. On the 1920s construction of "Bolshevism" in the US, see Erica J. Ryan, *Red War on the Family: Sex, Gender, and Americanism in the First Red Scare* (Philadelphia: Temple University Press, 2015): quotations on 18. I use the term *antiradical* here with reference to how historian Michael Cohen uses the term *radical* to signal a vein of early twentieth-century popular culture in which opposition to the "newly consolidated corporate ruling class" responded to the concerns of various left-wing factions including "industrial unionism, socialism, populism, progressivism, anarchism, black radicalism, feminism, and anti-militarism": Michael Cohen, "'Cartooning Capitalism': Radical Cartooning and the Making of American Popular Radicalism in the Early Twentieth Century," *International Review of Social History* 52, no. S15 (December 2007): 35–58, quotation on 36.

6. "Mighty project" quotation sourced from Famous Players–Lasky Corporation, "Paramount Short Subjects: One-Reel Subjects," *Moving Picture World*, June 28, 1919, 1862, https://archive.org/details/mopicwor40chal/page/n533; see also Famous Players-Lasky Corporation, *The Story of the Famous Players-Lasky Corporation* (New York: Famous Players-Lasky Corporation, 1919), 22, https://archive.org/details/storyoffamouspla00para/page/22/; for Franklin Lane and Thomas Marshall quotations from December 1919, see "Movies vs. Bolshevism Campaign Is Planned," *Indianapolis Star*, December 28, 1919, A5, https://www.proquest.com

/docview/756474006/13FDAB9F281A471EPQ/1. On the Americanism Committee of the Motion Picture Industry, see Stanciu, "Making Americans," 30–31; on framings of anti-Bolshevism of the project, see "Scheme to Fight National Unrest through Movies," *Atlanta Constitution*, January 12, 1920, 1, https://www.proquest.com/docview/497888449; for "combat Bolshevism" quotation, see "Government Enlists Film Aid," *Variety*, December 26, 1919, 222, https://www.proquest.com/docview/1505641284. On the dearth of productions related to Lane's project, see Larry Ceplair, "The Film Industry's Battle against Left-Wing Influences, from the Russian Revolution to the Blacklist," *Film History* 20 (2008): 399–411, see 403.

7. On the defining characteristics of managerial capitalism, see Alfred D. Chandler Jr., "The Emergence of Managerial Capitalism," *Business History Review* 58, no. 4 (Winter, 1984): 473–503, quotation on 473. On industrialization and immigration, see Stephen Meyer, "Adapting the Immigrant to the Line: Americanization in the Ford Factory, 1914–1921," *Journal of Social History* 14, no. 1 (1980): 67–82. On the "new" immigration wave, see James R. Barrett, "Americanization from the Bottom Up: Immigration and the Remaking of the Working Class in the United States," *Journal of American History* 79, no. 3 (1992): 996–1020, https://doi.org/10.2307/2080796; see also Lisabeth Cohen, *Making a New Deal: Industrial Workers in Chicago, 1919–1939* (Cambridge: Cambridge University Press, 2014), https://hdl.handle.net/2027/heb.00088. On immigrants and Americanization, see Meyer, "Adapting the Immigrant to the Line"; also Allison D. Murdach, "Frances Kellor and the Americanization Movement," *Social Work* 53, no. 1 (2008): 93–95. On citizenship training, see Gary Gerstle, "The Politics of Patriotism: Americanization and the Formation of the CIO," *Dissent* 33 (Winter, 1986), 84–92, quotation on 85. On Americanization as industrial socialization, see Jennifer Daryl Slack, "Media and the Americanization of Workers: *The Americanization Bulletin*, 1918–1919," in *The Critical Communication Review*, vol. 1, *Labor, the Working Class, and the Media*, ed. Vincent Mosco and Janet Wasko (Norwood, NJ: Ablex Publishing Corp., 1983), quotation on 28.

8. On traveling salesmen and the adaptation of their techniques, see Walter A. Friedman, *Birth of a Salesman: The Transformation of Selling in America* (Cambridge, MA: Harvard University Press, 2005), especially 157–59. On "scientific advertising," see Peggy J. Kreshel, "Advertising Research in the Pre-Depression Years: A Cultural History," *Journal of Current Issues and Research in Advertising* 15, no. 1, (Spring 1993): 59–75, quotation on 61, https://doi.org/10.1080/10641734.1993.10504995. For more on Scott, see Edmund C. Lynch, "Walter Dill Scott: Pioneer Industrial Psychologist," *Business History Review* 42, no. 2 (Summer 1968): 149–70, which discusses Scott's application of psychological theories to advertising problems on 151–52.

9. Walter D. Scott, "The Psychology of Advertising," *Atlantic*, January 1904, 29–36, https://www.theatlantic.com/magazine/archive/1904/01/the-psychology-of-advertising/303465/. On magazine advertising trends, see Kreshel, "Advertising Research in the Pre-Depression Years," and Richard W. Pollay, "The Subsidizing

NOTES TO PAGES 36–38

Sizzle: A Descriptive History of Print Advertising, 1900–1980," *Journal of Marketing* 49 (Summer 1985): 24–37; see also Stole, *Advertising on Trial*, 16–17. On Scott's activities during the First World War, see Lynch, "Walter Dill Scott: Pioneer Industrial Psychologist," 160–65. On the Committee on Public Information, see Robert Jackall and Janice M. Hirota, *The Image Makers: Advertising, Public Relations and the Ethos of Advocacy* (Chicago: University of Chicago Press, 2000), 21–22. On George Creel, see Steven J. Ross, *Working-Class Hollywood: Silent Film and the Shaping of Class in America* (Princeton, NJ: Princeton University Press, 1998). Of note is Ross's (125) observation that Creel's personal politics were progressive, but his choice to use the CPI to promote "class harmony" was a strategic decision toward the overall goal of raising wartime morale and civilian support.

10. On silent film and language, see Stanciu, "Making Americans," 4 For Lane's speech, see Franklin Knight Lane, "The Living Flame of Americanism," *Current History* 14, no. 4 (1921): 608–10. A print advertisement in the *New York Times* promoting the essay's publication in *Current History* claimed that it was "heretofore unpublished": see "Display Ad 50—No Title," *New York Times (1857–1922)*, June 30, 1921, 10, https://www.proquest.com/docview/98409634. The speech was reportedly first delivered "just after the Armistice and at the outset of the Americanization movement," placing its initial performance somewhere around the beginning of 1919: see Rollo La Verne Lyman and Howard Copeland Hill, eds., *Literature and Living Book Three* (New York: Charles Scribner's Sons, 1925), retrieved from https://www.google.com/books/edition/Literature_and_Living/En80LpdWmFwC; and Elizabeth J. Sherwood and Dorothy Goodman, eds., *Readers' Guide to Periodical Literature*, vol. 5, *1919–1921* (New York: H. W. Wilson Company, 1922), retrieved from https://www.google.com/books/edition/Readers_Guide_to_Period ical_Literature/k5lAAQAAMAAJ; "aglow with sacred fire" quotations from US Department of the Interior, "Americanization Speech of Hon. Franklin K. Lane at Hotel Astor, New York," in *America, Americanism, Americanization* (Washington, DC: Government Printing Office, 1919), 4. On affective attunement, see Papacharissi, *Affective Publics*, 118.

11. On anticommunism, Richard Gid Powers in *Not without Honor: The History of American Anticommunism* (New York: Free Press, 1995) notes that the anticommunist forces of the 1920s included organizers from Jewish, Black, Catholic, and leftist communities—see 44–67.

12. On traditions of place promotion, see Stephen V. Ward, *Selling Places: The Marketing and Promotion of Towns and Cities, 1950–2000* (New York: E & FN Spon Press/Routledge, 1998), especially chapter 2.

13. On Frank Branch Riley, see "Famed Westerner to Be Speaker at Big Convention: Oregon Celebrity among Notable Names upon Chicago Programme," *San Francisco Chronicle (1869–Current File)*, June 4, 1921, 6, retrieved from https://www .proquest.com/docview/365922543; see also "Oregonian to Give Series of Lectures Here on Northwest: Frank Branch Riley Will Address Rotarians and Nature Study

212   NOTES TO PAGES 39-40

Club," *Indianapolis Star (1907–1922)*, January 5, 1922, 7, retrieved from https://
www.proquest.com/docview/741478562. On the history of the National Association
of Real Estate Boards, see Paige Glotzer, "Exclusion in Arcadia: How Suburban
Developers Circulated Ideas about Discrimination, 1890–1950," *Journal of Urban
History* 41, no. 3 (2015): 479–94. On Riley's advocacy for limiting immigration, see
S. S. Walstrum, "The Convention of Realtors at Chicago," *Commerce and Finance*
30 (July 27, 1921): quotation on 1075, retrieved from https://books.google.com
/books?id=9_M9AQAAMAAJ&pg=PA1075&lpg=PA1075. On Riley's promotion of the Northwest to national and international audiences, see "Northwest Offers Large Market for Products of Factories of Cincinnati Industries: Portland Attorney Who Is to Speak at Forum, Forecasts Much Trade with Far East," *Cincinnati
Enquirer (1872–1922)*, March 3, 1922, 9, retrieved from https://www.proquest.com
/docview/865492144. On the American Travel Bureau, see "Hotels Favor Travel
Bureau," *San Francisco Examiner (1902–2007)*, November 28, 1923), 7, retrieved
from https://www.proquest.com/ docview/2148778423.

14. On federal funding for roads in parks and quotation from the president
of the American Automobile Association, see "Congress Authorizes $7,500,000
Budget for Road Building: Movement for Improved Highways in National Parks
Supported by the A.A.A.," *Austin Statesman (1921–1973)*, May 18, 1924, A15, retrieved from https://www.proquest.com/docview/1643859894. On tourism industry
appeals to Congress, see "National Aid Is Urged for 'Seeing U.S.' Tours: Meeting
in March Will Call on Congress to Create $5,000,000 Fund," *New York Herald
Tribune (1926–1962)*, February 20, 1927, D13, retrieved from https://www.proquest
.com/docview/1113691882.

15. C. F. Hatfield quotations sourced from "Americans in Europe Lavish: Over
Billion and a Half Spent in Year by Tourists," *Los Angeles Times*, March 25, 1927, 14,
retrieved from https://www.proquest.com/docview/161954322. For an example of
"see America First" rhetoric, see "Seek to Turn Tide of Travel," *Detroit Free Press*,
June 29, 1930, 14, retrieved from https://www.newspapers.com/image/97467399/.
On "America First" rhetoric, see Sarah Churchwell, *Behold America: A History of
America First and the American Dream* (New York: Bloomsbury Publishing, 2018),
quotation on 54.

16. On Marvin's positions regarding immigrants, see *Immigration from Countries
of the Western Hemisphere: Hearings before the Committee on Immigration and Naturalization, House of Representatives, Seventieth Congress, First Session, on H.R. 6465,
H.R. 7358, H.R. 10955, H.R. 11687. February 21 to April 5, 1928. Hearing no. 70.1.5*, retrieved from https://books.google.com/books?id=dEOOAAAAMAAJ, Statement
of Fred R. Marvin, executive director of the Key Men of America and the American Hour Broadcasting Committee, New York City, March 3, 1928, 643–61; see esp.
646. On the American Hour Broadcasting Committee, see "Muncie Radio Station
Helps 'Sell America to Americans': WLBC Member of American Hour Broadcasting Committee—First Address Will Be Heard Monday Night," *Star Press* (Muncie,

NOTES TO PAGES 41–43

IN), January 22, 1928, 20; quotations in this paragraph sourced from 20, https://www.newspapers.com/clip/14920323/22-jan-1928-wlbc-broadcast-of-american/.

17. "Prominent citizens" phrasing sourced from "Woman Senator Aids Patriotic Campaign," *Baltimore Sun*, March 11, 1928, MR12, retrieved from https://www.proquest.com/docview/543581740. On Smith's appearance on KFWB, see "Wilbur's Speech on Radio: Mission of Modern Navy as Seen by Secretary Read to Stimulate Interest in Things American," *Los Angeles Times (1923–1995)*, March 8, 1928, retrieved from https://www.proquest.com/docview/161996805/. For more on the Better America Federation, see Edwin Layton, "The Better America Federation: A Case Study of Superpatriotism," *Pacific Historical Review* 30, no. 2 (1961): 137–47, https://doi.org/10.2307/3636698. On Mary Logan Tucker's political activism, see Kirsten Marie Delegard, *Battling Miss Bolsheviki: The Origins of Female Conservatism in the United States* (Philadelphia: University of Pennsylvania Press, 2012), 87–88, https://www.jstor.org/stable/j.ctt3fhgwx, and on her radio appearance, see "Radio Spreads Patriotism: National Society Head Commends Campaign against Falsifying of American History," *Los Angeles Times (1923–1995)*, March 29, 1928, A11, retrieved from https://www.proquest.com/docview/162101573/. For a critical review of a broadcast in the series, see "On the Air Today: Listening in with the Enquirer's Reviewer," *Cincinnati Enquirer (1923–2009)*, April 5, 1928, quotation on 8, retrieved from https://www.proquest.com/docview/1882996397/.

18. On consumer activism, see Cohen, *A Consumer's Republic*, and Stole, *Advertising on Trial*. On New Deal policies, see Jonathan Levy, *Ages of American Capitalism: A History of the United States* (New York: Random House, 2021), especially chapter 13. On business opposition, see Phillips-Fein, *Invisible Hands*, in particular Phillips-Fein's account of organizations such as the American Liberty League as well as the National Association of Manufacturers and the Chamber of Commerce of the United States during the 1930s, 16–22.

19. Glickman, *Free Enterprise*, quotation on 69. Wendy L. Wall, *Inventing the American Way: The Politics of Consensus from the New Deal to the Civil Rights Movement* (New York: Oxford University Press, 2008), quotation on 41.

20. On corporate backing for the Crusaders and their pivot from Prohibition, see Dewey L. Fleming, "Lobby Probes Victor in Fight with Hearst," *Baltimore Sun*, April 9, 1936, 1, 7, retrieved from https://www.newspapers.com/image/373893782/ and https://www.newspapers.com/image/373893927/. Quotations describing the Crusaders' positioning sourced from "Crusaders Fight to Defeat Sinclair Poll," *Courier-Journal* (Walnut Creek, CA), October 25, 1934, 5, retrieved from https://www.newspapers.com/image/744270223/ ("toward Fascism . . ."), and "Yountville News: Are Working Hard," *St. Helena (CA) Star*, October 26, 1934, 6, retrieved from https://www.newspapers.com/image/626956295/ ("pledged to fight . . ."). For Van Dyke remarks, see "Crusaders to Carry Forward 'California for Californians' Campaign throughout State," *Van Nuys (CA) Register*, November 8, 1934, 9, https://www.newspapers.com/image/700708424/. On the involvement of the motion

picture industry in the campaign to defeat Sinclair, see also Donald L. Singer, "Upton Sinclair and the California Gubernatorial Campaign of 1934," *Southern California Quarterly* 56, no. 4 (1974): 375–406, see 393–94.

21. For Crusaders rhetoric about its enemies, see "Crusaders Organized," *Los Angeles Times*, June 11, 1935, quotation on 12, retrieved from https://www.newspapers.com/image/380642675/. For Crusaders rhetoric about the threat of socialization, see "Call to Arms Sounded by Crusaders in Effort to Get Sound Government," *Concord (CA) Transcript*, October 17, 1935, 1, 8, quotation on 8, retrieved from https://www.newspapers.com/image/745145023/ and https://www.newspapers.com/image/745145055. On the American Economic Foundation and Chairman Fred Clark's role as the "voice of the Crusaders," see R. S. Pierrepont Jr. "Economic Illiteracy Leads to National Disunity," *Journal of Business Education* 23, no. 5 (1948): 11–12. For Clark quotation, see Randall M. Fisher, "Modern Business Speaking: A Rhetoric of 'Conventional Wisdom,'" *Southern Journal of Communication* 30, no. 4 (1965): 327–34, 334.

22. On World's Fairs, see Robert W. Rydell, *All the World's a Fair: Visions of Empire at American International Expositions, 1876–1916* (Chicago: University of Chicago Press, 1984), and Robert W. Rydell, *World of Fairs: The Century-of-Progress Expositions* (Chicago: University of Chicago Press, 1993). On Creel's political contest with Sinclair, see Singer, "Upton Sinclair and the California Gubernatorial Campaign of 1934." For Creel's essay promoting the Golden Gate International Exhibition, see George Creel, "Selling America to Americans," *Pacific Coast Review* 10, no. 10 (October 1937): 17–19. For Creel's commentary on artists, see 17. Muralists hired for the project included Diego Rivera, a Mexican painter and political radical (see Diego Rivera Mural Project, "Golden Gate International Expo," retrieved June 30, 2021, from https://riveramural.org/ggie/).

23. Quotations sourced from Creel, "Selling America to Americans," 17 and 19.

24. Busch quotations: "Anheuser-Busch Campaign Aims to Sell America to Americans," *Muncie Morning Star*, October 22, 1938, 11, retrieved from https://www.newspapers.com/image/252108043.

25. On the campaign, see "Anheuser-Busch Campaign," *Muncie Morning Star*, 11. On the film *Reflecting Our Confidence in the Future of America*, see Library of Congress, *Catalog of Copyright Entries Part 1, Group 3: Dramatic Compositions, Motion Pictures* (US Government Printing Office, 1939), retrieved from https://archive.org/details/catalogofcopyrig121libr/page/122/mode/2up; for claims of positive reception and audience size, see Roland Krebs and Percy J. Orthwein, *Making Friends Is Our Business: 100 Years of Anheuser-Busch* (St. Louis: Anheuser-Busch, Inc, 1953), quotation on 220. Quotation regarding a "normal and enduring market" sourced from "Anheuser-Busch Campaign," 11. On New Thought and business culture, see Dawn Hutchinson, "New Thought's Prosperity Theology and Its Influence on American Ideas of Success," *Nova Religio: The Journal of Alternative and Emergent Religions* 18, no. 2 (2014): 28–44, quotation on 38.

NOTES TO PAGES 47–55

26. On the role of syndicated columnists as influences on public opinion, see Philip Glende, "Westbrook Pegler and the Rise of the Syndicated Columnist," *American Journalism* 36, no. 3 (2019): 322–47, https://doi.org/10.1080/08821127.2 019.1644081. On Boake Carter's popularity and eventual cancellation, see David Culbert, "U.S. Censorship of Radio News in the 1930s: The Case of Boake Carter," *Historical Journal of Film, Radio, and Television* 2, no. 2, (1982): 173–76, https://doi .org/10.1080/01439688200260131, and Elizabeth A. Fones-Wolf, *Waves of Opposition: Labor and the Struggle for Democratic Radio* (Urbana: University of Illinois Press, 2006).

27. For Carter's initial claims of a lack of selling America, see Boake Carter, "Sell America to Us-Diplomatic Visitations—Self-Preservation," *Boston Globe*, December 22, 1938, 27, https://www.newspapers.com/image/431797805/. For subsequent expansion of this claim, see Boake Carter, "But—Says Boake Carter," *Palm Beach (FL) Post*, December 26, 1938, 26, 1, 2, quotations on 1, https://www.newspa pers.com/image/130224415/.

28. On the US Chamber of Commerce's political claims and concerns, see Stole, *Advertising on Trial*, 161.

29. Benjamin De Casseres, "The March of Events," *San Francisco Examiner*, November 21, 1939, 10, retrieved from https://www.newspapers.com/image/458048636/.

Chapter Three

1. I draw on the notion of professional jurisdiction as outlined by Andrew Abbott in *The System of Professions: An Essay on the Division of Expert Labor* (Chicago: University of Chicago Press, 1988).

2. Carey, *Taking the Risk Out of Democracy*; Richard S. Tedlow, "The National Association of Manufacturers and Public Relations during the New Deal," *Business History Review* 50, no. 1 (1976): 25–45; Wall, *Inventing the American Way*; Jennifer Delton, *The Industrialists: How the National Association of Manufacturers Shaped American Capitalism* (Princeton, NJ: Princeton University Press, 2020).

3. Frank W. Fox, *Madison Avenue Goes to War: The Strange Military Career of American Advertising, 1941–1945*, (Provo, UT: Brigham Young University Press, 1975); Fones-Wolf, *Selling Free Enterprise*; Robert Griffith, "The Selling of America: The Advertising Council and American Politics, 1942–1960," *Business History Review* 57, no. 3 (1983): 388–412; Stole, *Advertising at War*; see also Inger L. Stole, "Advertising America: Official Propaganda and the U.S. Promotional Industries, 1946–1950," *Journalism and Communication Monographs* 23, no. 1 (2021): 4–63.

4. Stuart Hall, "The Rediscovery of 'Ideology': Return of the Repressed in Media Studies," in *Culture, Society, and the Media*, ed. M. Gurevich, T. Bennett, J. Curran, and J. Woollacott, 56–90 (London and New York, Methuen, 1982), quotations on 76.

NOTES TO PAGES 55–58

5. On the shift toward public relations techniques, see Carey, *Taking the Risk Out of Democracy*. On the NAM during the Depression, see Tedlow, "The National Association of Manufacturers and Public Relations during the New Deal," 28–32 On Roosevelt's Business Advisory and Planning Council, see Robert M. Collins, "Positive Business Responses to the New Deal: The Roots of the Committee for Economic Development, 1933–1942," *Business History Review* 52, no. 3 (Autumn 1978): 369–91, 370.

6. Roland Marchand, *Creating the Corporate Soul: The Rise of Public Relations and Corporate Imagery in American Big Business* (Berkeley: University of California Press, 1998), quotations on 204, 206.

7. On the American Liberty League, see Phillips Fein, *Invisible Hands*. On the NAM 1933 memo, see Tedlow, "The National Association of Manufacturers and Public Relations during the New Deal," quoting a memo from Robert L. Lund, chairman of the board of the NAM, in 1933; quotations on 31. On lawmakers' wariness of the NAM in the 1910s, see Edgar Lane, "Some Lessons from Past Congressional Investigations of Lobbying," *Public Opinion Quarterly* 14, no. 1 (January 1, 1950): 14–32, as cited in Carey, *Taking the Risk Out of Democracy*. On NAM publicity budgets and labor legislation passed in the early/mid-1930s, see Delton, *The Industrialists*, especially 110–11. On senate investigations in the aftermath of the Wagner Act, see Jerold S. Auerbach, "The LaFollette Committee: Labor and Civil Liberties in the New Deal," *Journal of American History* 51, no. 3 (December 1964): 435–59. For an example of labor press coverage of the NAM, see "La Follette Committee Exposes Cleveland Associated Industries," *CIO News*, April 9, 1938, 6, accessed via https://archive.org/details/mdu-labor-057485/page/n85/mode/2up.

8. Wall, *Inventing the American Way*, see 58–60. On the National Electric Light Association, see Oreskes and Conway, *The Big Myth*, especially 49–66.

9. On the NAM's strategic claim that free enterprise was inseparable from civil liberties, see Wall's discussion of the "Tripod of Freedom" in *Inventing the American Way*, 59, and also Oreskes, Conway, and Tyson, "How American Businessmen Made Us Believe." For NAM's self-positioning as interpreter, see National Association of Manufacturers, *Experts All: Who's Who behind Industry's Public Information Program* (leaflet) (New York: National Association of Manufacturers, circa 1939), quotations on 2 and 21, Hagley Museum and Archives Digital Archive, https://digital.hagley.org/LMSS_1411_OS848_04_003 (physical item location in National Association of Manufacturers Records, Series 34, Box OS4, Folder "Miscellaneous NIIC Material, 1938–1940"). "High powered" quotation sourced from "The NAM—They Also Serve," *CIO News*, August 6, 1938, 6, accessed via https://archive.org/details/mdu-labor-057485/page/n221/mode/2up. Per the feature in *The CIO News*, which cited NAM promotional materials in addition to the multimedia discussed here the NAM also sponsored "You and Your Nation's Affairs," a syndicated column written by economists; a series of slidefilms to be shown to workers; newspaper advertisements; a speakers bureau; and surveys conducted by Elmo Roper.

NOTES TO PAGES 58–62

10. On the extent of the NAM campaign, see Beder, *Free Market Missionaries*, 15–20; Wall, *Inventing the American Way*, 53–58; Andrew L. Yarrow, "Beyond Civics and the 3 R's: Teaching Economics in the Schools," *History of Education Quarterly* 48, no. 3 (August 2008): 397–431; and NAM, *Experts All*, "industry's first national advertising campaign" quotation on 8, see 19 on booklets, press service, and newsletters. See also "The NAM—They Also Serve," *CIO News*. While *American Family Robinson* failed to gain major network distribution, another sponsored entertainment program, DuPont's *Cavalcade of America*, did pass muster at NBC and aired for a total of twenty years on its radio and television networks. On both *American Family Robinson* and *Cavalcade of America*, see Willam L. Bird, *"Better Living": Advertising, Media, and the New Vocabulary of Business Leadership, 1935– 1955* (Evanston, IL: Northwestern University Press, 1999). On *Men and Machines*, see "Machine 'Lectures' in Own Defense: New Device Gives Illustrated Talk for Manufacturers, Upholding Power Age," *New York Times*, July 23, 1936, 24, https:// www.proquest.com/docview/101817640. For details on NAM films and digitized copies of the films, see *Let's Go America! A Screen Editorial* (Audio Productions and the National Industrial Council, 1936), https://www.loc.gov/item/2018601241/; *Frontiers of the Future* (Audio Productions and the National Industrial Council, 1937), https://archive.org/details/Frontier1937; and *America Marching On* (Audio Productions and the National Industrial Council, 1937), https://archive.org/details /america_marching_on. On the fifteen million audience figure, see NAM, *Experts All*, 11. On the titles of NAM films, see Bird, *"Better Living,"* 131 and NAM, *Experts All*, 12. The films were distributed in the name of the National Industrial Council, an umbrella group of local and national trade organizations sponsored by the NAM, as Delton notes in *The Industrialists*, 110: see "Business Men to Meet: National Industrial Council to Convene Here Today," *New York Times*, December 5, 1938, 30, https://www.proquest.com/docview/102484392.

11. NAM, *Experts All*, quotation on 3.

12. W. F. Kruse, "The Business Screen—Some Demands Made by and upon It," *Journal of the Society of Motion Picture Engineers* 27, no. 4 (October 1936): 431–39, quotations on 432; "The Sign of Good Showmanship: The Power of Films to Sell" (Modern Talking Pictures advertisement), *Business Screen* 1, no. 1 (January 1938): quotations on 13.

13. On "minute movies" as a term of art for theatrical advertisements, see General Screen Advertising, "We Tip Our Hat to Business Screen [advertisement]," *Business Screen* 1, no. 1 (January 1938): 10, and "Film Forum," *Business Screen* 1, no. 1 (January 1938): 11. For NAM public relations claims about its use of film, see James P. Selvage, Letter to the Editor, *Business Screen* 1, no. 1 (January 1938): 9; for the editorial comment responding to Selvage, see "Film Forum: A Department of Letters," *Business Screen* 1, no. 1 (January 1938): 9.

14. Creel, "Selling America to Americans," quotation on 17.

15. On consumer activism, see Cohen, *A Consumer's Republic*; on critiques of the advertising industry and legislation, see Stole, *Advertising on Trial*, 29–30 and 152–57.

218   NOTES TO PAGES 63–66

16. For the AAAA/ANA list of critiques, see "Meeting of the ANA-AAAA Steering Committee re: Joint Meeting of the Two Associations [meeting minutes]" (September 24, 1941), Thomas D'Arcy Brophy Papers, Wisconsin Historical Society: Box 9, Folder 6; quotations on 4. For additional context on how these criticisms shifted as the nation moved to war footing, see Stole, *Advertising at War*, 36.

17. See Stole, *Advertising at War*, chapter 1 on the FTC and other governmental organizations seen as threats to the advertising industry. On "attacks" rhetoric, see "ANA-AAAA Joint Committee Meeting to Discuss a Joint Meeting of the Two Associations on the Attacks on Advertising at AAAA Headquarters [enclosure to September 22, 1941, correspondence from Frederic R. Gamble to Thomas D'Arcy Brophy]" (September 19, 1941), 1, Thomas D'Arcy Brophy Papers, Wisconsin Historical Society: Box 9, Folder 6.

18. On Barton's 1940 speech, see "Barton Attacks New Deal Plot on Free Press-Radio," *Daily Sentinel-Tribune* (Bowling Green, OH), February 15, 1940, 1, https://www.newspapers.com/image/883569458. For West's remarks, see Paul B. West, "An Opportunity to Do a Vitally Necessary Job for Advertising and for the National Welfare [memorandum: enclosure to September 11, 1941, correspondence from Frederic R. Gamble to Thomas D'Arcy Brophy]" (September 2, 1941), Thomas D'Arcy Brophy Papers, Wisconsin Historical Society: Box 9, Folder 6; quotations on 1 and 2. For concerns about the branding system, see Paul B. West, "Prospectus of a Joint Meeting Sponsored by ANA and 4 A's [enclosure to September 22, 1941, correspondence from Frederic R. Gamble to Thomas D'Arcy Brophy]" (n.d., but prepared for, and presented as an appendix to, meeting minutes dated September 19, 1941); quotation on 1nB, Thomas D'Arcy Brophy Papers, Wisconsin Historical Society: Box 9, Folder 6.

19. On doxa, see Richard Swedberg, "Folk Economics and Its Role in Trump's Presidential Campaign: An Exploratory Study," *Theory and Society* 47 (2018): 1–36; quotations on 9 and 10.

20. Swedberg, quotations on 4, 11.

21. Swedberg, quotations on 7. My claim that the advertising industry positioned its insiders as economic experts is not to say that the doxa of advertising industry leaders was as epistemically robust as the expert knowledge of economists, yet nor is it to reify the economic discipline's claims to objectivity. Expert knowledge is itself a social construct. Some fields of expert knowledge are systematic to the extent that they rely on scientific processes such as testing, replication, and peer review in order to create internal consistency (but, as Ian Hacking might point out, these standards of knowledge production are, themselves, social in nature). The economics discipline is at once socially constructed and systematic in its production of knowledge. The practical nature of doxa makes it something closer to knowledge supported by anecdote.

22. Swedberg observes that it is possible to turn away from framing a group or its attitudes as ignorant by asking about "the structures that make up 'the ignorance'";

NOTES TO PAGES 66–69

see "Folk Economics," 9n9. With apologies for the awkwardness of the neologism, I choose *folk expertness* to emphasize the social, cultural, and institutional actions and policies that a supposed expertise makes possible, in contrast to the typical usage of *folk expertise* to signify informally acquired skills and knowledge.

23. "Prospectus of Special Joint Meeting: Association of National Advertisers Inc. and American Association of Advertising Agencies" (n.d.), quotations on 3, Thomas D'Arcy Brophy Papers, Wisconsin Historical Society: Box 9, Folder 6. On approval at the meeting for public interest projects as a publicity strategy, see Griffith, "The Selling of America," 390.

24. Marchand, *Creating the Corporate Soul*, quotation on 320; on the founding of the Advertising Council, see also Stole, "Advertising America," and Griffith, "The Selling of America."

25. On official information agencies prior to the US entry into the war, see Sydney Weinberg, "What to Tell America: The Writers' Quarrel in the Office of War Information," *Journal of American History* 55, no. 1 (June 1968): 73–89, see 73–75. On the OFF as "clearinghouse," see Allan M. Winkler, *The Politics of Propaganda: The Office of War Information, 1942–1945* (New Haven, CT: Yale University Press, 1978), quotation on 23; see also 55 on the relationship between the OFF and OWI. On OFF activities as "psychological warfare," see Chesly Manly, "It's Highly Paid Work—Molding Public Opinion," *Chicago Daily Tribune*, May 13, 1942, 3, quotation on 3, https://www.proquest.com/docview/176668755. MacLeish quoted in Winkler, *The Politics of Propaganda*, 23. On the OFF's goals and perceived shortcomings, see Winkler, *The Politics of Propaganda*, 24. On Dyke's appointment, see Stole, *Advertising at War*, 58–59. On the OWI's founding, see Lewis Wood, "Feud within OWI Is Spreading Far," *New York Times*, April 18, 1943, E10, quotation on E10, https://www.proquest.com/docview/106664030.

26. On the mission of OWI, see Christof Decker, "Fighting for a Free World: Ben Shahn and the Art of the War Poster," *American Art* 33, no. 2 (Summer 2019): 87. On OWI's leadership and size, see Walter Trohan, "U.S. Propaganda Costs Jump to 60 Million a Year," *Chicago Daily Tribune*, October 19, 1942, 6, https://www.proquest.com/docview/176848180. On OWI divisions and their duties, see A. H. Feller, "OWI on the Home Front," *Public Opinion Quarterly* 7, no. 1 (1943): 55–65, quotation on 61, Radio Bureau figures 63. The Bureau of Campaigns was renamed the Bureau of Program Coordination in spring of 1943.

27. For press coverage of OWI, see Manly, "It's Highly Paid Work"; Trohan, "U.S. Propaganda Costs"; and John D. Morris, "The OWI on the Domestic Radio Front," *New York Times*, January 31, 1943, X9, https://www.proquest.com/docview/106525139. Kent quotations from Frank R. Kent, "The Great Game of Politics: Most Heavily Advised," *Wall Street Journal*, July 6, 1942, 4, https://www.proquest.com/docview/131399968.

28. On the OWI focusing on public relations in place of news, see Winkler, *The Politics of Propaganda*, quotations on 53, 54.

220   NOTES TO PAGES 69–71

29. Frank Fox uses this phrase to describe the advertising industry in Fox, *Madison Avenue Goes to War*, 65. Fox examines how, unlike the unflinching and emotionally arresting war advertising created by copy director Walter Weir of Lord and Thomas, "most war advertising worked oppositely toward catharsis and the expurgation of guilt. It gave readers to understand that the symbolic act of buying bonds or donating blood was of such consequence in the war's social economy as to require little else." I borrow Fox's phrase, inspired by his evocative observation, that many copy writers failed to capture the moment, suggesting that "advertising had too long represented the voice of affirmation in American life to speak of death so unsmilingly." Fox's observations attuned me to larger promotional patterns of affirmation common to economic education media.

30. On the founding of the Advertising Council, see Stole, "Advertising America," 14. Quotations in this paragraph sourced from John Benson, Thomas D'Arcy Brophy, F. R. Feland, William G. Palmer, William Reydel, and Walter Weir, "The Place of Advertising in a War Economy" (August 26, 1942), 1, Thomas D'Arcy Brophy Papers, Wisconsin Historical Society: Box 10, Folder 5. On tax deduction as government subsidy, see Stole, *Advertising at War*, quotation on 53.

31. On Advertising Council techniques and advertisement types including "all-out" campaigns, see Jackall and Hirota, *Image Makers*, 41–42, quotation on 41. On institutional advertising strategies meant to keep companies in consumers' minds despite limited products to sell, see Thomas D'Arcy Brophy, Correspondence to Raymond Browne (January 13, 1943), Thomas D'Arcy Brophy Papers, Wisconsin Historical Society: Box 1, Folder 6. See also Benson et al., "The Place of Advertising in a War Economy."

32. "Expert and disinterested" (3) and "real arsenal of democracy" (14) quotations from Benson et al., "The Place of Advertising in a War Economy." "Good citizen" quotation from Frederic R. Gamble, "Advertising after the War" (May 1, 1942), 3, Thomas D'Arcy Brophy Papers, Wisconsin Historical Society: Box 10, Folder 5.

33. On political pressures and reorganization at the OWI, see Weinberg, "What to Tell America," 83–84. "Huge costs" quotation from Arthur Krock, "New OWI Magazine Irks Congressional Groups," *New York Times*, February 14, 1943, E3, https://www.proquest.com/docview/106534882. On personnel changes at the Domestic Branch, see also Winkler, *The Politics of Propaganda*, 63. On resignations from OWI under Cowles, see Lewis Wood, "Writers Who Quit OWI Charge It Bars 'Full Truth' for 'Ballyhoo,'" *New York Times*, April 16, 1943, 1, https://www.proquest.com/docview/106674273. On Cowles's assumptions about the public's interest in "columns of type" and his affinity for the War Advertising Council, see Winkler, *The Politics of Propaganda*, 39–40; quotation on 40.

34. Cowles statements sourced from "OWI Division Head Ousted," *Washington Post*, April 10, 1943, 1, https://www.proquest.com/docview/151654560. See also "14 OWI Officials Quit; Protest Admen's Policy," *Chicago Daily Tribune*, April 11, 1943, 8, https://www.proquest.com/docview/176853720. On writers' response, see

"14 OWI Officials Quit," 8. On Cowles's defense of industry collaboration, see Ben W. Gilbert, "OWI Slashes Output of Pamphlets after 14 Writers Resign," *Washington Post*, April 11, 1943, 8, https://www.proquest.com/docview/151689548. Voluntary industry participation in messaging would come to be coordinated by the Advertising Council across multiple campaigns by the end of the war; see War Advertising Council, "War Advertising Council Home Front Campaigns" (June 15, 1945), Poster US 7625, Poster collection, Hoover Institution Library and Archives, https://digitalcollections.hoover.org/objects/41596.

35. On the writers' perspective on the role of advertising techniques, see "Sole Aim Is Facts, Says Davis of OWI," *New York Times*, April 15, 1943, 9, quotation on 9, https://www.proquest.com/docview/106653102. "Too gloomy" quotation from "False Ballyhoo Is OWI's Creed, Say 15 Who Quit," *Chicago Daily Tribune*, April 16, 1943, 11, https://www.proquest.com/docview/176658574. "High pressure promoters" quotation from Wood, "Writers Who Quit OWI Charge It Bars 'Full Truth,'" 13.

36. "Grimmer side" (82) and "patriotic fervor" (82–83) quotations from Weinberg, "What to Tell America." For Wall's characterization of "upbeat" materials at OWI, see Wall, *Inventing the American Way*, quotation on 117. On Shahn's resignation, see Decker, "Fighting for a Free World."

37. On the position of the advertising industry after the war, see Fox, *Madison Avenue Goes to War*, and Inger L. Stole, "The Fight against Critics and the Discovery of 'Spin,'" in *The Routledge Companion to Advertising and Promotional Culture*, ed. Matthew P. McAllister and Emily West (New York: Routledge. 2015), 39–52, see in particular 48. On the political implications of the resignations, see Wall, *Inventing the American Way*, quotation on 118. On "emotionalizing facts," see Victor J. Viser, "Winning the Peace: American Planning for a Profitable Postwar World," *Journal of American Studies* 35 (2001): 111–26, quotation on 112; Viser cites a 1945 speech written by the Advertising Council's first chairman, James Webb Young, whose notes for another speech delivered the following day read: "we found that what we knew about emotionalizing facts, and about other devices for getting action, would bring results that agencies of government had despaired of achieving." James Webb Young, "What Advertising Learned from the War [speech transcript prepared for presentation at the Annual Meeting of the Central Council of the American Association of Advertising Agencies, Continental Hotel, Chicago]" (December 12, 1945), 5, Thomas D'Arcy Brophy Papers, Wisconsin Historical Society: Box 3, Folder 5.

38. On the council's vision for the postwar period and the need for persuasion, see "The Council Looks Ahead [memo attached to correspondence dated October 16, 1944, from T. S. Repplier to All Directors and Sponsor Members of the War Advertising Council]" (n.d.), quotation on 2, Thomas D'Arcy Brophy Papers, Wisconsin Historical Society: Box 1, Folder 6. For more on the Advertising Council's transition to peacetime, see Jackall and Hirota, *The Image Makers*, 47–48.

222 NOTES TO PAGES 73–75

39. On the council's administration of the radio plan, see Advertising Council, "The New Radio Allocation Plan [undated attachment to correspondence from H. W. Roden, Stuart Peabody, and Lee H. Bristol on behalf of the Advertising Council to Watson Vanderploeg (November 29, 1945)]," Thomas D'Arcy Brophy Papers, Wisconsin Historical Society: Box 1, Folder 7; "public service advertising is good business" quotation from 2–3. The classification of PSAs as prospectively serving the public interest—if they were "devoted to a non-profit cause" and if the airtime was donated by the broadcaster rather than paid for by a sponsor— was formalized in the FCC's Blue Book: see Federal Communications Commission, *Public Service Responsibility of Broadcast Licensees* (report) (Washington, DC, March 7, 1946), 55, https://hcinonline.org/HOL/P?h=hein.intprop/fccpsrbl0001&i=59. On the history of the FCC and the Blue Book, see Victor Pickard, "The Battle over the FCC Blue Book: Determining the Role of Broadcast Media in a Democratic Society, 1945–8," *Media, Culture & Society* 33, no. 2 (2011): 171–91. On expanding council services to nonprofit organizations, see James Webb Young, "The Advertising Council at Work," Address delivered at the Hotel Statler, Washington DC (September 18, 1946), Thomas D'Arcy Brophy Papers, Wisconsin Historical Society: Box 3, Folder 5.

40. "Making facts simple" quotation from Young, "What Advertising Learned from the War," 4; all other quotations in this paragraph from Advertising Council, "The New Radio Allocation Plan," 3.

41. Bruce Barton, Correspondence to Thomas D'Arcy Brophy (September 19, 1946), quotations on 1 and 2, Thomas D'Arcy Brophy Papers, Wisconsin Historical Society: Box 1, Folder 1.

42. James Webb Young, Correspondence to Bruce Barton (September 24, 1946), Thomas D'Arcy Brophy Papers, Wisconsin Historical Society: Box 1, Folder 7. See also James Webb Young, "A Re-examination and Appraisal of the Peacetime Program of the Advertising Council [presentation notes]" (April 11, 1947), 1, Thomas D'Arcy Brophy Papers, Wisconsin Historical Society: Box 1, Folder 8.

43. See Young, "A Re-examination and Appraisal of the Peacetime Program of the Advertising Council," 9, for a description of "drop-in" content as prewritten copy in an editorial style.

44. On the establishment of the council as a nonprofit organization, see Thomas D'Arcy Brophy, Correspondence to Ted Repplier with attachment from assistant Engle (September 25, 1946), Thomas D'Arcy Brophy Papers, Wisconsin Historical Society: Box 1, Folder 7. On philanthropy in the postwar period, see Nicholas J. Duquette, "Founders' Fortunes and Philanthropy: A History of the U.S. Charitable-Contribution Deduction," *Business History Review* 93, no. 3 (Autumn 2019): 553–84. Repplier quotations on campaign kits sourced from Staley Jones, "Gallery: Ted Repplier, The Unhappy Worrier," *Advertising & Selling* (December 1946), n.p., Thomas D'Arcy Brophy Papers, Wisconsin Historical Society: Box 3, Folder 5. "Campaigns for economic and political education" quotation sourced

NOTES TO PAGES 77–84

from Young, "A Re-examination and Appraisal of the Peacetime Program of the Advertising Council," 6.

Chapter Four

1. William H. Whyte, *Is Anybody Listening? How and Why Business Fumbles When It Talks with Human Beings* (New York: Simon and Schuster, 1952), quotations on 7, 10, and vii.

2. Whyte, quotations on 10, 11, 12.

3. Whyte, 7. On prior decades' advocacy, see also Tedlow, "The National Association of Manufacturers and Public Relations during the New Deal."

4. On individual companies' sponsorship of films, see Bird, *"Better Living,"* in particular chapter 7. On the Advertising Council's participation in promoting private enterprise, see Griffith, "The Selling of America"; Wall, *Inventing the American Way*; Stuart J. Little, "The Freedom Train: Citizenship and Postwar Political Culture, 1946–1949," *American Studies* 34, no. 1 (Spring 1993): 35–67. Inger Stole's *Advertising at War* surveys the links between the AAAA, ANA, and the Advertising Council, mentioning the Smock Report (see 166–70).

5. "Summary: Joint ANA-AAAA Committee on Improvement of Public Understanding of Our Economic System" (n.d., circa March 1950), Thomas D'Arcy Brophy Papers, Wisconsin Historical Society: Box 10, Folder 2.

6. On the formation of the committee, its tasks, its name change, personnel, funding, and facility, see "Summary: Joint ANA-AAAA Committee on Improvement of Public Understanding of Our Economic System," and Paul B. West, Correspondence to T. S. Repplier (September 2, 1947,), 2, Thomas D'Arcy Brophy Papers, Wisconsin Historical Society: Box 9, Folder 8. "In the interests of the American people" and "less vulnerable" quotations from Jack Smock, "Joint ANA-AAAA Committee on Improvement of Public Understanding of Our Economic System, Report on the Activities of the Research and Creative Committees to Twenty-Ninth Annual Convention of American Association of Advertising Agencies, Hotel Waldorf-Astoria, New York City" (April 17, 1947), 2, Thomas D'Arcy Brophy Papers, Wisconsin Historical Society: Box 9, Folder 7.

7. On doxa, see Swedberg, "Folk Economics."

8. Smock, "Joint ANA-AAAA Committee on Improvement of Public Understanding of Our Economic System, Report [. . .]," quotations from 3, 6.

9. Smock, quotations on 9, 13; see also Glickman, *Free Enterprise*, 74–75, for an account of how the metaphor of government as referee or umpire was in circulation by the 1930s.

10. Smock, "Joint ANA-AAAA Committee on Improvement of Public Understanding of Our Economic System, Report [. . .]," quotations on 24, 25–26, 27; De Casseres, "The March of Events," 10.

224   NOTES TO PAGES 84–88

11. Lund quotation cited in S. Alexander Rippa, *Education in a Free Society: An American History* (New York: Longman, 1997), 240, which sources the quote on 250n18 to National Association of Manufacturers, "Proceedings of the Fortieth Annual Convention of the Congress of American Industry held on 4–5 December 1935, at the Hotel Commodore in New York City" (New York: Association, n.d.), 25–26. Young quotation from Young, "What Advertising Learned from the War," 4.

12. While Lewenstein focuses on the rhetoric of popular science in the midcentury period, and not on corporate public relations, the dynamic in play was notably similar. See Bruce V. Lewenstein, "The Meaning of 'Public Understanding of Science' in the United States after World War II," *Public Understanding of Science* 1 (1992): 45–68, quotation on 45–46. Tedlow, "The National Association of Manufacturers and Public Relations during the New Deal," 31n19.

13. On the publicity for the Freedom Train, see Thomas D'Arcy Brophy, "Progress Report to the Board of Trustees of the American Heritage Foundation" (September 4, 1947), 12, images located between 14 and 15, Thomas D'Arcy Brophy Papers, Wisconsin Historical Society: Box 17, Folder 5. On Freedom Train stops and attendance rates, see Little, "The Freedom Train," 35. Wall, *Inventing the American Way*, quotation on 201.

14. On Advertising Council involvement in the American Heritage program, see Brophy, "Progress Report to the Board of Trustees of the American Heritage Foundation," "program of public education" quotation on 12. On the campaign as a counterpoint to socialism, see Griffith, "The Selling of America," and also Wall, *Inventing the American Way*. Shugrue quotations on 18 of J. Edward Shugrue, "Freedom Is Everybody's Business," *Business Screen* 9, no. 1 (1948): 18–19.

15. On the Freedom Train's downplaying of conflict, see Wall, *Inventing the American Way*, quotations on 201–2. On labor power after the Second World War, and for quotation from Reuther, see Nelson Lichtenstein, *State of the Union: A Century of American Labor* (Princeton, NJ: Princeton University Press, 2002); Reuther quotation on 103.

16. On personnel and institutions involved in the development of the exhibit, see Little, "The Freedom Train," 39–41. On the Advertising Council's acceptance of the American Heritage campaign, see Young, "A Re-examination and Appraisal of the Peacetime Program of the Advertising Council [presentation notes]," 8; and also Little, "The Freedom Train," 40; and Griffith, "The Selling of America," 398–99. On Brophy, see Wall, *Inventing the American Way*, 177–78.

17. On characterization of the Freedom Train as "moderately pro-business," see Little, "The Freedom Train," 39. Mortimer quotation from Charles G. Mortimer, "Democracy's Newest Weapon [speech to the Conference of 100 Business Leaders, Statler Hotel, Washington DC]" (October 27, 1947), 2, Thomas D'Arcy Brophy Papers, Wisconsin Historical Society: Box 1, Folder 8. "Track and locomotive" quotations from "Meeting of Joint ANA-AAAA Committee on Improvement of Public Understanding of Our Economic System [meeting minutes]" (July 30, 1947),

NOTES TO PAGES 90–92

6, Thomas D'Arcy Brophy Papers, Wisconsin Historical Society: Box 9, Folder 7. See also Wall, *Inventing the American Way*, 211, which cites correspondence from Brophy to Don Belding dated June 2, 1947, that made a similar point.

18. Fri quotation from James L. Fri, "Trade Associations in Our Time," *Business Screen* 9, no. 1 (February 1948): 17. For Link's perspective on the exhibit, see Link, "How to Sell America to the Americans," quotations 20 and 21. "Croaking prophets" quotation from Wilding Picture Productions, "Everybody Is busy . . . [print advertisement]," *Business Screen* 9, no. 1 (1948, February): 5.

19. Shugrue, "Freedom Is Everybody's Business," 19, quotations on 19; on Shugrue's directorship, see "J. Edward Shugrue, Ex-Director with American Heritage Foundation [obituary]," *New York Times*, August 18, 1977, 24, https://www .proquest.com/docview/123435759; James McCabe, "Changing the Conversation in Detroit: Norman Rockwell's Four Freedoms and the Four Freedoms War Bond Show," in *Enduring Ideals: Rockwell, Roosevelt and the Four Freedoms*, ed. Stephanie Haboush Plunkett and James J. Kimble (New York: Abbeville Press Publishers, 2018). Bolte quotations from Major General Charles L. Bolte, "The American Heritage," *Business Screen* 9, no. 1 (February 1948): 16.

20. On industrial films, see "Well Produced Films Serve Vast Audience," *Business Screen* 9, no. 1 (February 1948): 22, quotations on 22. On government as referee, see "Five Fundamental Features of Our Economy," *Business Screen* 9, no. 1 (February 1948): 23. Editors' comments about the slidefilm quoted from 22, "This Is Our Problem," *Business Screen* 9, no. 1 (February 1948): 22.

21. On the duration of the campaign, see Robert H. Zeiger, "The Paradox of Plenty: The Advertising Council and the Post-Sputnik Crisis," *Advertising and Society Review* 4, no. 1 (2003), and Griffith, "The Selling of America." On the campaign, see also Beder, *Free Market Missionaries*, 32–42.

22. On Joint Committee on Improvement requests for Advertising Council support, see "Minutes of Meeting: Board of Directors and Sponsor Members, The Advertising Council, Inc. [meeting minutes]" (January 3, 1947), especially 3, Thomas D'Arcy Brophy Papers, Wisconsin Historical Society: Box 2, Folder 7. On Hoffmann, Shishkin, and Shuster's involvement in winning Public Advisory Committee approval, see Advertising Council, "Proposed Program for Better Understanding of Our Economic System" (April 9, 1947), 1, Advertising Council Papers, University Library at the University of Illinois, Records Group 13/2/219, Box 12; on the membership of the Public Advisory Committee, see also Michael Amrine, "Memorandum to Members of Press and Radio [press release]" (April 17, 1947), Thomas D'Arcy Brophy Papers, Wisconsin Historical Society: Box 9, Folder 7, which additionally lists the members of the Public Advisory Committee.

23. Quotations in this paragraph from 1 of Advertising Council, "Proposed Program for Better Understanding of Our Economic System" (April 9, 1947), Advertising Council Papers, University Library at the University of Illinois, Records Group 13/2/219, Box 12.

226   NOTES TO PAGES 92–96

24. Young, "A Re-examination and Appraisal of the Peacetime Program of the Advertising Council [presentation notes]," 6; Association of National Advertisers and American Association of Advertising Agencies, "To the Advertising Council, Inc.: A Program for Better Understanding of Our Economic System" (n.d.), Thomas D'Arcy Brophy Papers, Wisconsin Historical Society: Box 9, Folder 7: quotations on "more" wealth "to share" on 4, quotations on the "American system" and "complicated mechanisms" on 1, on preventing destructive effects of business cycles on 3, quotation on unemployment on 3.

25. On the council commencement of the campaign, see Charlie G. Mortimer, Correspondence to Thomas D'Arcy Brophy (April 10, 1947), Thomas D'Arcy Brophy Papers, Wisconsin Historical Society: Box 1, Folder 8. On Chamber of Commerce publicity around the Smock Report, see "Meeting of Steering Committee, Joint ANA-AAAA Committee on Improvement of Public Understanding of Our Economic System [meeting minutes]" (April 30, 1947), 1, Thomas D'Arcy Brophy Papers, Wisconsin Historical Society: Box 9, Folder 6. On the rationale for the *Miracle of America* booklet, see Advertising Council, "Chronological History of American Economic System Campaign" (n.d.), quotation on 5, Advertising Council Papers, University Library at the University of Illinois, Records Group 13/2/219, Box 12.

26. On the Joint Committee on Improvement as official sponsor, see "Steering Committee, Joint ANA-AAAA Committee on Improvement of Public Understanding of Our Economic System [meeting minutes]" (May 9, 1947), 2, Thomas D'Arcy Brophy Papers, Wisconsin Historical Society: Box 9, Folder 7. For booklet copy, see Advertising Council, *The Miracle of America*, 4th ed. (New York: Advertising Council, 1950), 19. On the question of the Advertising Council raising funds for the full range of Joint Committee on Improvement projects, see "Minutes of Meeting: Board of Directors, The Advertising Council, Inc. [meeting minutes]" (May 15, 1947), quotation on 4, Thomas D'Arcy Brophy Papers, Wisconsin Historical Society: Box 2, Folder 7. On the decision that the Advertising Council would not raise funds for Program One, see "Meeting of the Joint ANA-AAAA Committee on Improvement of Public Understanding of Our Economic System [meeting minutes]" (May 20, 1947), see 2 in particular, Thomas D'Arcy Brophy Papers, Wisconsin Historical Society: Box 9, Folder 7. On seeing the council as "one of several means to an end," see "Steering Committee, Joint ANA-AAAA Committee on Public Understanding of Our Economic System [meeting minutes]" (June 10, 1947), quotation on 3, Thomas D'Arcy Brophy Papers, Wisconsin Historical Society: Box 9, Folder 7.

27. For quotations on "higher productivity" and "more freedoms," see Advertising Council, "Proposed Program for Better Understanding of Our Economic System," 1; on productivity as an alternative to redistribution, see Fones-Wolf, *Selling Free Enterprise*, 5.

28. Jason Chambers, *Madison Avenue and the Color Line: African Americans in the Advertising Industry* (Philadelphia: University of Pennsylvania Press, 2008). See especially chapter 2, and on "special markets," see 61–64, quotation on 61.

NOTES TO PAGES 96–102

29. Advertising Council, *The Miracle of America*, 2.

30. Advertising Council, quotations on "more of everything" on 3, on "the greatest group of workers" on 7, on the American standard of living on 10, on individual freedom on 14.

31. Circulation figures from "Summary: Joint ANA-AAAA Committee on Improvement of Public Understanding of Our Economic System," 5. On campaign descriptions and corporate sponsors, see Advertising Council, "Chronological History of American Economic System Campaign," 14, and on polling data, 16.

32. For Wells's reported figures on Program One, see M. Jones, "Community Drives in 150 New Plants: 360 Companies Now Sponsor 'American Way' Programs, Says Project Director," *New York Times*, June 5, 1949, F1, https://www.proquest.com/docview/105863042. On the scope of Program One activities, see "Summary: Joint ANA-AAAA Committee on Improvement of Public Understanding of Our Economic System," 3–4.

33. On George S. Benson, see L. Edward Hicks, *Sometimes in the Wrong but Never in Doubt: George S. Benson and the Education of the New Religious Right* (Knoxville: University of Tennessee Press, 1994), Robbie Maxwell, "'A Shooting Star of Conservatism': George S. Benson, the National Education Program, and the 'Radical Right,'" *Journal of American Studies* 53, no. 2 (2019): 372–400, and Robbie Maxwell, "The Emergence of a Pioneer Conservative: George S. Benson and the Politics of America's 'Great Interior' in the 1930s and 1940s," *Journal of Contemporary History* 53, no. 4 (2016): 714–39, quotation on 717. On Benson's advocacy of "economy" and reduced spending, see "Editorial: The Dance of the Billions," *Los Angeles Times*, July 13, 1941, A4, https://www.proquest.com/docview/165164829; and Henry N. Dorriss, "Doughton Denies Tax 'Shenanigans,'" *New York Times*, May 16, 1941, 39, https://www.proquest.com/docview/105569000. On Benson's criticism of the CCC, see "Asks U.S. to Cut Expenditures in Civilian Fields," *Chicago Daily Tribune*, August 6, 1941, 24, https://www.proquest.com/docview/176651844; Robert C. Albright, "College Cheaper than CCC: George Calls for Leadership to Cut Nondefense Spending," *Washington Post*, August 22, 1941, 1, quotation on CCC costs on 1, https://www.proquest.com/docview/151417549; on Benson's other comparisons of CCC costs and college costs, see "College Head Calls NYA and CCC Units Hindrance to War," *Chicago Daily Tribune*, April 15, 1942, 11, https://www.proquest.com/docview/176676986; and "Nondefense Economies Spiked on a Point of Order," *Washington Post (1923–1954)*, August 26, 1941, 1, https://www.proquest.com/docview/151429922. On Williams's criticisms of Benson, see "NYA Head's Slap at Patriotism Hit in Senate: Aubrey Williams Branded 'Arrogant Bureaucrat,'" *Chicago Daily Tribune*, February 4, 1942, 2, quotation on 2, https://www.proquest.com/docview/176848772. On dissolution of federal programs, see Winkler, *The Politics of Propaganda*, 65–66.

34. On Benson's Rotary Club speech, see "Calls Federal Plans a Threat to U.S. Rights," *Chicago Daily Tribune*, May 9, 1943, 6, quotations on 6, https://www.proquest.com/docview/176732621. On California Taxpayer Association appearance,

see "Taxpayer Group Hears Free Enterprise Plea," *Los Angeles Times*, March 27, 1946, A2, quotations on A2, https://www.proquest.com/docview/165657422.

35. On the funding and production of *Make Mine Freedom*, see Caroline Jack, "Fun and Facts about American Business: Economic Education and Business Propaganda in an Early Cold War Cartoon Series," *Enterprise & Society* 16, no. 3 (2015): 491–520. On Joint Committee on Improvement members, see Advertising Council, "Chronological History of American Economic System Campaign," 1; see also West, Correspondence to T. S. Repplier, 3. On Sutherland's interactions with Johns-Manville executives, see John Sutherland, Correspondence to George S. Benson (October 9, 1946), file B-057, "John Sutherland Correspondence 1947" folder, George Benson Papers, Ann Cowan Dixon Archives and Special Collections, Harding University. On inclusion of ideas from the Smock Report in the film, see "Meeting of the Joint ANA-AAAA Committee on Improvement of Public Understanding of Our Economic System [meeting minutes]," (June 2, 1948), quotations on 2, Thomas D'Arcy Brophy Papers, Wisconsin Historical Society: Box 10, Folder 1.

36. An account of the initial discussion between Wells, Belding, and Benson may be found in Ted M. Altman, "The Contributions of George Benson to Christian Education" (PhD diss., North Texas State University, 1971), 68, https://digital.library.unt.edu/ark:/67531/metadc164505/m2/1/high_res_d/nd_00543.pdf. On Harding's role in enacting Program One, see George S. Benson, Undated memorandum included as an appendix to "Meeting of the Joint ANA-AAAA Committee on Improvement of Public Understanding of Our Economic System [meeting minutes]" (January 6, 1949), especially 1 and 2, Thomas D'Arcy Brophy Papers, Wisconsin Historical Society: Box 10, Folder 1, and also Ken Wells, Correspondence to Thomas D'Arcy Brophy (January 26, 1949), 2, Thomas D'Arcy Brophy Papers, Wisconsin Historical Society: Box 8, Folder 4. For press coverage of the Freedom Forum, see Brendan M. Jones, "Community Drives in 150 New Plants: 360 Companies Now Sponsor 'American Way' Programs, Says Project Director," *New York Times*, June 5, 1949, F1, https://www.proquest.com/docview/105863042. On Benson's use of the Smock Report, referred to here as "The Joint Committee Creative Report" in the Freedom Forums, see Don Belding, Memo to Thomas D'Arcy Brophy, Enclosure A (May 16, 1949), 1, Thomas D'Arcy Brophy Papers, Wisconsin Historical Society: Box 8, Folder 4. On the division of funding and job roles for the Freedom Forums, see "Meeting of the Joint ANA-AAAA Committee on Improvement of Public Understanding of Our Economic System [meeting minutes]" (January 6, 1949), 3, Thomas D'Arcy Brophy Papers, Wisconsin Historical Society: Box 10, Folder 1. For Wells's remarks about Harding College, see Wells, Correspondence to Thomas D'Arcy Brophy (January 26, 1949), quotation on 1.

37. On Freedom Forum corporate attendees, see Ken Wells, Correspondence to Thomas D'Arcy Brophy (February 24, 1949), Thomas D'Arcy Brophy Papers, Wisconsin Historical Society: Box 8, Folder 4. On featured speakers and guests,

NOTES TO PAGES 104–105

see "Harding College to Help Implement Plant and Plant-Community Program of Joint ANA-AAAA Committee," *AAAA Bulletin*, no. 1706 (February 18, 1949): 2, Thomas D'Arcy Brophy Papers, Wisconsin Historical Society: Box 8, Folder 4. On the political leanings of *Counterattack*, see A. J. Bauer, "Journalism History and Conservative Erasure," *American Journalism* 35, no. 1 (2018): 2–26. On the Chicago Employers' Association's tradition of advocacy for open shops, see Andrew W. Cohen, "The Racketeer's Progress: Commerce, Crime, and the Law in Chicago, 1900–1940," *Journal of Urban History* 29, no. 5 (2003): 519–630, 58. In 2021 Millikan's name was removed from buildings on the campus he founded due to his association with the eugenics movement, which was described by Caltech's Committee on Naming and Recognition as "sexist, racist, xenophobic, and inexcusable by any standard." See California Institute of Technology Media Relations, "Caltech to Remove the Names of Robert A. Millikan and Five Other Eugenics Proponents from Buildings, Honors, and Assets," *Caltech*, January 15, 2021, https://web .archive.org/web/20240124201926/https://www.caltech.edu/about/news/caltech-to -remove-the-names-of-robert-a-millikan-and-five-other-eugenics-proponents. For Belding's report to the Joint Committee on Improvement, see Belding, Memo to Thomas D'Arcy Brophy, Enclosure A, 2. On the end of the relationship with Harding College, see Faustin J. Solon, Frederic R. Gamble, and Paul B. West, "Statement of the Joint ANA-AAAA Committee on Improvement of Public Understanding of Our Economic System [attachment to correspondence from R. L. Scheidker to Thomas D'Arcy Brophy, March 3, 1950]" (n.d.), Thomas D'Arcy Brophy Papers, Wisconsin Historical Society: Box 10, Folder 2. On Harding's profile in the 1960s, see Maxwell, "A Shooting Star of Conservatism," 381–83. See also Hicks, *Sometimes in the Wrong but Never in Doubt*, 62–63.

38. On AAAA preference for a third party, see "Meeting of Operations Committee, AAAA [meeting minutes]" (September 8, 1948), see 9, Thomas D'Arcy Brophy Papers, Wisconsin Historical Society: Box 8, Folder 9. On the Joint Committee on Improvement's shift to a "creative and plans board," see "Meeting of the Joint ANA-AAAA Committee on Improvement of Public Understanding of Our Economic System [meeting minutes]" (January 6, 1949), 4.

39. The form of the "slidefilm" was a set of prepared slides, presented on a strip of film (also known as filmstrips); sound slidefilms came with a recorded voiceover. On slidefilms, see "Slidefilms a 'New' Medium," *Business Screen* 2, no. 9 (1948): 19.

40. On *This Is Our Problem*, see American Association of Advertising Agencies, *Bulletin*, no. 1951 (March 7, 1952), Thomas D'Arcy Brophy Papers, Wisconsin Historical Society: Box 10, Folder 2. On accomplishments related to Programs One and Two, see "Meeting of Research Group, Joint ANA-AAAA Committee on Improvement of Public Understanding of Our Economic System [meeting minutes]" (January 24, 1952), Thomas D'Arcy Brophy Papers, Wisconsin Historical Society: Box 10, Folder 2. On accomplishments related to Program Three, see "Summary: Joint ANA-AAAA Committee on Improvement of Public Understanding of Our

Economic System," 5–6. On Freedoms Foundation statements about the organization's goals and its links to an undeveloped educational program, see Brendan M. Jones, "Awards to Fortify American Way Designed to Match Nobel Prizes," *New York Times*, June 2, 1949, 1, https://www.proquest.com/docview/105615422/. On the Freedoms Foundation, see Kevin M. Kruse, *One Nation under God: How Corporate America Invented Christian America* (New York: Basic Books, 2015), 69–72, quotation on 72; on the links between corporate advocacy and public demonstrations of religious faith, see especially chapter 5, in which Kruse documents the Advertising Council's "Religion in American Life" campaign, launched shortly after the late 1940s "American Economic System" campaign, 130–38.

41. On committee assessments of the projects' influence on public opinion, see "Memorandum to the Research Group of the Joint ANA-AAAA Committee" (February 27, 1952), Thomas D'Arcy Brophy Papers, Wisconsin Historical Society: Box 10, Folder 2. On Psychological Corporation study results, see "Fourth Meeting of the Research Group, Joint ANA-AAAA Committee on Improvement of Public Understanding of Our Economic System [meeting minutes]" (March 3, 1952), quotations on 1, Thomas D'Arcy Brophy Papers, Wisconsin Historical Society: Box 10, Folder 2. On Opinion Research Corporation study results, see "Fifth Meeting of the Research Group, Joint ANA-AAAA Committee on Improvement of Public Understanding of Our Economic System [meeting minutes]" (March 10, 1952), quotations on 1, 2, Thomas D'Arcy Brophy Papers, Wisconsin Historical Society: Box 10, Folder 2.

42. Regarding the Brookings Institution's assessments of advertising as a technique for economic education, see C. W. McKee and H. G. Moulton, *A Survey of Economic Education* (Washington, DC: Brookings Institution, 1951), 57. On economic education media as propaganda, see Richard Braddock, "Films for Teaching Mass Communication," *English Journal* 44, no. 3 (1955): 156–67, quotation on 166.

43. On the question of whether the Joint Committee on Improvement should continue, see "Meeting of the Joint ANA-AAAA Committee on Improvement of Public Understanding of Our Economic System [meeting minutes]" (January 6, 1949). On the misinformation framing as possibly counterproductive, see undated memo, stamped as received July 22, 1952, 14, Thomas D'Arcy Brophy Papers, Wisconsin Historical Society: Box 10, Folder 2. On the Joint Committee on Improvement's waning leadership role, see "Meeting of Joint ANA-AAAA Committee on Improvement of Public Understanding of Our Economic System [meeting minutes]" (July 14, 1952), 3, Thomas D'Arcy Brophy Papers, Wisconsin Historical Society: Box 10, Folder 2.

44. On market segmentation for Programs One and Two and the question of whether Program Three should be handled by the advertising industry, see "Meeting of Joint ANA-AAAA Committee on Improvement of Public Understanding of Our Economic System [meeting minutes]" (n.d., marked received July 22, 1952), 16, Thomas D'Arcy Brophy Papers, Wisconsin Historical Society: Box 10, Folder 2.

NOTES TO PAGES 107–111

On the shift to focus on marketing, see the Joint ANA-AAAA Committee on Understanding of the Economic System, Memorandum (meeting minutes) (June 15, 1955), Thomas D'Arcy Brophy Papers, Wisconsin Historical Society: Box 10, Folder 2.

Chapter Five

1. On JCEE's rejection of "management-run" economic education programs, see Fones-Wolf, *Selling Free Enterprise*, 206.

2. On the CED's founding goals, vision, institutional lineage, and membership, see Robert M. Collins, "Positive Business Responses to the New Deal: The Roots of the Committee for Economic Development, 1933–1942," *Business History Review* 52, no. 3 (Autumn, 1978): 369–91.

3. On the CED's policy positions, see Fones-Wolf, *Selling Free Enterprise*, 204–6, quotation on 206; "Tax Cut of Billions Declared Possible: Economic Committee Businessmen Take View Opposite to Truman," *Los Angeles Times*, January 8, 1950, 35, retrieved from https://www.proquest.com/docview/166038562; and also "Controls Branded Peril to Economy: Flexible Wage-Price Ceilings Are Urged by Committee for Economic Development," *New York Times*, December 2, 1951, 65, retrieved from https://www.proquest.com/docview/112091747.

4. On Benton's contributions to the CED, see Collins, "Positive Business Responses to the New Deal," 384–88; on shared values between the two factions of economic education in the 1940s and 1950s, see Fones-Wolf, *Selling Free Enterprise*, quotation on 206.

5. On CED reluctance to prompt questions about their impartiality, see "Meeting of Joint ANA-AAAA Committee on Improvement of Public Understanding of Our Economic System [meeting minutes]" (July 1, 1948, quotation on 2, Thomas D'Arcy Brophy Papers, Wisconsin Historical Society: Box 10, Folder 1. On business outreach to schools, see Fones-Wolf, *Selling Free Enterprise*, 197–204. On NELA and the public scandal around its influence campaigns, see Oreskes and Conway, *The Big Myth*, 54–57. On the NAM "textbook controversy," see S. Alexander Rippa, "The Textbook Controversy and the Free Enterprise Campaign, 1940–1941," *History of Education Journal* 9, no. 3 (Spring 1958): 49–58; Rippa, *Education in a Free Society*, 242–45 and Oreskes and Conway, *The Big Myth*, 99–100.

6. On education and politics, see Ronald Lora, "Education: Schools as Crucible," in *Reshaping America: Society and Institutions, 1945–1960*, ed. Robert H. Bremner and Gary W. Reichard (Columbia: Ohio State University Press, 1982): 223–60, quotations on 226–27.

7. G. Derwood Baker, "The Joint Council on Economic Education," *Journal of Educational Sociology* 23, no. 7 (1950): 389–96, quotations on 391; see also M. L. Frankel, "The Joint Council on Economic Education: The First Ten Years," *Bulletin*

of the National Association of Secondary-School Principals 42, no. 240 (1958): 124–28. On CED business-educational committee membership, see "Economic Development Group Studies Education Activities," *La Crosse [WI] Tribune*, March 3, 1949, 22, https://www.newspapers.com/image/510895261. The language of "economic understanding" surfaced in an announcement of the group's founding; see Baker, "The Joint Council on Economic Education," 393.

8. On the workshop's methods, see Baker, "The Joint Council on Economic Education"; on national income analysis, see Timothy Mitchell, "Economists and the Economy in the Twentieth Century," in *The Politics of Method in the Human Sciences: Positivism and Its Epistemological Others*, ed. George Steinmetz (Durham, NC: Duke University Press, 2005), 126–41, quotations on 130, 136, and 140; see 135–36 on concepts of the nation and 139–40 on branding and promotion.

9. On Paul Hoffman's work on the Marshall Plan, see Francis X. Sutton, "The Ford Foundation: The Early Years," *Daedalus* 116, no. 1 (1987): 41–91, quotation on 53. Folsom and Hoffman quotations sourced from Joseph A. Loftus, "New C.E.D. Head Calls for Unity to Keep Output, Employment High," *New York Times*, May 19, 1950, 16, retrieved from https://www.proquest.com/docview/111709627. On scientific anticommunism, see Michael Curtin, "The Discourse of 'Scientific Anti-Communism' in the 'Golden Age' of Documentary," *Cinema Journal* 32, no. 1 (Autumn 1992): 3–25, quotation on 5.

10. Conceptually, I see some resonance with journalism scholar Dan Hallin's analysis of journalistic discourses during the Vietnam War: Hallin found that newspaper journalists were likely to practice "journalistic virtues" of objectivity, falling within what he calls the "sphere of legitimate controversy," whereas television reports tended more to stick to the "sphere of consensus," casting the war in terms of "good" and "evil." See Daniel C. Hallin, *The Uncensored War: The Media and Vietnam* (Berkeley: University of California Press, 1989), 115–21, quotations on 116, 188.

11. On the JCEE's 1950 workshop offerings, see "Summer Workshops: Economic Education Courses to Be Given for 700 Teachers," *New York Times*, April 2, 1950, 149, quotations on 149, retrieved from https://www.proquest.com/docview/111337059. On the JCEE's early 1950s growth and funding, see Benjamin Fine, "Joint Council's Workshops Help Public School Teachers Understand Economic Problems," *New York Times*, January 6, 1952, E9, https://www.proquest.com/docview/112250893/; see also "Learning Practical Economics," *New York Times*, April 3, 1955, E11, https://www.proquest.com/docview/113334140. On Hoffman's time at the Ford Foundation, see Francis X. Sutton, "The Ford Foundation: The Early Years." On funding for the JCEE in the 1950s, see Fine, "Joint Council's Workshops Help Public School Teachers Understand Economic Problems," E11; "Joint Council on Economic Education Trustees Newsletter" (January 1959), Box 14, Folder Trustee Newsletter, Joint Council on Economic Education Papers, Hoover Institution Library and Archives, Stanford University, Stanford, CA. On Ford Foundation support, see also Bess Furman, "Conference Spurs Econom-

NOTES TO PAGES 114–117

ics Study: Joint Council Is Told Schools Require Assistance from Community Groups," *New York Times*, May 10, 1951, 33, retrieved from https://www.proquest.com/docview/111803633.

12. Fred Turner, *The Democratic Surround: Multimedia and American Liberalism from World War II to the Psychedelic Sixties* (Chicago: University of Chicago Press, 2013), 201–2, quotation on 201. On the global implications of economic education, see "Report to the Trustees of the Ford Foundation," Ford Foundation (September 27, 1950), quotations on 13, 20–21, https://www.fordfoundation.org/wp-content/uploads/2015/05/1950-annual-report.pdf.

13. On economic education as a growing trend, see Daniel M. Burnham, "School Days: Business-Backed Groups Help Enliven, Expand High School Economics," *Wall Street Journal*, October 26, 1955, 1, retrieved from https://www.proquest.com/docview/132201622; also "Learning Practical Economics," *New York Times*, April 3, 1955, E11. On *I, Pencil*, see also Glickman, *Free Enterprise*, 182–88. On "How Our Business System Operates" (HOBSO) see Fones-Wolf, *Selling Free Enterprise*, 83–84 and 205.

14. Ryan Boyle, "A Red Moon over the Mall: The Sputnik Panic and Domestic America," *Journal of American Culture* 31, no. 4, (December, 2008): 373–82. Boyle quotes *Time* magazine's evocative description of Sputnik's beeps as "throaty" from its feature "Into the Orbit," *Time Magazine*, October 21, 1957, 50–51, https://content.time.com/time/subscriber/article/0,33009,937986,00.html. On the US Office of Education findings, see Benjamin Fine, "Soviet Education Far Ahead of U.S. in Science Stress," *New York Times*, November 11, 1957, 1, 11, retrieved from https://www.proquest.com/docview/114316648/.

15. Fine, "Soviet Education Far Ahead of U.S. in Science Stress," 11, quotation on 11.

16. On educational mandates, see Campbell F. Scribner, "'Make Your Voice Heard': Communism in the High School Curriculum, 1958–1968," *History of Education Quarterly* 52, no. 3 (August, 2012): 351–69, especially 357–58. On the social upheaval and questioning of US prosperity, see Boyle, "A Red Moon over the Mall: The Sputnik Panic and Domestic America."

17. For the initial editorial, see "Science and Our Society," *New York Times*, November 11, 1957, 28, retrieved from https://www.proquest.com/docview/114304044/. For Fersh's reply, see George L. Fersh, "Social Aspects of Science: Linking Science and Economics," *New York Times*, November 16, 1957, 18, quotation on 18, retrieved from https://www.proquest.com/docview/114114915.

18. On *Soviet Progress vs. American Enterprise*, see Harry Schwartz, "Briefing on Russia," *New York Times*, March 23, 1958, BR14, retrieved from https://www.proquest.com/docview/114611209. For Neal's comments, see "Economic Growth Called a Weapon," *New York Times*, June 8, 1958, 75, retrieved from https://www.proquest.com/docview/114585788; and "Free Economy Put Ahead of Soviets," *New York Times*, August 7, 1958, 16, retrieved from https://www.proquest.com

/docview/114407357. On the Purdue Opinion Poll, see Joan Beck, "Teen-Agers' Views on Free Enterprise: Ideas Less Socialistic than Decade Ago," *Chicago Daily Tribune*, March 6, 1958, C9, https://www.proquest.com/docview/182141817.

19. On the National Defense Education Act, see Arthur S. Flemming, "The Philosophy and Objectives of the National Defense Education Act," *Annals of the American Academy of Political and Social Science* 327, no. 1 (January 1, 1960): 132–38; Wayne J. Urban, *More than Science and Sputnik: The National Defense Education Act of 1958* (Tuscaloosa: University of Alabama Press, 2018), quotation on xi, see in particular chapter 4 on educational organizations' strategic use of the crisis.

20. On Bach (and the Ford Foundation's influences on graduate business study in the US), see Rakesh Khurana, *From Higher Aims to Hired Hands: The Social Transformation of Business Schools and the Unfulfilled Promise of Management as a Profession* (Princeton, NJ: Princeton University Press, 2007), especially chapter 6. On defining educational benchmarks for high school students, see "News Notes: Classroom and Campus; Yardsticks for Judging a School's Quality; Study of High School Economics," *New York Times*, November 13, 1960, E9, quotation on E9, https://www.proquest.com/docview/114929804. For Bach's comments on educational reform, see Fred M. Hechinger, "Economists Chart Teaching Reform: Education Survey Seeks to End 'Illiteracy' in Subject Found in High Schools," *New York Times*, March 6, 1961, 1, quotations on 1, retrieved from https://www.proquest.com/docview/115238948/.

21. On JCEE study materials, see "Economists Offer New Studies Plan," *New York Times*, October 6, 1961, 37, retrieved from https://www.proquest.com/docview/115247230. On *The American Economy*, see Joint Council on Economic Education, "The Case for Business Support of the Council's New Program for Improving Economic Education in the Secondary Schools: Visual Material Used in a Presentation to a Group of Business Leaders at a Dinner Given by Roger Blough and George Champion" (April 4, 1964), quotation on slide 14, Box 29, Folder Fund Raising 1964–67, Joint Council on Economic Education Papers, Hoover Institution Library and Archives, Stanford University, Stanford, CA. On Ford Foundation grants and national JCEE programs, see "Economists Offer New Studies Plan," 37. For press discourses comparing economic education to the reform of sciences education, see Hechinger, "Economists Chart Teaching Reform," quotation on 1.

22. National Task Force on Economic Education, *Economic Education in the Schools: A Report of the National Task Force on Economic Education* (New York: Committee for Economic Development, September 1961), quotations on 9, 13, and 14. On science and citizenship, see Audra J. Wolfe, *Freedom's Laboratory: The Cold War Struggle for the Soul of Science* (Baltimore, MD: Johns Hopkins University Press, 2018), 137–38, quotation on 138.

23. National Task Force on Economic Education, *Economic Education in the Schools*, quotations on 25, 71, 61. On Problems of Democracy courses, see Scribner, "Make Your Voice Heard," 354.

NOTES TO PAGES 120–124

24. On the authority of documents, see Matthew S. Hull, "The File: Agency, Authority, and Autography in an Islamabad Bureaucracy," *Language and Communication* 23 (2003): 287–314. JoAnne Yates and Wanda J. Orlikowski, "Genres of Organization Communication: A Structurational Approach to Studying Communication and Media," *Academy of Management Review* 17, no. 2 (1992): 299–326, quotation on 301.

25. Wanda J. Orlikowski and JoAnne Yates, "Genre Repertoire: The Structuring of Communicative Practices in Organizations," *Administrative Science Quarterly* 39, no. 4 (December 1994): 541–74, 542.

26. National Task Force on Economic Education, *Economic Education in the Schools*, quotations on 5, 9–10, 76. On assertions of independence, see "Should High Schools Teach Economics?," *Business Week*, October 7, 1961, 145–46, quotation on 145. Clipping sourced from Box 29, Folder American Economy TV Course, Joint Council on Economic Education Papers, Hoover Institution Library and Archives, Stanford University, Stanford, CA.

27. For the editorial, see "Statism for Sophomores," *Wall Street Journal*, December 6, 1961, 18, quotation on 18, retrieved from https://www.proquest.com /docview/132639676. For Bach's response, see George Leland Bach, "Dean Bach's Letter," *Wall Street Journal*, January 9, 1962, 18, quotations on 18, retrieved from https://www.proquest.com/docview/132846688. For the subsequent editorial comment, see "Review and Outlook: Teaching or Preaching?," *Wall Street Journal*, January 9, 1962, 18, quotation on 18, retrieved from https://www.proquest.com /docview/132788593.

28. On CED leadership's disagreement with the task force report, see Gene Currivan, "Economic ABC's Urged for Youth: Better Training of Teachers of Subject also Proposed," *New York Times*, March 19, 1962, 32, quotations on 32, retrieved from https://www.proquest.com/docview/115737220. For the CED statement, see "The C.E.D. Takes a Second Look," *Wall Street Journal*, March 20, 1962, 18, quotations on 18, https://www.proquest.com/docview/132754510.

29. For production information including sponsorship details, see Learning Resources Institute, "Approved Draft Prospectus for *The American Economy*: A Proposed Year Course on a Nationwide Television Network" (n.d.), 4, Box 29, Folder American Economy TV Course, Joint Council on Economic Education Papers, Hoover Institution Library and Archives, Stanford University, Stanford, CA.

30. Anna McCarthy, *The Citizen Machine: Governing by Television in 1950s America* (New York: New Press, 2010), quotation on 21. Learning Resources Institute, "Approved Draft Prospectus for *The American Economy*," quotation on 3. On the importance of knowledge and emotions, see Learning Resources Institute, "College of the Air: The American Economy [promotional brochure]," (New York: Learning Resources Institute, September 1962), 3–4, Box 29, Folder American Economy TV Course, Joint Council on Economic Education Papers, Hoover Institution Library and Archives, Stanford University, Stanford, CA.

236   NOTES TO PAGES 124–127

31. John R. Coleman and Kenneth O. Alexander, *The American Economy: College of the Air Television Study Guide* (New York: McGraw-Hill, 1962), iv, Box 39, Joint Council on Economic Education Papers, Hoover Institution Library and Archives, Stanford University, Stanford, CA. Perry J. Molinaro, "Educator Explains Whys of TV Course," *Pittsburgh Courier*, October 20, 1962, 17, quotation on 17, retrieved from https://www.proquest.com/docview/202489366.

32. For descriptions of the target audiences for the telecourse, see Learning Resources Institute (n.d.), "Approved Draft Prospectus for *The American Economy*," 2. On supporting materials, see Coleman and Alexander, *The American Economy: College of the Air Television Study Guide*, vi.

33. On the broadcast coverage and viewership of the series, see Phillip Saunders, "The Effectiveness of 'The American Economy' in Training Secondary School Teachers," *American Economic Review* 54, no. 4 (June 1964): 396–403, see 396. On topics covered, see Learning Resources Institute, "College of the Air: The American Economy." For review of the series premiere, see "Television Review: The American Economy," *Variety*, September 26, 1962, 31, quotation on 31, https://www.proquest.com/docview/1017092002.

34. On documentary television, see Curtin, "The Discourse of 'Scientific Anti-Communism' in the 'Golden Age' of Documentary," quotations on 5. On CBS publicity for both series, see "Radio-Television: Stanton Carries Torch via Closed-Circuit TV for Economics Specials," *Variety*, August 15, 1962, 38, quotation on 38, retrieved from https://www.proquest.com/docview/1032412780. For promotion of *Money Talks*, see Columbia Broadcasting System, "Week-Long Series on CBS: Money Talks [display advertisement]," *Wall Street Journal*, August 20, 1962, 5, retrieved from https://www.proquest.com/docview/132747895. On *Money Talks*, see John Shanley, "TV: Economic Series; 'Money Talks' starts 5 shows on CBS," *New York Times*, August 21, 1962, 67, https://www.proquest.com/docview/116168 774. See also "T.V. Spotlight: Series to Study US Economy," *Austin American [American-Statesman]*, August 19, 1962, E9, retrieved from https://www.proquest.com/docview/1609620347. On the framing of freedom as a foil to communism, see Curtin, "The Discourse of 'Scientific Anti-Communism' in the 'Golden Age' of Documentary," quotations on 8.

35. On the concept of flow, see Williams, *Television: Technology and Cultural Form*, quotation on 92. For the Union Carbide advertisement, see Union Carbide Corporation, "Let's Look at the Price of Eggs [advertisement]," Joint Council on Economic Education Records, Box 23, Folder 5, Hoover Institution Library and Archives. The advertisement appeared in many popular outlets including in *Scientific American*, September 1, 1962, 112.

36. On the announcement of DEEP and its initial distribution, see "News Notes: Classroom and Campus," *New York Times*, June 7, 1964, E11, https://www.proquest.com/docview/115804048, and Joint Council on Economic Education, "Developmental Economic Education Program: First Annual Report" (n.d., cov-

NOTES TO PAGES 128–131

ers September 1, 1964–December 31, 1965), Box 16, Joint Council on Economic Education Papers, Hoover Institution Library and Archives, Stanford University, Stanford, CA.

37. For fundraising rhetoric around economic education, see Joint Council on Economic Education, "The Case for Business Support of the Council's New Program for Improving Economic Education in the Secondary Schools: Visual Material Used in a Presentation to a Group of Business Leaders at a Dinner Given by Roger Blough and George Champion" (April 4, 1964), quotations on slide 3. See also slides 10 and 14.

38. Joint Council on Economic Education, quotation on slide 6, 7; emphasis in original.

39. Joint Council on Economic Education, quotation on slide 2; for budget details, see slide 25.

40. Fred M. Hechinger, "News of the Week in Education: Economics 'In,' " *New York Times*, February 14, 1965, E7, https://www.proquest.com/docview/116758016. Dorothy Townsend, "Experiment in Learning: See Billy, See Billy Sell; He's Studying Economics," *Los Angeles Times*, March 14, 1967, A6, quotations on A6, https://www.proquest.com/docview/155674271.

41. On inflation statistics, see World Bank, *Inflation, Consumer Prices for the United States* (FPCPITOTLZGUSA), retrieved from FRED, Federal Reserve Bank of St. Louis, https://fred.stlouisfed.org/series/FPCPITOTLZGUSA, September 30, 2020. On anti-inflation activism, see "Inflation: The Consumer Revolt," *Newsweek*, September 15, 1969, 74, 79, quotation on 74, https://www.proquest.com/docview/1866711131.

42. Joint Council on Economic Education, *Annual Report: Twentieth Anniversary Report, 1949/1969* (New York: Joint Council on Economic Education, 1969), quotation on 2; see also 10, Box 18, Joint Council on Economic Education Papers, Hoover Institution Library and Archives, Stanford University, Stanford, CA. On the American Bankers Association–affiliated film *Economic Stability*, see Joint Council on Economic Education, *Trustees Newsletter*, April 1970, 3, Box 14, Folder Trustee Newsletter, Joint Council on Economic Education Papers, Hoover Institution Library and Archives, Stanford University, Stanford, CA; and Lawrence S. Moss, "Film and the Transmission of Economic Knowledge: A Report," *Journal of Economic Literature* 17 (1979): 1005–19, reprinted in *American Journal of Economics and Sociology* 69, no. 1 (2010): 290–320. On Advertising Council anti-inflation campaigns, see Griffith, *The Selling of America*. On Advertising Council contributions and circulation in 1967 and 1968, see "A Good '68 for Ad Council," *Broadcasting*, June 23, 1969, 100, retrieved from https://worldradiohistory.com/Archive-BC/BC-1969/1969-06-30-BC.pdf.

43. Edwin Dale Jr., "The Dreadful Economic Choice That Faces Mr. Nixon," *New York Times Sunday Magazine* November 24, 1968, SM56, quotations on SM56, https://www.proquest.com/docview/118405462.

44. On Thompson's role in the campaign, see Associated Press. "Let's Not Be 'Piggy': Ad Campaign Aimed at Consumer; 'Spend More Prudently,'" *Cincinnati Enquirer*, August 10, 1969, 35, https://www.proquest.com/docview/1888359281/. Thompson quoted in Ray Nelson, "'Stop Inflation' Campaign Launched," *Herald-Journal* (Logan, Utah), September 23, 1969, 8, https://www.newspapers.com/image /687502076/.

45. Advertising Council, "4 out of 5 Americans Will Flunk This Piggy Test [advertisement]." As appearing in the *Brattleboro [VA] Reformer*, January 30, 1970, retrieved from https://www.newspapers.com/image/548383665/. For *New York Times* coverage, see Philip H. Dougherty, "Advertising: Council Will Battle Inflation," *New York Times*, July 10, 1969, 58, https://www.proquest.com/docview/118716405. On the roles of government and individuals in fighting inflation, see Advertising Council, "Let's All Be a Little Less Piggy. And Stop Inflation [display advertisement]," *Chicago Tribune*, September 7, 1969, C14, retrieved from https://www.pro quest.com/docview/169784557.

46. Joint Council on Economic Education, *Inflation Can Be Stopped: Steps for a Balanced Economy* (New York: Joint Council on Economic Education, 1969), quotations on 1, 12, 13, 27, Box 33, Folder Advertising Council Campaign 1969—A Failure, Joint Council on Economic Education Papers, Hoover Institution Library and Archives, Stanford University, Stanford, CA.

47. Joint Council on Economic Education, *Inflation Can Be Stopped: Steps for a Balanced Economy*, see 22, quotation on 26.

48. On the surcharge as a "war tax," see Albert R. Hunt, "Income-Tax Surcharge Expires Tonight, but Disputes over Its Effects Rage On," *Wall Street Journal*, June 30, 1970, 10, https://www.proquest.com/docview/133505235. On Nixon's advocacy for the surcharge, see Phillip Warden, "Nixon Aims Big Guns to Win Income Tax Surcharge Fight," *Chicago Tribune*, July 23, 1969, 5, retrieved from https://www.proquest.com/docview/175972479. On concerns about perceptions of bias, see Robert P. Keim, Correspondence to M. L. Frankel (June 24, 1969), 1, Box 33, Folder Advertising Council Campaign: A Failure, Joint Council on Economic Education Papers, Hoover Institution Library and Archives, Stanford University, Stanford, CA. On Nixon's arguments to Congress, see Associated Press, "Dems Press for Budget Trims as Surtax Price," *Ironwood [MI] Daily Globe*, March 27, 1969, 8, retrieved from https://www.newspapers.com/image/55079226/.

49. For Nixon's quoted comments, see Murray Seeger, "Madison Avenue Readies Attack on Inflation," *Los Angeles Times*, May 19, 1969, part 3, 10, retrieved from https://www.newspapers.com/image/383409401/. For representation of "government levers," see Joint Council on Economic Education, *Inflation Can Be Stopped: Steps for a Balanced Economy*, 14–15.

50. For James O'Hara's remarks, see US Congress, *Congressional Record* 115, part 11 (June 2, 1969): 14522–23, quotations on 14523, retrieved from https://www.con gress.gov/bound-congressional-record/1969/06/02/extensions-of-remarks-section.

NOTES TO PAGES 138–140   239

On concerns about political bias, see Nathaniel Goldfinger, Correspondence to M. L. Frankel (June 24, 1969), Joint Council on Economic Education Records Group, Box 33, Folder "Advertising Council Campaign 1969: A Failure," Hoover Institution Library and Archives, Stanford University, Stanford, CA. On avoiding further confusion between the Advertising Council and other organizations, see Keim, Correspondence to M. L. Frankel, 1. On the eventual wind-down of the surcharge, see Hunt, "Income-Tax Surcharge Expires Tonight, but Disputes over Its Effects Rage On," 10.

51. On the campaign's poor performance and negative public reception, see M. L. Frankel, Correspondence to Robert Keim (December 30, 1969), 1, Box 33, Folder "Advertising Council Campaign: A Failure," Joint Council on Economic Education Papers, Hoover Institution Library and Archives, Stanford University, Stanford, CA. Eda Finkel, "Letters from Courier News Readers: Resents Insult," *Courier-News* (Bridgewater, NJ), October 13, 1969, 22, retrieved from https:// www.newspapers.com/image/221981325/. For *Inflation Can Be Stopped* circulation figures, see Frankel, Correspondence to Robert Keim (December 30, 1969), 1, Box 33, Folder "Advertising Council Campaign: A Failure," Joint Council on Economic Education Papers, Hoover Institution Library and Archives, Stanford University, Stanford, CA. For Bowen quotation, see Philip G. Dougherty, "Advertising Council to Aid Ford's Drive," *New York Times*, October 9, 1974, 25, https://www.proquest .com/docview/120034543.

52. On Madden's concerns, see Carl H. Madden, Correspondence to M. L. Frankel (December 17, 1969, 2, Box 33, Folder "Advertising Council Campaign: A Failure," Joint Council on Economic Education Papers, Hoover Institution Library and Archives, Stanford University, Stanford, CA. The Benton and Bowles campaign copywriters' seeming lack of awareness about these issues would have been consistent with the firm's status as a relative latecomer to the countercultural creative wave that had swept the US advertising industry in the mid-1960s; on Benton and Bowles's position regarding countercultural forces in the advertising industry, see Thomas Frank, *The Conquest of Cool: Business Culture, Counterculture and the Rise of Hip Consumerism* (Chicago: University of Chicago Press, 1997), 102. On Frankel's concerns, see Frankel, Correspondence to Robert Keim (December 30, 1969), quotation on 2.

53. Chapter 3 examines Barton's concerns. See Barton, Correspondence to Thomas D'Arcy Brophy, quotations on 2. On the results of prior anti-inflation campaigns, see Elmer Roessner, "Business Today: A Nutty Campaign," *Johnson City [TN] Press*, July 18, 1969, 4, retrieved from https://www.newspapers.com/image/589968719/. On Barton's concerns, see Barton, Correspondence to Thomas D'Arcy Brophy, 2.

54. For Lee's comments, see Alfred McClung Lee, *Is Anybody Listening?* (book review), *American Journal of Sociology* 58, no. 4 (January 1953): 437–38, quotation on 437.

240   NOTES TO PAGES 140–143

55. For JCEE operations and DEEP implementation figures, see Joint Council on Economic Education, *Annual Report: Twentieth Anniversary Report, 1949/1969*, 1. On *The American Economy* circulation figures, see Joint Council on Economic Education, "A Status Report on 'The American Economy' TV Course, 1962–1970" (n.d.), Box 29, Folder American Economy TV Course, Joint Council on Economic Education Papers, Hoover Institution Library and Archives, Stanford University, Stanford, CA. On JCEE fundraising and contributors, see Joint Council on Economic Education, "Contribution Status Report (for the Fiscal Year Ending June 30, 1971) through December 31, 1970" (n.d.), Box 14, Joint Council on Economic Education Papers, Hoover Institution Library and Archives, Stanford University, Stanford, CA.

Chapter Six

1. On the campaign, see Philip H. Dougherty, "Council Shapes Huge Campaign," *New York Times*, December 4, 1975, 71, https://www.proquest.com/doc view/120541955/, and Beder, *Free Market Missionaries*, 65–69. On the goals of the campaign and for images of still and television advertisements, see Advertising Council, "Every American Ought to Know What It Says: A Public Service Campaign of the Advertising Council, Inc." (poster) (New York: Advertising Council, n.d.), quotation on top left, Advertising Council Papers, University Library at the University of Illinois, Records Group 13/12/219, Box 12, Communications: Advertising and Marketing Files, 1969–82, AES Reading Material folder.

2. For advertisement copy details across billboards, print ads, transit ads, and broadcast, see Advertising Council, "Every American Ought to Know What It Says: A Public Service Campaign of the Advertising Council, Inc." (poster). For critique of the campaign, see Bill Mandel, "What Is the Public Interest?," *San Francisco Examiner*, November 30, 1976, 25, https://www.newspapers.com/image/461032838.

3. Advertising Council, *The American Economic System . . . and Your Part in It* (New York: Advertising Council, 1976), quotation from foreword.

4. For 1978 circulation figures, see Philip H. Dougherty, "Advertising: Iroquois Beating Its Own Drum," *New York Times*, May 24, 1978, D22, https://www.proquest .com/docview/123694291. For funding details, see Advertising Council, "Highlights of Results and Progress: The Advertising Council's Public Service Campaign on the American Economic System" (October 1, 1977), 1, Advertising Council Papers, University Library at the University of Illinois, Records Group 13/2/305, Box 30, Washington Office Subject File, 1942–77, "American Economic System" folder. On distribution methods, see Advertising Council, *Public Service Advertising Bulletin* 52 (March/April, 1978): quotation on 2, Advertising Council Papers, University Library at the University of Illinois, Records Group 13/12/219, Box 12, Washington Office Subject File, 1942–77, "American Economic System" folder.

NOTES TO PAGES 143–147

5. For an example of Advertising Council assurances of avoiding bias, see Philip H. Dougherty, "Advertising: Campaign on Economy Weighed," *New York Times*, July 22, 1975, 58, https://www.proquest.com/docview/120321310.

6. On the Fairness Doctrine and avoidance of controversy, see Patricia Aufderheide, "After the Fairness Doctrine: Controversial Broadcast Programming and the Public Interest," *Journal of Communication* 40, no. 3 (Summer 1990): 47–72, see 52, and Wendy Melillo, *How McGruff and the Crying Indian Changed America: A History of Iconic Ad Council Campaigns* (Washington, DC: Smithsonian Books, 2013), quotations on 10; on FCC regulations, see Victor Pickard, "The Battle over the FCC Blue Book: Determining the Role of Broadcast Media in a Democratic Society, 1945–8," *Media, Culture & Society* 33, no. 2 (2011): 171–91, quotation on 172; on public interest obligations, see Aufderheide, "After the Fairness Doctrine," and Craig Lamay, "Public Service Advertising, Broadcasters, and the Public Interest," *Shouting to Be Heard: Public Service Advertising in a New Media Age* (report) (Menlo Park, CA: Henry J. Kaiser Family Foundation, 2002), 8.

7. On the simplification often seen in corporate-sponsored economic education materials, see also Waterhouse, *Lobbying America: The Politics of Business from Nixon to NAFTA*, 71. On categorization of producers and consumers, see Advertising Council, *The American Economic System . . . and Your Part in It* (New York: Advertising Council, 1976), 5. On the conflation of individuals and firms in neoliberal thought, see Wendy Brown, *Undoing the Demos: Neoliberalism's Stealth Revolution* (Brooklyn, NY: Zone Books, 2015), quotation on 27.

8. On inflation in the 1970s, see World Bank, *Inflation, Consumer Prices for the United States* (FPCPITOTLZGUSA); see also Patrick J. Akard, "Corporate Mobilization and Political Power: The Transformation of U.S. Economic Policy in the 1970s," *American Sociological Review* 57, no. 5 (1992): 597–615, quotation on 601.

9. On corporate profit rates, see Akard, "Corporate Mobilization and Political Power: The Transformation of U.S. Economic Policy in the 1970s." On consumer activism, increased regulation, and legislation in the 1970s, see Cohen, *A Consumer's Republic*, esp. 358–61, quotation on 358. On managerial sentiments of victimhood, see Akard, 601–2.

10. For Meeds's comments, see Lloyd Meeds, "A Legislative History of OSHA," *Gonzaga Law Review* 9, no. 2 (Winter 1974): 327–48, quotations on 329. On the influence of color television, see William D. Ruckelshaus, "Environmental Protection: A Brief History of the Environmental Movement in America and the Implications Abroad," *Environmental Law* 15, no. 3 (Spring 1985): 455–70, quotation on 456.

11. On rhetorics of besiegement, see also, Carey, *Taking the Risk Out of Democracy*; Fones-Wolf, *Selling Free Enterprise*; and Phillips-Fein, *Invisible Hands*, among others. For examples of executives' self-reports of their own position in 1970s US society, see Leonard Silk and David Vogel, *Ethics and Profits: The Crisis of Confidence in American Business* (New York: Touchstone/Simon and Schuster,

1976), quotations on 24, 27. For further discussion of the "intense anger and pessimism" expressed in *Ethics and Profits*, see Waterhouse, *Lobbying America*, 15–16, quotation on 16. On Mobil Oil's image advertising, see Vanessa Murphree and James Aucoin, "The Energy Crisis and the Media: Mobil Oil Corporation's Debate with the Media, 1973–1983," *American Journalism* 27, no. 2 (Spring 2010): 7–30, quotation on 9.

12. Milton Friedman, "A Friedman Doctrine: The Social Responsibility of Business Is to Increase Its Profits," *New York Times Magazine*, September 13, 1970, 32–33, 122, 124, 126, https://www.proquest.com/docview/117933451.

13. Friedman, quotation on 33.

14. For Powell's memo, see Lewis F. Powell Jr., "Confidential Memorandum: Attack on Free Enterprise System" (August 23, 1971), Washington and Lee School of Law Scholarly Commons, https://scholarlycommons.law.wlu.edu/powellmemo/1, quotations on 1, 2; on the memo as culmination of prior decades' free enterprise thought, see Glickman, *Free Enterprise*, 20, 22–44.

15. Powell Jr., "Confidential Memorandum: Attack on Free Enterprise System," quotations on 8, 25. On the organizational power of the memo, see Waterhouse, *Lobbying America*, 59–60.

16. On the reinvigoration of the FTC and its pursuit of the advertising industry, see Molly Niesen, "The Little Old Lady Has Teeth: The U.S. Federal Trade Commission and the Advertising Industry, 1970–1973," *Advertising and Society Review* 12, no. 4 (2012): n.p. For Seaman's comments, see J. Robert Moskin, *The Case for Advertising: Highlights of the Industry Presentation to the Federal Trade Commission* (New York: American Association of Advertising Agencies, 1973), 15–16. On the Advertising Council's concerns about the citizenry and national values in the 1950s, see Robert H. Zeiger, "The Paradox of Plenty: The Advertising Council and the Post-Sputnik Crisis," *Advertising and Society Review* 4, no. 1 (2003).

17. Loevinger's advocacy for the virtues of advertising went well beyond these comments—see, for example, Lee Loevinger, "The Politics of Advertising," *William & Mary Law Review* 15, no. 1 (Fall 1973): 1–31. On the freedom to persuade, see Moskin, *The Case for Advertising: Highlights of the Industry Presentation to the Federal Trade Commission*, quotation on 23.

18. For Dillon's remarks, see Moskin, *The Case for Advertising: Highlights of the Industry Presentation to the Federal Trade Commission*, 19.

19. For LaRoche's comments in favor of a campaign, see C. J. LaRoche, *Memo from C. J. LaRoche* (September 25, 1974), Records Group 13/2/220, Box 1, Advertising Council Papers, University Archives, University of Illinois, Urbana-Champaign. On wage-price controls, see Benjamin Waterhouse, "Mobilizing for the Market: Organized Business, Wage-Price Controls, and the Politics of Inflation, 1971–1974," *Journal of American History* 100, no. 2 (September 2013): 454–78, see 467–68.

20. For Dent's remarks, see Frederick B. Dent, "Statement of Request by the Secretary of Commerce Frederick B. Dent for an Advertising Council Campaign

NOTES TO PAGES 153–154 243

to Improve Public Understanding of and Knowledge about Our American Economic System" (October 23, 1974), Advertising Council Papers, University Archives, University of Illinois, Urbana-Champaign (Records Group 13/2/305, Box 24), quotations on 6; see also Frederick B. Dent, "Secretary Dent's Remarks to the Advertising Council, Chicago, Ill., October 23, 1974" as reproduced in the appendix of *Oversight Hearing on Commerce Department Payment to the National Advertising Council for the Promotion of the Free Enterprise System, Hearing before the Subcommittee of the Committee on Government Operations, House of Representatives, Ninety-fourth Congress, First Session, July 30, 1975* (October 21, 1975), 43–45, https://books.google.com/books?id=EwvRAAAAMAAJ. Appendixes to the transcript of the July 30, 1975, hearing on the Commerce Department's funding of the campaign suggest that the initial research was performed by Coordinated Research Interviewing Service (CRIS) prior to the official application for, and granting of, federal funds between December 1974 and March 1975; see US Congress, *Oversight Hearing on Commerce Department Payment to the National Advertising Council*. For Dent's remarks on "psychological conditions" contributing to inflation, see Brendan Jones, "Dent Says Goal Is to Ease Curbs," *New York Times*, July 10, 1973, 55, 59, quotation on 59, https://www.proquest.com /docview/119869660. For Burns's remarks, see Arthur F. Burns, "The Battle against Inflation," *New York Times*, August 16, 1974, 29, quotation on 29, https://www.pro quest.com/docview/120033956. On business advocates' resistance to arguments for economic controls on the basis of inflationary psychology, see Waterhouse, "Mobilizing for the Market," 474.

21. On CRIS's implementation of surveys, see Philip H. Dougherty, "Advertising: Simplifying the Dismal Science," *New York Times*, August 1, 1975, 54, https:// www.proquest.com/docview/120310227. On the survey questions, see Larry Isaacson and Helen Kelly, "The American Economic System (B): The Design of the Proposed Research" (New Haven, CT: Yale School of Management, 1978), exhibit 1-1 through exhibit 1-5, Advertising Council Papers, University Library at the University of Illinois, Records Group 13/2/220, Robert P. Keim Papers, 1967–87, Box 4, AES Yale School of Organization and Management Case Studies M14R through M23R folder. On sampling and demographics, see Compton Advertising, Research Department, "National Survey on the U.S. Economic System: A Study of Public Understanding and Attitudes; Summary of Principal Findings" (April 1975), 3–4, Advertising Council Papers, University Library at the University of Illinois, Records Group 13/2/305, Washington Office Subject File, 1942–97, "American Economic System" folder.

22. For public statements from the Advertising Council about the survey, see Advertising Council, "An Ad Council National Survey on the American Economic System" (promotional handout) (n.d.), n.p., Advertising Council Papers, University Library at the University of Illinois, Records Group 13/2/305, Washington Office Subject File, 1942–97, "American Economic System" folder.

23. On the public understanding of science as a rhetorical substitute for appreciation of scientists and industry, see Lewenstein, "The Meaning of 'Public Understanding of Science' in the United States after World War II." For Compton researchers' construction of demographic groups, see Compton Advertising, Research Department, "National Survey on the U.S. Economic System: A Study of Public Understanding and Attitudes; Summary of Principal Findings" (April 1975), quotation on 8. On managerial knowledge and subjectivity, see Nigel Thrift, *Knowing Capitalism* (London: SAGE Publications, 2005), quotation on 97.

24. For details of the contract with the Department of Commerce, see US Congress, *Oversight Hearing on Commerce Department Payment to the National Advertising Council for the Promotion of the Free Enterprise System, Hearing before the Subcommittee of the Committee on Government Operations, House of Representatives, Ninety-fourth Congress, First Session, July 30, 1975* (October 21, 1975), 52–55, https://books.google.com/books?id=EwvRAAAAMAAJ. For the final proposal, see Advertising Council, "Definitive Proposal to the U.S. Department of Commerce Submitted by the Advertising Council for an American Economic System Educational Campaign" (n.d.), quotation on 2, Advertising Council Papers, University Library at the University of Illinois, Records Group 13/2/305, Box 26, Washington Office Subject File, 1942–77 American Economic System—55 MPH, 1975, "American Economic System" folder. While the proposal itself is not dated, it incorporates proposed edits dated from April of 1975.

25. Bruce Howard, "The Advertising Council: Selling Lies," *Ramparts*, December 1974, 25–26, 28–32, quotation on 32.

26. On the public interest advertising movement, see Henry Weinstein, ". . . And Selling Truth," *Ramparts*, December 1974, 27, 64–65, quotation on 27. See also Philip H. Dougherty, "Advertising: Latest Rallying Cry," *New York Times*, September 26, 1973, 63, https://www.proquest.com/docview/119794600.

27. On dates of Fairness Doctrine as active policy, see Pickard, "The Battle Over the FCC Blue Book," 186. On Fairness Doctrine requirements, see Aufderheide, "After the Fairness Doctrine: Controversial Broadcast Programming and the Public Interest," 47. On activists' use of the Fairness Doctrine, see Philip H. Dougherty, "Advertising: 2 Views of Economic System," *New York Times*, March 15, 1976, 41, https://www.proquest.com/docview/123017905.

28. US Congress, *Oversight Hearing on Commerce Department Payment to the National Advertising Council for the Promotion of the Free Enterprise System, Hearing before the Subcommittee of the Committee on Government Operations, House of Representatives, Ninety-fourth Congress, First Session, July 30, 1975*, 1–57, retrieved from https://heinonline.org/HOL/Page?collection=congrec&handle=hein.cbhear/ohcnacfes0001&id=1&men_tab=srchresults; see in particular the exchange between Milligan and Rosenthal on 7.

29. US Congress, *Oversight Hearing on Commerce Department Payment to the National Advertising Council*, Howard J. Morgens quotation on 41, from his speech

NOTES TO PAGES 158–159   245

"The Profit Motive and the Public Interest" (n.d.), as reproduced in the appendix and cited on 2 of Rothenthal's opening statement; on discussion of Proctor and Gamble's ties to the Advertising Council, see 10. For Keim's later remarks, see Robert P. Keim, *A Time in Advertising's Camelot: The Memoirs of a Do-Gooder* (Madison, CT: Longview Press, 2002): 72–73, quotation on 72. For Rosenthal's characterization of the campaign, see US Congress, *Oversight Hearing on Commerce Department Payment to the National Advertising Council*, 35. On the General Accounting Office study, see Lucia Mouat, "Ad Council's Campaign Draws Counterattack," *Christian Science Monitor*, September 21, 1976, 4, quotation on 4, https://www.proquest.com/docview/511898651.

30. For press coverage comparing economics to science and technology, see Dougherty, "Campaign on Economy Weighed," quotation on 58. For Cummings's remarks to the press, see Dougherty, "Advertising: Simplifying the Dismal Science," quotation on 54, and for his remarks to the ANA, see Philip H. Dougherty, "Advertising: Council Shapes Huge Campaign," *New York Times*, December 4, 1975, 71, quotations on 71. On the planned launch schedule, see Advertising Council, "The Plan for a Major Public Service Mass Communication Program by the Advertising Council, Inc. to Help Create a Better Understanding of the American Economic System" (May 1976), Advertising Council Papers, University Library at the University of Illinois, Records Group 13/2/305, Box 28, Washington Office Subject File, 1942–77, "American Economic System" folder.

31. On the Peoples Bicentennial Commission, see Simon Hall, "'Guerrilla Theater . . . in the Guise of Red, White, and Blue Bunting': The People's Bicentennial Commission and the Politics of (Un-)Americanism," *Journal of American Studies* 52, no. 1 (2018): 114–36, quotation on 134; see also Eugene L. Meyer, "Bicentennial Commercialism: Red, White, Blue—and Green," *Washington Post, Times Herald*, August 15, 1972, A1, https://www.proquest.com/docview/148275772. For PBC's description of the campaign as "propaganda," see Dougherty, "Advertising: 2 Views of Economic System," quotation on 41. For press coverage of Rifkin, see James R. Dorsey, "People's Bicentennial Commission Invades Concord," *Nashua Telegraph*, April 18, 1975, 14; and Christopher B. Daly, "The Peoples Bicentennial Commission: Slouching towards the Economic Revolution," *Harvard Crimson*, April 28, 1975, n.p., https://www.thecrimson.com/article/1975/4/28/the-peoples-bicentennial -commission-pif-you/. On the competing launch events, see Philip H. Dougherty, "Advertising: Economic Drive Spurs Conflict," *New York Times*, April 22, 1976, 67. On previous PBC event takeovers, see Dorsey, "People's Bicentennial Commission Invades Concord," 14.

32. On the PBC's Bill of Rights stunt in Delaware, critiques of the PBC from the left, and adoption of the group's educational materials, see Tom Mathews and Jane Whitmore. "Up-to-the-Minutemen," *Newsweek*, May 19, 1975, 29, https:// advance.lexis.com/document/?pdmfid=1516831&crid=539445f3-6774-4ea3-ab32 -083f60c2ef7b. On *Common Sense II*, see Allan J. Mayer and Pamela Ellis Simons,

"Selling Free Enterprise," *Newsweek*, September 20, 1976, 74, https://www.pro quest.com/docview/1866702113; for the PBC's rhetoric about corporations, see Peoples Bicentennial Commission, "Results of a Nationwide Public Opinion Poll Conducted by Hart Research Associates for the Peoples Bicentennial Commission" (1975), n.p., Advertising Council Papers, University Library at the University of Illinois, Records Group 13/2/305, Box 24, Washington Office Subject File, 1942–77, "American Economic System" folder.

33. On sponsor organizations, see Americans for a Working Economy, *A Working Economy for Americans*, ed. Joan Bannon, Gar Alperovitz, Woodrow L. Ginsburg, Robert G. Harris, Roger Hickey, and Nat Weinberg (San Francisco: Public Media Center, 1977), inside cover. For Hickey's remarks about the counter-campaign, see Michael J. Connor, "Selling Capitalism: Ad Campaign That Seeks to Explain Workings of Free Enterprise System Stirs Controversy," *Wall Street Journal*, August 4, 1976, 32, quotation on 32, https://www.proquest.com/docview/596 57442. On the Public Media Center's plans to respond to the Advertising Council campaign, see "Fairness an Issue in Ad Council's New Campaign on U.S. economy?," *Broadcasting* 90, no. 17 (April 26, 1976): 39–40, https://www.proquest.com/docview/1016881321.

34. On network responses to the campaign, see Connor, "Selling Capitalism: Ad Campaign That Seeks to Explain Workings of Free Enterprise System Stirs Controversy," 32, and Dominic Sama, "'Peanuts' Ads Create a Furor," *Philadelphia Inquirer*, September 27, 1976, 8-B, https://www.proquest.com/docview/1843012108. On CBS and ABC responses, see Connor, "Selling Capitalism: Ad Campaign That Seeks to Explain Workings of Free Enterprise System Stirs Controversy," 32, and Philip H. Dougherty, "Advertising: NBC-TV to Run Economic Ads," *New York Times*, July 30, 1976, 61, https://www.proquest.com/docview/122862061. On NBC's response to PBC pressure, see Jack Egan, "NBC Won't Give Time to Counter Ad Council Spots," *Washington Post*, August 12, 1976, C1, https://www.proquest.com/pagepdf/146633256. On the Department of Commerce's refusal to fund the Public Media Center's campaign, see Robert S. Milligan, Correspondence from US Department of Commerce Deputy Assistant Secretary for Policy Development and Coordination to Roger Hickey of the Public Media Center (September 24, 1976), Advertising Council Papers, University Library at the University of Illinois, Records Group 13/2/305, Box 28, Washington Office Subject File, 1942–77, "American Economic System" folder.

35. For Tobin's remarks, see Louis M. Kohlmeier, "The Babel of Economic Advertising," *New York Times*, September 19, 1976, 117, quotation on 117, https://www.proquest.com/docview/122919134. For the comments from the American Economic Foundation spokesperson and from Bob Keim, see Mayer and Simons, "Selling Free Enterprise," 74. On the Advertising Council's insistence that the campaign was unbiased, see Dougherty, "Advertising: NBC-TV to Run Economic Ads," 61.

NOTES TO PAGES 161–163

36. For quotation on reviewers of the booklet, see Advertising Council, "The Plan for a Major Public Service Mass Communication Program by the Advertising Council, Inc. to Help Create a Better Understanding of the American Economic System," 3. On the participation of writers from the Department of Commerce, see Paul H. Weaver, "Corporations Are Defending Themselves with the Wrong Weapon," *Fortune*, June 1977, 186–90; 192, 194, 196; quotations on 188.

37. For the schema of consumers, producers, and governments, see Advertising Council, *The American Economic System—and Your Part in It* (Pueblo, CO: Advertising Council, 1976), quotations on 2 and 3.

38. Advertising Council, quotations on 2. Given the market fundamentalism that would come to dominate public discourse in the decades to follow, it is important to note that the booklet did pay some attention to labor power and state intervention in the economy: labor unions and government spending on social programs were given matter-of-fact, if somewhat superficial, treatment. A libertarian-oriented new conservatism was gathering momentum in such places as the Ozark Mountain region of Arkansas and in Orange County, California, but was not yet entrenched in policy circles on the national level (see Moreton, *To Serve God and Wal-Mart: The Making of Christian Free Enterprise*, and Lisa McGirr, *Suburban Warriors: The Origins of the New American Right* [Princeton, NJ: Princeton University Press, 2015]). That a publication of the Advertising Council, which positioned itself as an ally of free enterprise, allowed room for social programs and labor bargaining power in their description of the US economic system illustrates how the institutional discourse has shifted since the mid-1970s.

39. On scant coverage of discrimination, see Connor, "Selling Capitalism: Ad Campaign That Seeks to Explain Workings of Free Enterprise System Stirs Controversy," 32. On concerns about bias and avoided topics, see Nancy L. Ross, "Public Media Center Hits Economic System Spots," *Washington Post*, September 21, 1976, D9, quotation on D9, https://www.proquest.com/docview/146587623.

40. On the circulation of Public Media Center PSAs, see Americans for a Working Economy, "Working Economy Booklet Released" (press release) (n.d.), Advertising Council Papers, University Library at the University of Illinois, Records Group 13/2/305, Box 30, Washington Office Subject File, 1942–77, "American Economic System" folder. On booklet circulation figures, see Dominic Sama, "A Battle to Shape Your Thinking," *Philadelphia Inquirer*, June 6, 1977, 6-C, https://www.newspapers.com/image/172243108. On the contrast in values between the two booklets, see Niesen, "The Little Old Lady Has Teeth: The U.S. Federal Trade Commission and the Advertising Industry, 1970–1973," quotation n.p. For the Public Media Center booklet, see Americans for a Working Economy, *A Working Economy for Americans*, ed. Joan Bannon, Gar Alperovitz, Woodrow L. Ginsburg, Robert G. Harris, Roger Hickey, and Nat Weinberg (San Francisco: Public Media Center, 1977), quotations on 4 and 5. For Howard remarks, see Dougherty, "Advertising: Economic Drive Spurs Conflict," 67.

248   NOTES TO PAGES 163–168

41. Daniel Rodgers, *Age of Fracture* (Cambridge, MA: Belknap Press of Harvard University Press, 2011), quotations on 42, 76. For Lutz's critique, see William D. Lutz, "'The American Economic System': The Gospel According to the Advertising Council," *College English* 38, no. 8 (April 1977): 860–65.

42. See Advertising Council, *The American Economic System—and Your Part in It*, quotation on 18, and Americans for a Working Economy, *A Working Economy for Americans*, quotations on 10, 30.

43. Naomi Oreskes and Erik M. Conway, *The Big Myth: How American Business Taught Us to Loathe Government and Love the Free Market* (New York: Bloomsbury Publishing, 2023), quotations on 3.

44. On the wind-down on the active campaign, see Compton Advertising, "A National Survey of Public Knowledge and Attitudes toward the American Economic System and Related Economic Issues, Phase V" (1980), ii, Advertising Council Papers, University Library at the University of Illinois, Records Group 13/2/220, Box 4, Robert P. Keim Papers, 1967–87.

45. On the decline in organized criticism, see "Industries Advisory Committee Meeting [Summary of Meeting: Industries Advisory Committee of the Advertising Council]" (January 27, 1977), quotation on 5, Advertising Council Papers, University Library at the University of Illinois, Records Group 13/2/305, Box 30, Washington Office Subject File, 1942–77, "American Economic System" folder.

46. On the new "E.Q."-themed PSAs, see "Broadcast Advertising: Ad Council Alters Campaign to Skirt Equal-Time Issue," *Broadcasting* 93, no. 15 (October 10, 1977): 71, https://www.proquest.com/docview/1016886166. On approval by all three major networks, see Advertising Council, "Statement on the Advertising Council's Public Service Mass Communications Program to Help Create a Better Understanding of the American Economic System" (July 1977), Advertising Council Papers, University Library at the University of Illinois, Records Group 13/2/305, Box 30, Washington Office Subject File, 1942–77. On the updated Compton survey figures, see Philip H. Dougherty, "Advertising: Review of Agency Ties by Simmons; Economic Campaign Widens," *New York Times*, October 5, 1977, D5, https://www.proquest.com/docview/123432202, and "Council Ads Make Dent in Economic Illiteracy," *Editor & Publisher*, November 26, 1977, 18, quotations from Compton on 18, as reproduced in Advertising Council Papers, University Library at the University of Illinois, Records Group 13/2/305, Box 30, Washington Office Subject File, 1942–77, American Economic System folder.

47. On the economic and political shifts of the 1970s, see Akard, "Corporate Mobilization and Political Power: The Transformation of U.S. Economic Policy in the 1970s."

48. For Keim's remarks, see Connor, "Selling Capitalism: Ad Campaign That Seeks to Explain Workings of Free Enterprise System Stirs Controversy," 32.

49. For Keim's comments, see Keim, *A Time in Advertising's Camelot: The Memoirs of a Do-Gooder*, 72. For Kristol's comments, see Irving Kristol, "On

NOTES TO PAGES 169–174

'Economic Education,'" *Wall Street Journal*, February 18, 1976, 20, https://www
.proquest.com/docview/134097640; Samuelson quoted in Connor, "Selling Capitalism: Ad Campaign That Seeks to Explain Workings of Free Enterprise System Stirs
Controversy," 32. For O'Connor remarks, see Philip H. Dougherty, "Advertising:
Economic Campaign Is Assailed," *New York Times*, May 17, 1976, 46, quotation on
46, https://www.proquest.com/docview/122627989/.

50. On economic literacy, see Ronald A. Banaszak, "The Nature of Economic
Literacy: ERIC Digest No. 41" (Bloomington, IN: ERIC Clearinghouse for Social Studies/Social Science Education, 1987), https://www.ericdigests.org/pre-926
/nature.htm, quotation n.p. Scholars have problematized present-day notions of
economic and financial literacy, arguing that such notions are historically and culturally contingent: see, for example, Charlotta Bay, Bino Catasús, and Gustav Johed, "Situating Financial Literacy," *Critical Perspectives on Accounting* 25 (2014):
36–45.

51. On affect and storytelling, see Megan Boler and Elizabeth Davis, "Affect,
Media, Movement: Interview with Susanna Passionen and Zizi Papacharissi," in
Affective Politics of Digital Media: Propaganda by Other Means, ed. Megan Boler
and Elizabeth Davis (New York: Routledge, 2021), 53–68, quotation on 60.

Chapter Seven

1. On state mandates, see "Carolina Bill Bids Schools Give Class in Free Enterprise," *New York Times*, March 23, 1975, 40, https://www.proquest.com/doc
view/120451807/; on the range of state mandates, and the Florida mandates and
financing for the Florida CEE, see Dennis C. Brennan and Ronald A. Banaszak,
"A Study of State Mandates and Competencies for Economics Education: Center
for the Development of Economic Education" (University of the Pacific, Stockton,
CA, 1982), especially 5 and 10.

2. "Carolina Bill Bids Schools Give Class in Free Enterprise," quotation on 40.
For an example of the North Carolina CEE's activities in the state, see "Economic
Education Proposal Outlined," *Asheville [NC] Citizen-Times*, August 13, 1976, 13,
https://www.newspapers.com/image/ 199119099. For the Powell Memo, see Lewis F.
Powell Jr., "Confidential Memorandum: Attack on Free Enterprise System."

3. For detailed findings including the distinctions between free enterprise education, economic education, and consumer education, see Brennan and Banaszak,
"A Study of State Mandates," quotations on 5. On the Center for the Development
of Economic Education at University of the Pacific, see Brennan and Banaszak, 2.

4. On economic education projects in Oklahoma, see Joseph Egelnof, "Education Group Aims to End Youths' 'Economic Illiteracy,'" *Chicago Tribune*, April 8,
1973, A15, https://www.proquest.com/docview/169297995. On Democratic lawmakers' sponsorship of the Oklahoma Economic Education Act, see "Allard,

Terrill Co-Author Economic Education Bill," *Okmulgee [OK] Daily Times*, February 1, 1974, 6, https://www.newspapers.com/image/749632157; on the passage of the law and the Oklahoma City Chamber of Commerce's support of it, see Jim Killackey, "Chamber behind Education All the Way," *Daily Oklahoman* (Oklahoma City, OK), November 10, 1974, 113, https://www.newspapers.com/im age/452371467. For Scheer's comments, see Mickey Sandlin, "CSU Teacher Praises Economic Education," *Daily Oklahoman*, April 26, 1976, 9, https://www.newspa pers.com/image/451819555.

5. For Silk's article featuring Bach, see Leonard Silk, "Economic Studies, a Growth Industry," *New York Times*, October 5, 1975, 207, https://www.proquest .com/docview/120287358. For Silk's commentary on the JCEE's *Master Curriculum Guide*, see Leonard Silk, "Economic Educators Cite Clashes in Goals," *New York Times*, July 28, 1976, 41, 43, quotations on 43, https://www.proquest.com/doc view/122867557. For press reports of a shift to the right, see Ann Crittenden, "The Economic Wind's Blowing to the Right—For Now," *New York Times*, July 16, 1978, F1, quotation on F1, https://www.proquest.com/docview/123629433.

6. For Coleman's remarks on fundraising troubles compared to other programs, see Crittenden, "The Economic Wind's Blowing to the Right," quotation on F1.

7. Darrell R. Lewis and Donald Wentworth, *Games and Simulations for Teaching Economics* (booklet) (Joint Council on Economic Education, June 1971), Box 38, Joint Council on Economic Education Papers, Hoover Institution Library and Archives, Stanford University, Stanford, CA.

8. Lewis and Wentworth, *Games and Simulations for Teaching Economics*: on citations of Twelker and Sprague, see 3; quotations on 5.

9. On the Junior Achievement's after-school programs, see Joseph J. Francomano, Wayne Lavitt, and Darryl Lavitt, *Junior Achievement, A History: A Personal Account of Managing Change from Drill Press to Computer* (Colorado Springs, CO: Junior Achievement, 1988). I have written elsewhere about Junior Achievement and its use of computer games for simulation: see Caroline Jack, "Meaning and Persuasion: The Personal Computer and Economic Education," *IEEE Annals of the History of Computing* 38, no. 3 (July–September 2016): 6–9.

10. For the Teen Environment Report's description of youth malaise, see Robert Johnston Company, "The Teen Environment, Based on a Study of Growth Strategies for Junior Achievement" (New York: Robert Johnston Company, March 1980), 9–11, quotation on 11; emphasis in original, Junior Achievement Papers, Box 16, Folder 25, Ruth Lilly Special Collections and Archives, IUPUI University Library, Indiana University–Purdue University Indianapolis.

11. For an overview of Applied Economics, see D. Oberman and J. Seeley, "Applied Economics Evaluation Report" (Ann Arbor, MI: Formative Evaluation Research Associates, December 1989), Junior Achievement Papers, Box 51, Folder 2, Ruth Lilly Special Collections and Archives, IUPUI University Library, Indiana University–Purdue University Indianapolis. On the 1984 study of Applied Economics, see Janet E. Wright and John A. Seeley, "Applied Economics Full Pilot

NOTES TO PAGES 179–184

Evaluation: A Comparison of Applied Economics with Regular Economics" (Ann Arbor, MI: Formative Evaluation Research Associates, September 1984), on student outcomes, see 11, Junior Achievement Papers, Box 51, Folder 1, Ruth Lilly Special Collections and Archives, IUPUI University Library, Indiana University–Purdue University Indianapolis.

12. On corporate funding figures for education in 1979, see Margaret Price, "Education Is Failing Industry," *Industry Week*, July 13, 1981, https://advance.lexis.com/document/?pdmfid=1516831&crid=ea634a15-0e22-4843-b232-b28fd91004e5. On critics of corporate-sponsored classroom materials in the interwar period, see Inger Stole, *Advertising on Trial*, 127–36. For Harty's critiques of state mandates, see Sheila Harty, *Hucksters in the Classroom: A Review of Industry Propaganda in Schools* (Washington, DC: Center for the Study of Responsive Law, 1979), quotations on 78, 86.

13. For an example of corporate sponsors' defense of their materials, see the comments of the spokesperson for Dry Dock Bank in Ralph Blumenthal, "Big Business as Schoolmaster," *New York Times*, January 23, 1980, C1, C12, https://www.proquest.com/docview/121370761.

14. For critiques of financial literacy education, see Bay, Catasús, and Johed, "Situating Financial Literacy," and Chris Arthur, "Consumers or Critical Citizens? Financial Literacy Education and Freedom," *Critical Education* 3, no. 6 (July 15, 2012): 1–25, retrieved from https://ices.library.ubc.ca/index.php/criticaled/article/view/182350. On the Community Reinvestment Act, see Helaine Olen, *Pound Foolish: Exposing the Dark Side of the Personal Finance Industry* (New York: Portfolio/Penguin, 2012), 203. On ideological shifts and the dissolution of the Soviet Union, see Gary Gerstle, *The Rise and Fall of the Neoliberal Order: America and the World in the Free Market Era* (New York: Oxford University Press, 2022).

15. Deborah Stead, "Corporate Classrooms and Commercialism," *New York Times*, January 5, 1997, A4, quotation on A4, https://www.nytimes.com/1997/01/05/education/corporate-classrooms-and-comercialism.html. In 2018, *Washington Post* personal finance columnist Michelle Singletary highlighted an alternative financial literacy program that refuses funding from financial industry donors, but such programs are less common than finance industry–affiliated programs; see Michelle Singletary, "Who Do You Want to Teach Your Children about Money?," *Washington Post*, January 4, 2018, https://www.washingtonpost.com/news/get-there/wp/2018/01/04/who-do-you-want-to-teach-your-children-about-money/.

Conclusion

1. On the midcentury distribution of *Make Mine Freedom*, see Jack, "Fun and Facts about American Business: Economic Education and Business Propaganda in an Early Cold War Cartoon Series."

2. Simon Brown, "The New Deficit Model," *Nature Nanotechnology* 4 (October 2009): 609–11, quotation on 609.

3. On political orders, see Gary Gerstle, *The Rise and Fall of the Neoliberal Order: America and the World in the Free Market Era* (New York: Oxford University Press, 2022), quotations on 2. On the ideological shift in economic imaginaries toward centering market forces, see Daniel Rodgers, *Age of Fracture* (Cambridge, MA: Harvard University Press, 2011).

4. On the orientation toward markets of thinkers associated with neoliberalism, and the shift from ambivalent to more polarized attitudes toward markets, see Angus Burgin, *The Great Persuasion: Reinventing Free Markets since the Depression* (Cambridge, MA: Harvard University Press, 2012), see, for example, 154. On neoliberalism and abstraction, see Kim Phillips-Fein, "The History of Neoliberalism," in *Shaped by the State: Toward a New Political History of the Twentieth Century*, ed. Brent Cebul, Lily Geismer, and Mason B. Williams (Chicago: University of Chicago Press 2019), 347–62, quotation on 351.

5. On "laissez-faire capitalism," see Gary Gerstle, "The Rise and Fall(?) of America's Neoliberal Order," *Transactions of the RHS* 28 (2018): 241–64, quotations on 246. On elements of neoliberalism, see Daniel Rodgers, "The Uses and Abuses of Neoliberalism," *Dissent* 65, no. 1 (Winter 2018): 78–87.

6. On market fundamentalism, see Rodgers, "The Uses and Abuses of Neoliberalism," quotation on 82.

7. On the threat of communism as a pressure toward compromise, see Gerstle, *The Rise and Fall of the Neoliberal Order*, 11–12, quotations on 12.

8. On narcotizing dysfunction, see Paul F. Lazarsfeld and Robert K. Merton, "Mass Communication, Popular Taste, and Organized Social Action," in *Media Studies: A Reader*, 2nd ed., ed. Paul Marris and Sue Thornham (New York: New York University Press), 18–29, quotation on 22–23, and Peter Simonson and Gabriel Weimann, "Critical Research at Columbia: Lazarsfeld's and Merton's 'Mass Communication, Popular Taste, and Organized Social Action," in *Canonic Texts in Media Research: Are There Any? Should There Be? How about These?*, ed. By Elihu Katz, John Durham Peters, Tamar Liebes, and Avril Orloff (Malden, MA: Polity Press, 2003), see 23.

Index

Page numbers followed by *f* refer to figures.

Abbott, Andrew, 53

Acland, Charles R., 5

advertising: nature of, 35; perceived attacks on, 63, 66; public service, 69

advertising campaigns, economic education and, 152, 157, 158, 169. *See also specific campaigns*

Advertising Council (Ad Council): affirmative style and, 69, 71–72, 76, 190; anti-inflation campaigns, 130–32, 136, 138–40, 165; Barton and, 74, 75, 139; Benton and Bowles and, 131, 132; criticisms of, 54, 155–56; economic education and, 136–37, 152, 153, 157, 158, 169; expertise and, 55, 70, 74–76, 188, 189; freedom and, 5, 164–65; Freedom Train and, 86–88, 89f; Joint Committee on Improvement and, 92–94, 100; names for, 67, 72, 73; Nixon and, 136, 137; patriotism and, 72, 88; postwar jurisdictional claims, 72–76; PSAs and, 55, 67, 72–73, 79, 131, 138, 141–44, 156, 159, 160, 165–67, 169–71, 186; Public Advisory Committee, 75, 92; representations of race in campaign materials and, 96, 141–42; "voice of affirmation" and, 69–72; World War II and, 69, 76, 193. *See also* "American Economic System" campaign (1970s) (Advertising Council); "American Economic System" campaign (postwar) (Advertising Council)

advertising executives, 55, 56, 65, 71, 109, 150–52. *See also* business executives

advertising techniques, 36, 66, 69–72, 74, 106

affect: affirmative style and, 191–94; in economic education media, 23–26; patriotism and, 112, 191–93

affective attunement, 36, 170

affective postures, 23, 25, 111, 170, 193

affective publics, 26

affective tenor, 23, 24

affirmative style, 69, 71, 196, 197; Advertising Council and, 69, 71–72, 76, 190; affect and, 191–94; of "American Economic System" campaign, 100, 169; capitalism and, 25; economic education and, 79, 183, 184, 191–95; limitations of, 98; *Miracle of America* and, 98, 100; nature of, 8; private enterprise and, 8, 9, 48–49, 113, 169, 183, 191, 192; promotional nationalism and, 8, 9, 30, 45, 51–53, 76, 107, 111, 123, 183, 190, 191, 195, 196; "selling America to Americans" and, 30, 31, 40, 42, 45, 51, 169; US history and, 9, 25. *See also* "voice of affirmation"

Akard, Patrick J., 146

"America first" (slogan), 38–40

American Association of Advertising Agencies (AAAA), 62, 63, 186; leaders, 63, 65–67, 69, 75, 81, 186; meeting with ANA in Hot Springs, 66. *See also* Joint ANA-AAAA Committee on Improvement of Public Understanding of Our Economic System (Joint Committee on Improvement)

American economic system: economic education and, 81–83; economic

254 INDEX

American economic system (*cont.*)
understanding and, 152–54, 166 (*see also* economic understanding); Joint Committee on Improvement and, 82, 83; *Miracle of America* and, 98; nature of, 97; Smock Report and, 80–84; terminology, 80, 81, 84, 186

American Economic System . . . and Your Part in It, The (Advertising Council booklet): capitalism and, 17–18, 161, 162; contrasted with other booklets, 145, 162–64; distribution of, 18, 143; freedom and, 17–18, 162, 165; limitations and criticisms of, 161, 162, 164; overview of, 142–43, 161–62, 169–71, 187; taxonomy of, 161–62

"American Economic System" campaign (1970s) (Advertising Council), 141, 145, 193; affirmative style of, 169; business interests' support for, 145; economic education and, 190; in historical context, 171; overview of, 171; Public Media Center and, 156, 159–60; purpose of, 144, 167; resistance to and criticisms of, 155–60, 166

"American Economic System" campaign (postwar) (Advertising Council), 91–100, 193; advertisements to support, 95f, 96f, 97f, 98f; affirmative style of, 100; American Heritage Foundation and, 91, 92; economic education and, 94; Joint Committee on Improvement and, 79–80, 83, 91–94, 106; *Miracle of America* and, 94, 100, 186; overview of, 91, 186; purpose of, 193; signature slogan of, 94, 134; Smock Report and, 91, 94, 104

American economy. *See* economy of United States

American Economy, The (TV course), 119, 140, 175–76; Cold War media flows and, 123–30

American Heritage Foundation, 86–91; Freedom Train and, 86–91; Joint Committee on Improvement and, 86, 88

American Hour Broadcasting Committee, 40, 41, 185

American identity. *See* national identity

American in the Making, An (film), 32

Americanism, 32, 43, 90; film industry and, 32, 34; Lane and, 33–36, 39, 45; New Deal

and, 186; notions of, 48, 50; Red Scare and, 32, 35, 50, 185

Americanism campaigns, 33f, 90

Americanization, 25, 30, 32, 34–36, 45, 50, 185, 192

American Liberty League, 56, 57

American Midwest, 37, 38

Americans for a Working Economy, 159, 165, 167

American way of life, 23, 93; NAM and, 53, 58, 59f; terminology, 81

American West, 37–39, 44, 185

Anderson, Benedict, 26, 27

Anheuser-Busch advertising campaign, 45–46, 46f, 47f, 193

anticommunism, 127, 167, 193, 196; capitalism and, 48, 113, 118; CED and, 112, 118; of Crusaders, 43; in film, 102; Harding College and, 101; JCEE and, 112, 140; notions of, 187; objectivity and, 126, 127; private enterprise and, 42–43, 118, 123; Red Scare and, 37; "selling America to Americans" and, 42–43. *See also* scientific anticommunism

anti-inflation campaigns: Advertising Council/JCEE, 130–32, 136, 138–40, 165; Benton and Bowles and, 131–32, 134, 138, 139. *See also* inflation: efforts to reduce

antiradicalism: Crusaders and, 43, 44; national identity and, 50; New Deal and, 41, 42, 185; place-making and, 37–42, 50; use of term, 209n5

Applied Economics (JA curriculum), 178

appreciation, 85, 154

Aronczyk, Melissa, 7

Association of National Advertisers (ANA), 112–13; CED and, 109, 110, 112; leaders, 63, 65–67, 69, 75, 81; meeting with AAAA in Hot Springs, 66, 186. *See also* Joint ANA-AAAA Committee on Improvement of Public Understanding of Our Economic System (Joint Committee on Improvement)

Aucoin, James, 147

audience: in economic education media, 22–23, 25–27; internal and external, 22–23; managerial, 182

Aufderheide, Patricia, 144, 156

automobiles, 39

INDEX

Bach, George Leland ("Lee"), 117, 175; JCEE and, 117–18; National Task Force on Economic Education and, 117, 118; *Wall Street Journal* and, 122–23

Baker, G. Derwood, 110–11

Banaszak, Ronald A., 168, 173–74

Barrett, James R., 34

Barton, Bruce, 63, 64, 74, 75, 139

BBDO (Batten, Barton, Durstine and Osborn), 63, 74

Belding, Don, 81, 103, 104

Benson, George S., 79, 101–2; characterization of, 101, 102; Harding College and, 79, 101–4; Joint Committee on Improvement and, 102–4; Smock Report and, 103

Benton, William, 109

Benton and Bowles, 131–32, 134, 138, 239n52; anti-inflation campaigns and, 131–32, 134, 138, 139

Berman, Elizabeth Popp, 8

"big government": citizens and, 101; opposition to, 165

Bird, William, 79

"Blue Book" (FCC report), 73, 144

Bolshevism, 32, 34

Bolte, Charles L., 90

Boyle, Ryan, 115

Brennan, Dennis C., 173–74

Brookings Institution, 105–6

Brophy, Thomas D'Arcy, 86, 88, 93

Brown, Simon, 184

Brown, Wendy, 145

Burant, Jim, 5

Burgin, Angus, 195

Burns, Arthur F., 153

Busch, Adolphus, III, 45, 46, 46f

business, American system of. *See* American economic system

Business Advisory and Planning Council (Roosevelt administration), 56

business as usual, 183

business executives, 19–22, 28, 146, 147. *See also* advertising executives

Business Screen (journal), 28, 60–61, 89–91

California Crusaders, 43, 48, 186

Campbell, Colin, 24, 165

Campbell-Ewald, 58

capitalism, 20, 56, 161–62; and *The American Economic System . . . and Your Part in It*, 17–18, 161, 162; anticommunism and, 48, 113, 118; Carter on, 48, 49; economic education, economic understanding, and, 1, 2, 21; freedom and, 17–18, 20, 57, 125, 149, 175, 184, 187, 195–97; Glickman on, 21; JCEE and, 112, 113, 118, 189, 190; Link on, 28, 29; National Task Force on Economic Education on, 118, 121, 122; neoliberalism and, 195–96; patriotism and, 1, 37; Powell Memo and, 149, 151; "selling America to Americans" and, 28, 29, 42, 45 (*see also* "selling America to Americans"); terminology, 195–96. *See also* free enterprise; managerial capitalism; private enterprise

Carey, Alex, 30, 32, 53

cars, 39

Carter, Boake, 48–49, 193

cartoons, 33f, 102, 181

Case for Advertising, The, 150, 151

Ceplair, Larry, 34

Chamber of Commerce of the United States. *See* US Chamber of Commerce

Chambers, Jason, 96

Chandler, Alfred D., Jr., 34

Churchwell, Sarah, 39–40

Civilian Conservation Corps (CCC), 101–2

civil liberties, 49–50; advertising and, 70; corporations and, 162; private enterprise and, 4, 15–17, 58, 63, 169, 187. *See also* liberty, democracy and

Clark, Fred G., 43–44

Cohen, Lizabeth, 29, 146

Cohen, Michael, 209n5

Cold War, 90, 125; CED and, 116, 118; JCEE and, 107, 108, 112, 114–16, 118. See also *American Economy, The* (TV course); Sputnik crisis

Coleman, John R., 125–27, 175–76

Collins, Robert M., 108

Commerce Department. *See* US Department of Commerce

Committee for Economic Development (CED): *The American Economy* and, 121, 126–27; anticommunism, 112, 118; business-educational committee, 111; Cold War and, 116; early history, 108; "economic citizenship" and, 108–13; finances, 113, 126–28, 140; goals, 108; JCEE and, 108, 110–12, 116–18, 128, 140;

Committee for Economic Development (CED) (*cont.*)

leadership, 108, 109, 112, 121; moderate and conciliatory stance, 108, 109; NAM and, 109, 110, 112, 118; National Task Force on Economic Education and, 117, 118, 120–23; research and policy committee, 123

Committee on Public Information (CPI), 36, 188, 192

communism, 196. *See also* anticommunism; Bolshevism

Compton Advertising, 153, 154, 157, 158, 166

computerized simulation games, 176–78

conservatism, 195; state mandates and, 173–76

content marketing, 3

Conway, Erik M., 17, 57, 110, 165, 196

corporate executives. *See* advertising executives; business executives

corporate social responsibility, 145–52

Cowles, Gardner, Jr., 70–72

Creel, George, 36, 44–45, 61, 192

Creel Committee. *See* Committee on Public Information (CPI)

Crusaders, 43–44; California chapter, 43, 48, 186

Culbert, David, 48

Cummings, Barton O., 158

Curtin, Michael, 112, 126, 127

Davis, Archie K., 136

Davis, Elmer, 67, 68, 70

Davison, W. Phillips, 22

De Casseres, Benjamin, 49–50, 83, 193

Decker, Christof, 72

deficit model, 184

Delton, Jennifer, 53–54, 57

democracy, 19, 70, 87, 88, 109, 155; *The American Economic System . . . and Your Part in It* and, 164, 165, 170–71; complications of markets and, 165–71; definitions of, 114, 162; education system, economic education, and, 113–15, 117–21, 124, 125, 129–31, 140; liberty and, 15, 165, 183, 184; managerial capitalism and, 29, 81; market fundamentalism and, 170–71; *A Working Economy for Americans* and, 162–64

Dent, Frederick Baily, 152–53

Developmental Economic Education Program (DEEP), 127, 129, 130, 140

Dillon, Tom, 151

doxa. *See* economic doxa

Du Pont family, 43

economic, uses of term, 7

"economic citizenship," CED and, 108–13

economic development. *See* Committee for Economic Development (CED)

economic doxa, 64, 65, 76, 81, 84, 85, 183, 218n21; expertise and, 64–65, 84–86, 218n21; primary vs. secondary, 64

economic education: approaches to, 107, 112–14, 118, 189; as blanket term, 4; citizenship and, 120, 124–25, 131, 140; as misnomer, 78; rationales for, 109, 117, 154, 170; in schools, 106–7, 118–20, 175, 180; state mandates for, 173–74, 178–79

Economic Education Act of 1974, 174

Economic Education in the Schools (National Task Force on Economic Education report), 118–23, 129, 131

economic education media, 10, 196; affirmative style and, 79, 183, 184, 191–95; audience, affect, and imaginaries in, 22–27; central contradiction of, 19–21; computers, simulation, and, 176–80; constructing postwar, 80–86 (*see also* Smock Report); democracy and, 113–15, 117–21, 124, 125, 129–31, 140; expertise and, 59–60, 62, 84, 85, 182, 183, 188, 189; inflation and contradictions of, 130–40; managerial capitalism and, 4, 187, 194; patriotism and, 10, 23, 25, 184; private enterprise and, 15, 18–21, 23, 173, 176, 182–85, 187–92; promise of, 83; and romance of business, 14; scientization of, 183–84, 188–91; simulation and games in, 176–78; as sponsored media, 3; teaching economic concepts, 177; uses and meanings of term, 1–2, 4

economic literacy, 105, 106, 122, 129, 130, 168–69, 180

economics, applied. *See* Applied Economics (JA curriculum)

economic style of reasoning, 8

economic systems, 82. *See also specific systems*

INDEX

economic understanding, 104, 111; advertising campaign to promote, 152, 157, 158, 169; Advertising Council and, 136–37, 152, 153, 157, 158, 169; advertising industry and, 65; effects of, 21, 114; Ford Foundation and, 114; media campaigns and, 20; Nixon and, 136–37

economy: balanced (see *Inflation Can Be Stopped* [JCEE booklet]); notion of, 7

economy of United States: defining principles of, in Smock Report, 82; power vs. freedom in, 160–65

education: corporate funding for, 179; economic (*see* economic education media); media as *educational*, 2; Soviet educational system, 115

educational reform, 115. *See also* Sputnik crisis

E. I. Du Pont de Nemours and Company (DuPont), 15

emotions: attitudes and, 106; emotional experiences, 104; emotionally literate subject, 178; facts and, 51, 72, 124; judgments and, 117; in persuasive appeals, 25, 28, 29, 35, 37, 45, 50, 63, 112, 150, 188, 191–92; publics and, 56. *See also* affect

Employment Act of 1946, 134, 134f

Environmental Protection Agency (EPA), 147

ephemeral films, 182

ephemeral media, 5–6, 7, 14, 181

"E.Q." (Economic Quotient), 166

executive officers. *See* advertising executives; business executives

expertise, 20–22, 65, 66, 135; Advertising Council and, 55, 70, 74–76, 188, 189; doxa and, 64–65, 84–86, 218n21; economic education and, 59–60, 62, 84, 85, 182, 183, 188, 189; folk, 66, 219n22; NAM and, 53–55, 59–60, 62, 85, 188–89; scientization, media, and, 188–89; Swedberg on, 64–65, 218nn21–22

Experts All (NAM booklet), 59–60, 189

Fairness Doctrine, 156, 159, 167; revocation of, 180

Federal Communications Commission (FCC). *See* "Blue Book"; Fairness Doctrine

Federal Trade Commission (FTC), 62, 150

feeling, structures of, 24, 194. *See also* affect

Feller, Abraham H., 67–68

felt experience, 39, 50

Fersh, George L., 116

film, 32; ephemeral films, 182 (*see also* ephemeral media); Prelinger and, 3; sponsored, 3. *See also specific films*

film industry: Americanism and, 32, 34; Lane and, 33–34, 36, 41, 192

"financial literacy," 180. *See also* economic literacy

Finkel, Eda, 138

folk expertise, 66, 219n22

folk knowledge. *See* managerial folk knowledge

Folsom, Marion B., 112, 117

Fones-Wolf, Elizabeth A., 54, 94, 109

Ford Foundation, 114; funding from, 113, 117, 119, 129, 140

Fox, Frank W., 54, 220n29

Frankel, M. L. ("Moe"), 117, 130, 137, 138, 179

freedom, 87; Advertising Council and, 5, 164–65; and *The American Economic System . . . and Your Part in It*, 17–18, 162, 165; capitalism and, 17–18, 20, 57, 125, 149, 175, 184, 187, 195–97; idea of, 15–19, 164–65; political, 115; vs. power in American economy, 160–65; types of, 92, 94. *See also* liberty, democracy and

Freedom Train (traveling exhibit), 86–91, 186; Advertising Council and, 86–88, 89f; American Heritage Foundation and, 86–91; Rededication Week, 86, 87, 90

free enterprise: Carter and, 48–49; Glickman on, 21, 30, 42; "great free enterprise campaign," 77, 105; perceived attacks on free enterprise system, 149, 173; uses and meanings of term, 4, 42, 87, 149. *See also* capitalism; private enterprise

free enterprise promotional nationalism, 107, 123, 129. *See also* promotional nationalism

free-market system, 155, 175

Fri, James, 89

Friedman, Milton, 138, 147–48, 150, 151, 175, 190, 195

Friedman, Walter A., 35

Friedman Doctrine, 148, 151

Frontiers of the Future (film), 61

General Motors (GM), 43, 148
Gerstle, Gary, 35, 180, 195, 196
Glende, Philip M., 48
Glickman, Lawrence B., 9, 149; on free enterprise, 21, 30, 42
Glotzer, Paige, 38
Great Depression, 41–42, 185
Griffith, Robert, 54, 79

Hacking, Ian, 8
Hall, Simon, 158
Hall, Stuart, 3–4, 26, 55, 182
Harding College: Freedom Forums, 100–104; George Benson and, 79, 101–4; Joint Committee on Improvement and, 101, 103–4
Harty, Sheila, 179
Hatfield, C. F., 39
Hickey, Roger, 159
Hirota, Janice M., 36
Hoffmann, Paul G., 92, 112, 113
Hofstadter, Richard, 8
Hot Springs (Virginia), joint meeting of AAAA and ANA in, 66
Howard, Ted, 163
Hucksters in the Classroom (Harty), 179
Hull, Matthew S., 120
Hutchinson, Dawn L., 47

imaginaries, in economic education media, 24, 27
immigrant labor, 37, 39
immigrants, 27; anti-immigration sentiments and, 38, 40, 41; assimilating, 32, 34; Lane and, 34, 36, 37
immigration waves, 34–35
income tax surcharge, 136–38
indivisibility thesis, 17, 196
inflation: causes of, 74, 134, 139 (see also inflationary psychology); and contradictions of economic education, 130–40; efforts to reduce, 74, 137–40, 165 (see also anti-inflation campaigns; Inflation Can Be Stopped [JCEE booklet]); government and, 131, 132, 134, 136–39; impact of, 113, 134, 139, 145, 146, 152, 166
inflationary psychology, 131, 132, 136–37, 153
Inflation Can Be Stopped (JCEE booklet), 132–38; Advertising Council and, 137;

distribution of, 138; images and text from, 133f, 134f, 135f; Miracle of America and, 132–33, 145; overview of, 132, 135–36
interwar period, 41, 54–56; Advertising Council, NAM, AAAA/ANA, and, 188–89; motion picture industry during, 192; US economic system during, 82. See also New Deal; "selling America to Americans"
isolationism, 39
It's Everybody's Business (cartoon film), 15–18, 16f, 17f

Jackall, Robert, 36
Jasanoff, Sheila, 27
JA Worldwide. See Junior Achievement (JA)
job safety legislation, 146–47
John Sutherland Productions, 15, 102
Joint ANA-AAAA Committee on Improvement of Public Understanding of Our Economic System (Joint Committee on Improvement), 95, 98, 100; Advertising Council and, 92–94, 100; "American Economic System" campaign and, 79–80, 83, 91–94, 106; American Heritage Foundation and, 86, 88; Brophy and, 86, 88; CED and, 109; creation of, 81; George Benson and, 102–4; Harding College and, 101, 103–4; later focus on marketing, 106; in 1950s, 106; overview of, 80; programs, 80, 83, 92–94, 101–4, 106; projects, 105; Research and Creative Committees, 80; Smock Report and, 80–83, 85, 91, 93, 100–101, 103, 105, 106; terminology, 80, 81
Joint Council on Economic Education (JCEE): The American Economy and, 126–27, 140; anticommunism and, 112, 118, 140, 155, 186–87, 189, 190, 193; Bach and, 117–18; CED and, 108, 110–12, 116–18, 128, 140; Cold War and, 107, 108, 112, 114–16, 118; contrasted with other groups, 112–13; executive committee of, 128, 129; founding and early history of, 108, 110–11, 113; and ideologies of space race, 113–18; Inflation Can Be Stopped, 132–38, 133f, 134f, 135f; influence of, 114; leaders of, 114–17; in media, 114, 116;

National Task Force on Economic Education and, 117, 118; overview of, 107–8, 110–14, 118; promotional nationalism and, 129, 136, 186–87, 189–90; purpose of, 107, 112, 113, 118; redesigning education, 117; special committees of, 119; workshops by, 113, 114

Junior Achievement (JA), 176–79

jurisdiction, professional, 11, 53, 55, 67, 68, 72, 74, 76, 196

Keim, Robert ("Bob") P., 137, 138, 157, 158, 160, 168

Kent, Frank R., 68, 69

Kreshel, Peggy, 35

Kristol, Irving, 168

Kruse, Kevin M., 105

Kruse, W. F., 60

laissez-faire capitalism, 195

LaMay, Craig, 144

Lane, Franklin Knight, 36, 192; Americanism and, 33–36, 39, 45; film industry and, 33–34, 36, 41, 192; immigrants and, 34, 36, 37; "mighty project of selling America to Americans," 37; national identity and, 34, 36

Lange, Dorothea, 58–59

LaRoche, Chester J., 152

Lazarsfeld, Paul F., 197

Lee, Alfred McClung, 139

Lewenstein, Bruce V., 85

Lewis, Darrell R., 176–78

liberty, democracy and, 15, 165, 183, 184. *See also* civil liberties; freedom

Link, Henry C., 28–29, 89–90, 149

literacy vs. illiteracy, 32. *See also* economic literacy

Little, Stuart J., 79, 86, 88

Loevinger, Lee, 151

Lora, Ronald, 110

Lund, Robert, 84

Lynch, Edmund C., 36

MacLeish, Archibald, 67, 68

Madden, Carl H., 138

Make Mine Freedom (cartoon film), 102, 181

managerial anxiety, 145–52

managerial audience, 182

managerial capitalism, 9, 48, 50, 75, 154; Advertising Council and, 167; democracy and, 81; economic education and, 4, 187, 194; freedom, liberty, and, 75, 147; history of, 34–35; Joint Committee on Improvement and, 80; motion picture industry and, 31–37; overview of, 20, 34, 81; patriotism and, 34, 81; "selling America to Americans" and, 31, 34, 48; Smock Report and, 80, 81

managerial culture, 20, 22, 23, 145, 148

managerial folk knowledge, 62–66, 153, 154, 188; economic education as project of, 84; Smock Report and, 81, 82, 84

manufacturers, 63, 66. *See also* National Association of Manufacturers (NAM)

Marchand, Roland, 56, 66

market crash of 1929, 41, 55; aftermath of, 55. *See also* interwar period

market economy, 17, 83. *See also* private enterprise

market forces, 169–71

market fundamentalism, 169–71, 196

market ideologies, 169, 171

Marshall, Thomas, 34

Marvin, Fred R., 40, 41

Marxism, 173

Mauney, William Kemp, 173

Maxwell, Robbie, 101

McCarthy, Anna, 124

media effects, 204n7

Meeds, Lloyd, 146–47

Melillo, Wendy, 144

Men and Machines (NAM filmstrip), 58–59

Merton, Robert K., 197

Meyer, Stephen, 34

Midwest (United States), 37, 38

Milligan, Robert S., 157, 160

Miracle of America (Advertising Council booklet): affirmative style and, 98, 100; "American Economic System" campaign and, 94, 100, 186; distribution of, 100; drafting of, 93; *Inflation Can Be Stopped* and, 132–33, 145; overview, 93, 95, 96–98, 100; text of, 99f

misinformation, 106

Mitchell, Timothy, 7, 111–12

Modern Talking Picture Service, 60, 61f

morale, politics of, 41–50

Mortimer, Charles G., Jr., 88
Murphree, Vanessa, 147

narcotizing dysfunction, 197
National Association of Manufacturers (NAM), 57–58, 62, 85, 112, 188; and "American Way," 53, 58, 59f; campaigns, 57–59, 75; CED and, 109, 110, 112, 118; expertise and, 53–55, 59–60, 62, 85, 188–89; films, 32, 58–61; literature, 58–60, 188–89; mass media and, in New Deal period, 53, 56–57, 62
National Chamber Foundation, 131, 137
National Defense Education Act, 116–18
National Electric Light Association, 57, 110
national identity, 10, 34, 61, 62; anticommunism as part of, 43; antiradicalism, felt experience, and, 50; economic education and, 14, 23; of immigrants, 36; private enterprise and, 19, 41, 42, 88, 100, 184, 185, 193, 194, 197; promotional nationalism and, 184, 185; public service and, 185; rhetoric of, in 1910s, 32; "selling America to Americans" and, 39, 42, 45, 192; Whyte and, 77–78
nationalism, 40, 41. *See also* patriotism; promotional nationalism; "selling America to Americans"
National Labor Relations Act of 1935 (Wagner Act), 57
National Task Force on Economic Education, 119, 121, 122, 124, 127; aims and agenda of, 117–19, 121, 124; *The American Economy* and, 125–27; Bach and, 117, 118; background and early history of, 117, 118; on capitalism, 118, 121, 122; CED and, 117, 118, 120–23; criticisms of, 175; *Economic Education in the Schools*, 118–23, 129, 131; JCEE and, 117, 118; in media, 119, 122, 123
Neal, Alfred C., 116
neoliberalism, 194–98; neoliberal political order, 195–97
New Deal, 30, 185; antiradicalism and, 41, 42, 185; NAM and, 53, 56–62; opposition to, 41–43, 53, 56–57, 62, 101, 147, 181, 185–86; political order, 185, 195–97; and politics of morale, 41–43; promotional nationalism and, 56, 102, 185–86; selling America and, 41; Smock Report and, 82

Niesen, Molly, 150, 162
Nixon, Richard, 136–38
Nye, David E., 27

objectivity: anticommunism and, 126, 127; scientific, 118
Occupational Safety and Health Administration (OSHA), 146–47
O'Connor, Neal, 168
Office of Facts and Figures (OFF), 67
Office of War Information (OWI), 73, 75; assessments of, 68–70; early history of, 67–68; founding of, 67, 68; media coverage of, 68; purpose of, 67; "voice of affirmation" and, 70–72
O'Hara, James, 137
Oklahoma City, 174
Olen, Helaine, 180
"ordinary people," 64
Oreskes, Naomi, 17, 57, 110, 165, 196
organizational communication, 120–21
Orlikowski, Wanda J., 120–21
ostensible audience, 22
"Our American Heritage" campaign, 87. *See also* American Heritage Foundation
Outdoor Advertising Association of America, 58

Papacharissi, Zizi, 26, 36, 170
parks, national, 39
patriotism, 96; Advertising Council and, 72, 88; affect and, 112, 191–93; capitalism, private enterprise, and, 1, 10, 34, 37, 81, 88, 105; economic education and, 10, 23, 25, 184; film industry and, 34; Freedom Train and, 86, 88; New Deal policies and, 56; PBC and, 158; promotional nationalism and, 37, 184, 185, 191; "selling America to Americans" and, 37, 40, 188, 193 (*see also* "selling America to Americans"); Uncle Sam and, 133; during war and peacetime, 34. *See also* nationalism
Peoples Bicentennial Commission (PBC), 158–60
persuasive media, 2
Phillips-Fein, Kim, 2, 195
Pickard, Victor, 144
"piggy" advertisements (Advertising Council), 132, 134, 138; piggy test, 132, 133f
political freedom. *See* freedom

INDEX 261

postwar period. *See* "American Economic System" campaign (postwar) (Advertising Council); World War II: aftermath of

Powell Memo (1971), 149–51; capitalism and, 149, 151; private enterprise and, 149, 173

power vs. freedom, and American economy, 160–65

Prelinger, Rick, 3, 4

private enterprise, 1, 4; affirmative style and, 8, 9, 48–49, 113, 169, 183, 191, 192; anticommunism and, 42–43, 118, 123; economic education and, 15, 18–21, 23, 173, 176, 182–85, 187–92; freedom, liberty, and, 4, 15–18, 58, 63, 169, 187; national identity and, 19, 23, 41, 88, 100, 184, 185, 193, 194, 197; patriotism and, 10, 88, 105; persuasive media and attitudes about, 2; Powell Memo and, 149, 173; promotional culture and, 1; promotional nationalism and, 9, 145, 184–87; "selling America to Americans" and, 192–93. *See also* capitalism; free enterprise

Proctor and Gamble, 157

productivity, "the better we produce — the better we live" slogan and, 94, 134

promotional expertise, 86. *See also* expertise

promotional nationalism, 7–11, 79, 88, 90; affirmative style and, 8, 9, 30, 45, 51–53, 76, 107, 111, 123, 183, 190, 191, 195, 196; and construction of private enterprise as free, 184–87; free enterprise, 107, 123, 129; JCEE and, 129, 136, 186–87, 189–90; NAM's vision of, 58; nature of, 184; neoliberalism and, 187, 195; New Deal and, 56, 102, 185–86; patriotism and, 37, 184, 185, 191; private enterprise and, 9, 145, 184–87; "selling America to Americans" and, 37, 45, 51, 52 (*see also* "selling America to Americans")

propaganda, 139; advertising and, 168. *See also* Harding College: Freedom Forums

public interest, 20, 66, 69, 74, 140, 144, 198; constructing publics and, 152–55; serving, 11, 71, 161, 168

public interest advertising (movement), 13, 156, 158–59, 167

"publicity boys," 68, 69; home-front messaging in wartime, 66–69

Public Media Center, 156, 157, 159–60; "American Economic System" campaign and, 156, 159–60; PSAs and, 156, 159–60, 162. *See also* Americans for a Working Economy

public service advertisements (PSAs), 66, 72, 73, 152–53, 186; Advertising Council, 55, 67, 72–73, 79, 131, 138, 141–44, 156, 159, 160, 165–67, 169–71, 186; Public Media Center and, 156, 159–60, 162

radical, 209n5. *See also* antiradicalism

reasoning, styles of, 8

Rededication Week (Freedom Train), 86, 87, 90

Red Scare, 37; Americanism and, 32, 35, 37, 50, 185; first Red Scare, 185

Reflecting Our Confidence in the Future of America (film), 45–46, 47f

Repplier, Ted S., 75

Riley, Frank Branch, 38

Rippa, S. Alexander, 110

Roche, James, 148

Rodgers, Daniel, 163–64, 195–96

Roosevelt, Franklin D., 56. *See also* New Deal

Rosenfeld, Sophia, 21

Rosenthal, Benjamin, 155–57

Ryan, Erica J., 32

Samuelson, Paul A., 117, 168

Scheer, Lorraine, 174, 179

scientific advertising, 25, 35, 192

scientific anticommunism, 112, 118, 123, 126, 140, 145, 171, 176, 193; JCEE's, 118, 155, 186–87, 189, 190, 193

scientific objectivity, 118

scientific reasoning, styles of, 8

scientization, 21; different forms of in different historical moments, 20–21; of economic education, 183–84, 188–91; and rhetoric of selling, 31

Scott, Walter Dill, 35–37, 45, 50, 60, 192

Scribner, Campbell, 116, 120

Seaman, Alfred, 150

"selling America to Americans," 29–32, 192; affirmative style and, 30, 31, 40, 42, 45, 51, 169; American identity and, 39, 42, 45, 192; anticommunism and, 42–43; antiradicalism and, 37–42, 50; capitalism

"selling America to Americans," (*cont.*)
and, 28, 29, 42, 45; "How to Sell America
to the Americans" (Link), 28–29 (*see
also* Link, Henry C.); managerial capitalism and, 31, 34, 48; patriotism and, 37, 40,
188, 193; place-making, antiradicalism,
and, 37–42, 50; promotional nationalism
and, 37, 45, 51, 52
Selvage, James P., 60
Shahn, Ben, 72
shareholder theory, 148
Shugrue, J. Edward, 87, 90
Shuster, George N., 92
Silk, Leonard, 175
simulation and games in economic education, 176–78
Sinclair, Upton, 43, 44
Slack, Jennifer Daryl, 35
Smith, Leroy F., 40
Smock, Jack, 91–94, 100, 103
Smock Report, 92–94, 98, 103, 149, 181, 182,
189; American economic system and,
80–84; "American Economic System"
campaign and, 91, 94, 104; constructing
postwar economic education, 80–86;
Harding College and, 193; influence of,
104–6; Joint Committee on Improvement and, 80–83, 85, 91, 93, 100–101, 103,
105, 106; managerial capitalism and, 80,
81; managerial folk knowledge and, 81,
82, 84; overview of, 81–82, 85; *This Is
Our Problem* and, 91, 104
social imaginaries, in economic education
media, 24, 27
Soviet Union: economic system, 120, 122;
educational system, 115; scientific and
technological advances, 115, 116. *See
also* Bolshevism; Cold War; space race;
Sputnik crisis
space race, 113–18
sponsored media, 3, 4; importance of, 3–7
Sprague, Hall T., 177
Sputnik crisis, 115–18, 129, 130, 150
Stanciu, Cristina, 32, 36
Stanton, Frank, 126
Stole, Inger L., 7, 11, 22, 29, 49, 54, 62, 69,
72, 79
structures of feeling, 24, 194
Sun Oil, 43
Sutherland, John, 102

Sutton, Francis X., 112
Swedberg, Richard, 64–65, 81, 218nn21–22

taxation, 101, 102, 137; income tax surcharge,
136–38
Taylor, M. Brook, 7–9
Tedlow, Richard S., 53, 56–57, 85
television, 18, 124–27; color, 147; influence
of, 19
third-person effect (communication theory),
22
This Is Our Problem (AAAA-ANA
slidefilm), 91, 104
Thompson, T. S., 131–32
Thrift, Nigel, 153
Tobin, James, 160
Tucker, Mary Logan, 40–41
Turner, Fred, 114
Twelker, Paul A., 177

Uncle Sam, 44, 95, 97–98, 99f, 133
Union Carbide, 127, 128f
Urban, Wayne J., 117
US Chamber of Commerce: anticommu-
nism and, 49; anti-inflation campaigns
and, 130, 131, 136–39; *It's Everybody's
Business* and, 15–16, 18; Smock Report
publicized by, 93
US Department of Commerce, 155, 160, 161
US economy. *See* economy of United States
"useful" media, 5

values, US's national, 42, 87, 123
Van Dyke, W. S., 43, 48
violence, mass media and, 19
"voice of affirmation": advertising as representing, 220n29; Advertising Council,
OWI, and, 69–72. *See also* affirmative
style
voluntarism, 83

Wagner Act, 57
Wall, Wendy L., 11, 42, 53, 57, 58, 72, 79, 86,
87
Wall Street crash of 1929, 41, 55. *See also*
interwar period
War Advertising Council. *See* Advertising
Council (Ad Council)
Ward, Stephen V., 38
Warshaw, Isadore, 6–7

INDEX 263

Wasson, Haidee, 5
Waterhouse, Benjamin C., 22–23, 149,
152
Weinberg, Sydney, 70–72
Wells, Kenneth, 81, 101, 103, 104
Wentworth, Donald, 176–78
West (United States), 37–39, 44, 185
West, Paul B., 63–65, 93
Wheeler-Lea Act, 62, 63
Whyte, William H., 77–78, 105
Williams, Aubrey, 101–2
Williams, Raymond, 19–20, 24, 127, 183,
194
Winkler, Allan M., 68–69
Wolfe, Audra J., 120

Working Economy for Americans, A (Public
Media Center booklet), 162–65
World's Fairs, 44
World War I, 32, 35, 192
World War II, 56, 69, 72, 193; Advertising
Council and, 69, 76, 193; aftermath of,
25, 110; educational resources and, 110;
US's entry into, 66. *See also* Office of
War Information (OWI)

Yates, JoAnne, 120–21
Young, James Webb, 74–75, 84, 92, 93
Your America (film series), 33–34

Zeiger, Robert H., 150